For TSA – who, at different times in her life, has
been a thief, a thug, an assassin and a maniac.
But, fortunately for me, has never once forgotten
how to be a true friend. Thank you.

CONTENTS

FROM ZERO TO HERO

'Maybe one day I'll be able to know I did a great job while I'm on set, but I'm not there yet. I was still just really embarrassed and full of anxiety that I was blowing it the whole time.'
Chris Pratt, after completing work on
GUARDIANS OF THE GALAXY – HUFFINGTON POST

There's a moment, just after the halfway point in *Guardians of the Galaxy*, when the titular band of misfits – who have only just managed to put aside their differences and form a very uneasy alliance – appear to be falling apart. This most unlikely gang of intergalactic heroes – consisting of a deluded space pirate, a female assassin, a vengeful warrior, a genetically mutated talking racoon and a walking tree – faces a seemingly insurmountable challenge, hopelessly outnumbered and vastly outgunned. It is at this crucial moment when their leader, Peter Quill (aka Star-Lord) – a half-human, half-alien bounty hunter – steps up and proclaims, 'I have a plan.' Immediately shot down by the rest of the team, he reasserts himself with, 'I have *part* of a plan,' only to face further derision. On finally being asked, 'What percentage?' he adamantly counters, 'I don't know: twelve per cent.' Taken at face value, it's not exactly the most rousing speech you're likely to hear, much less the rallying cry of the hero in a potential franchise-launching, $170 million action movie. It leaves you wondering if the speech Mel Gibson delivered as William Wallace in 1995's *Braveheart* would have inspired the gathered clans of Scottish freedom fighters quite as much if he'd demanded only 12 per cent of his freedom from the English oppressors, or what the amassed followers of the Reverend Martin Luther King Jr would have made of his not-quite-so-stirring, 'I have twelve per cent of a dream' speech. The fact that the actor in the role of Peter Quill is Chris Pratt – at that point best known for playing likeable but dim-witted, overweight slobs, such as Andy Dwyer in the television comedy series *Parks and Recreation* – makes the scene all the more incongruous.

Just over a decade earlier, Chris entered the acting profession with a similarly shaky plan but his strategy was undoubtedly one that fell a few percentage points short of twelve. After charming his way onto a movie set, via a stint living rough in a converted van and working as a waiter in Hawaii, Chris accumulated an enviably eclectic acting CV in a relatively short period of time. It ranged from the broadest of comedies to a handful of more serious dramas, including several 'Best Friend' roles opposite the likes of Channing Tatum and Vince Vaughn, to supporting roles in three 'Best Picture' Oscar-nominated features working alongside some of Hollywood's most acclaimed filmmakers and actors, including Kathryn Bigelow, Philip Seymour Hoffman, Brad

Pitt and Jessica Chastain. In under five years Chris went from headlining a gross-out comedy, which bordered on soft porn and contained virtually no laughs whatsoever (*Deep in the Valley*) to becoming the lead in the US's highest-grossing movie of 2014 (*Guardians of the Galaxy*). As he entered 2015, he was enjoying the prospect of headlining three very different movie franchises well into the next decade and beyond, with roles already confirmed in sequels to *Guardians* and *The Lego Movie* and his future in the *Jurassic World* saga largely dependent on his ability to outrun a genetically modified mega-dinosaur. While all this is undeniably impressive, the really extraordinary achievement is that he has done all of this without seeming overexposed or turning into the typically Hollywood-created, egocentric nightmare.

Much of his 'down to earth' charm and good humour can be attributed to his working-class roots, his close-knit family upbringing and, more recently, his relationship with the comedienne and actress Anna Faris. The strength of Chris and Anna's marriage is noteworthy and comes as a direct consequence of their ability to work together and successfully navigate the pressures and pitfalls associated with their shared profession – Anna already had a very successful film career when they met and, with her ongoing role in the sitcom *Mom*, she continues to be one of America's most consistently funny comediennes. But surviving – and, indeed, thriving – within an industry fuelled by gossip, rumour and scandal is not easy. Their obvious stability as a couple probably has more to do with their apparent decision to shun much of the glitz and glamour, as well as the intrusive media coverage which inevitably follows the type of sustained success they have experienced in Hollywood. While Chris and Anna may have all the obvious characteristics necessary to become a typical 'Hollywood Power Couple', they have shown little interest in exploiting their success to feed their own fame or celebrity status. Unlike Hollywood's other 'golden couples', Brad Pitt and Angelina Jolie (Brangelina) or Ben Affleck and Jennifer Garner (Beniffer), Chris and Anna are rarely photographed leaving star-studded industry events or fashionable celebrity hang-outs and, besides, Chranna is probably the worst superstar couple name... ever. Instead, the couple seem much more interested in spending their free time at home together, raising their son, Jack.

Fiercely protective of their privacy, they have chosen to shield Jack from minute-by-minute media coverage and unsolicited paparazzi attention in a manner that Kanye West and Kim Kardashian's baby daughter North might only dream about.

But behind the image of Chris as the devoted family man, with the apparently easy-going attitude and slacker personality he has portrayed so successfully in multiple roles, there is someone who wants to be seen as something more; someone determined to prove himself as an accomplished, all-round actor. Initially – perhaps fuelled by that 'twelve per cent of a plan' – his career aspirations were limited and it seemed unlikely he would progress beyond bit parts and walk-ons, seemingly unwilling or unable to shift from first gear. As an untrained actor, he remained unconvinced about his own versatility, constantly undermining himself with doubts as to his abilities and satisfied to carve out a respectable niche using his admittedly formidable skills as a naturally comedic performer.

Chris had seemingly found the perfect outlet for his talents on US television in 2009, with the character of Andy Dwyer – *Parks and Recreations*' lovable bonehead – and he would serve as one of the show's key players throughout its seven-year run. But despite his own misgivings and being constantly told by casting directors that he didn't have 'The It Factor', he never stopped auditioning for lead parts. However, soon after failing to win a string of high-profile jobs, with his confidence understandably dented, he decided to focus more directly on one type of role. As a character actor, aiming predominantly at supporting roles, he insisted on being the best he could possibly be in whatever parts he could land. It was this distinct shift in focus that led him to a greater understanding of his rare power as an actor. He now approached each job with renewed dedication, leading to the creation and portrayal of a wide range of characters, while still striving to find truth and something recognisably connected to his own spirit and personality in every one. Whatever the role, he went the extra mile. Whether that preparation involved extensive research, learning new skills, or the type of physical transformation that required massive weight gain or crash-dieting, he showed he was a hundred per cent committed to every project and the individual character he had been hired to play. This newfound clarity helped him deliver a series of supporting – but often scene-stealing – performances in a string of successful comedies, while simultaneously highlighting his evolving versatility in some quietly understated dramatic roles. Chris's apparent willingness to challenge himself and defy people's expectations of him as an actor led to a rapid increase in his stock as a relatable and – far more importantly in terms of success in the movie industry – a bankable leading man. And, finally, when it comes to Hollywood at least, it never hurts to show the world you've got killer abs, even if it does come via a 'my brother made me do this' photo on Instagram.

CHAPTER ONE

MONKEY BOY

'I got pretty good at falling... I learned by falling on my ass in front of people.'
CHRIS PRATT, ON HIS FIRST 'PUBLIC PERFORMANCES'
AS PART OF HIS HIGH-SCHOOL FOOTBALL TEAM –
THE BIG LEAD

In late September 2014, a couple of months after *Guardians of the Galaxy* had opened big at the US box office, the movie's lead, Chris Pratt, was beginning to reap some of the rewards associated with headlining the summer's biggest money maker. He found himself gearing up to host the season premiere of America's long-running satirical comedy sketch show *Saturday Night Live (SNL)* – the show that launched the careers of many of his own comedy idols, including Chevy Chase, Mike Myers and Will Ferrell, as well as his *Parks and Recreation* co-star Amy Poehler. Interviewed by his former hometown's local newspaper, *The Lake Stevens Herald*, about his recent success and what impact it was having, he admitted that it made him appreciate the town where he'd grown up more than ever. Chris described Hollywood – the place he now calls home – as 'kind of a ruthless town', before bemoaning a lifestyle in which 'you just float around like a gypsy'. He admitted that it was far removed from his own Lake Stevens' upbringing and the actor was quick to point out, 'I cling really tightly to my roots,' before stressing, 'I think that portion of my life, like [with] anybody, it really defines who you are.' He was keen to acknowledge the influence his childhood home had on him, while his unwillingness to leave behind the values it instilled in him has made an indelible mark on his basic character and beliefs. His easy-going temperament and affable persona have, in turn, informed the irresistibly relatable, everyman characters he has brought to life for the last decade and which have subsequently catapulted him to the top of his profession.

Arriving on 21 June 1979, Christopher Michael Pratt was the third child born to Dan and Kathy Pratt, following his brother Cully and a sister, Angie, and his birth would complete the close-knit family unit. As working parents, Dan and Kathy were very much a product of their time – Dan was the main breadwinner who, despite chasing whichever job opportunity he felt would earn him the most money, sometimes struggled to keep his family afloat in a time of widespread economic upheaval and uncertainty, and Kathy made her own contribution by taking part-time jobs in addition to raising the couple's three children. The 1970s had been a very turbulent time for the average working-class American and, as the country headed into a new decade, things didn't exactly look promising. Although it had come to an end in the mid-1970s, the Vietnam War had been a costly twenty-year blunder, which had far-reaching effects on the US economy. By 1979 inflation and unemployment had rocketed and whole families were forced to uproot and relocate to find work wherever they could. It would seem that Dan Pratt was what you might call 'a jack of all trades' and had learned to turn his hand to almost anything in order to earn an honest wage. Around the time of his youngest son's birth, the family had settled in Virginia, in an area known as The Iron Range of Minnesota, where Dan took advantage of the job opportunities thrown up by the region's dwindling – but still profitable – iron-mining industry. But the work was hard, with diminishing returns, and he was forced to keep moving further afield to find work. Utilising his experience in iron ore, he turned his hand to gold mining, taking advantage of the 1970s 'gold boom', which had seen the price of an ounce of gold rise from $35 to more than $800 in a decade. And when Chris was just two years old, Dan uprooted the entire Pratt family once again, settling in far-flung Alaska for the next few years. Chris told *GQ* that they only moved on once his father figured it was too dangerous to raise kids there 'because there's fuckin' bears and shit everywhere'.

The family then embarked on a seemingly endless pilgrimage around America to find gainful employment. Over the next five or six years they lived in nearly twenty different homes. In an interview with *Men's Fitness*, Chris later described his father's compulsion to keep on moving as 'chasing dreams' and this restlessness continued until the family eventually settled in Lake Stevens, a prosperous, rural district of Washington state. This last move brought to an end the constant upheaval of changing schools, making and losing new friends and the general state of limbo that Chris and his siblings had been experiencing over the last few years, giving the entire Pratt family some much-needed stability. In comparison to the harsh climate and isolation of Alaska and the transient nature of their early childhood, Lake Stevens must have seemed like an Eden-like paradise to Chris, Cully and Angie and it wasn't long before they were exploring their new surroundings and taking advantage of everything the area had to offer.

Putting down more permanent roots in a flourishing and prosperous community like Lake Stevens proved to be a shrewd move and it wasn't long before Dan and Kathy had found regular work. Dan was quickly accepted in the town as a reliable handyman and was soon putting his versatile skills to good use. He turned his hand to construction and maintenance work, which led to remodelling numerous houses in the area. Keen to make her own contribution and integrate herself into the local community, Kathy took a job at the town's Safeway supermarket. It suited her to be at the heart of town life. And there was nowhere better to catch up on local gossip or make new friends than working at the checkout of the local store. It was a job she held for many years, only moving on when a vacancy opened up on the same store's fresh-meat counter. Although money was coming into the house on a more regular basis, every dollar was earmarked for essentials such as food and household bills. While Chris would later admit to cutting holes in his Reebok trainers to make room for his growing feet, unable to replace them or buy a bigger pair, no one in the family seemed to complain about a lack of money or worry about the future.

Dan soon had a gang of hunting and fishing buddies, while the supermarket where Kathy worked was an obvious social hub, and Chris and his brother and sister quickly settled in at school. Unsurprisingly, after many years travelling from place to place, the Pratts had become a particularly close-knit family, content in each other's company and capable of making their own entertainment. Over the years they had learned to rely solely on each other and, subsequently, they would happily spend a great deal of their free time together as a family. Chris told the *Huffington Post* about the family taking a holiday cruise when he was about twelve years old and how entering a dance competition onboard the ship with his brother resulted in the pair scooping third prize. He recalled, 'In terms of dancing, I loved Michael Jackson, some *Saturday Night Fever*, a little early hip-hop,' before admitting, 'I was the guy who would enter a dance contest in eighth grade and just do the Running Man for twenty minutes.'

It was a relatively simple and contented life, one that would have an effect on Chris's overall personality, instil a general lack of cynicism and help him maintain a wide-eyed innocence – until he eventually moved to Los Angeles, at least! Perhaps joking a little, he later told one reporter from the *New York Times*, 'I definitely benefited growing up in a household that lacked any critical-thinking skills,' before emphasising his point with a firm 'Really!' One of Kathy's favourite pastimes was bingo and Chris often accompanied his mother, with the added incentive of being allowed to keep his own winnings and spend the money however he chose. On one particular occasion he remembered winning $300 in a local bingo tournament and spending every penny of his windfall on comic books. In the *Los Angeles Times* he joked, 'I had no overhead at twelve, so three hundred bucks was all disposable income.' He recalls how he took home a sizeable collection of the latest titles, which included *Ghost Rider*, *Batman*, *New Amazing Spider-Man*, *Spawn* and even one containing a certain mismatched group of space freaks known as *The Guardians of the Galaxy*!

Chris's love of comic books had less to do with following the fantastical adventures of a particular superhero or character than his love of the actual artwork contained within the pages. He told the *LA Times*, 'In our household we were big into arts and creating things ... we would trace and copy and draw pictures.' He went on to explain, 'I would try to copy these exceptional artists who could just draw male and female figures and the outfits and the hair and the guns and the wild worlds,' before adding, 'Our walls were covered with comic-book murals.' Chris was particularly obsessed with monkeys and, when he wasn't drawing them, he was collecting them, as he told the *Daily Mirror*: 'Every time I'd see one I'd buy one, little stuffed monkeys,' and he admitted, 'My nickname in school was Monkey Boy.' As well as monkeys, he loved to collect baseball cards, something he hoped would eventually translate into becoming a shrewd investment for the future, telling *The Big Lead* website in 2011, 'I still have a bone to pick with baseball cards. I thought for sure I'd be putting myself through college on baseball cards.' Around his early teens he had also started to show an interest in music, singling out rock acts Pantera and Faith No More as the type of bands he listened to most as a teenager, before his eclectic tastes expanded to include The Beatles and hip-hop and rap acts such as Mos Def and 2Pac. Later in life he would also count several more traditional country artists, including Garth Brooks, Keith Urban, Brooks & Dunn, George Strait and Eric Church, among his favourite artists and he cites Elvis Presley and Johnny Cash as his musical heroes. He says he picked up a guitar when he was sixteen years old and has played ever since. While his performances as the frontman of Mouse Rat – the band co-founded by his *Parks and Recreation* character, Andy Dwyer – would disguise his skills as a guitarist and singer later in life, he actually became a fairly accomplished guitarist, with an almost spiritual reverence for the instrument. In recent times, while shopping to upgrade his current guitar, he told *Men's Fitness* he was looking for 'the guitar that I will play for the next fifty years.' Chris explained that he was torn between buying new or second-hand, saying, 'Guitars evolve with the sounds of the music that is played on them.'

He went on to theorise that the sound produced by the same instrument owned by a blues enthusiast in the humid bible belt and one which had belonged to a rock guitarist from the considerably drier LA area would be completely different. 'It's like getting a house that's haunted,' he elaborated, 'The spirit of the previous player can be heard in the guitar... If I buy it new, fifty years from now, it'll only be my ghost in there.' It would seem that the last thing he wanted was for his guitar's legacy to be Mouse Rat's crowning glories 'Sex Hair' or '5,000 Candles in the Wind'.

Back in his teens, although he may have harboured dreams of

becoming a famous rock star, he was much more of an outdoorsy type. And the family's move to Lake Stevens would solidify and nurture this particular passion into a life-long obsession.

Situated nearly 50km north of Seattle on the US West Coast, Lake Stevens shares its name with the stretch of fresh water it almost completely surrounds. Covering almost a thousand acres of land, with an eight-mile circumference, the lake is an oasis of breathtaking natural beauty and the region is home to several national parks and flanked by a vast area of protected forestland and mountainous wilderness. Almost immediately on arrival, Chris started to take a keen interest in nature and wildlife – which would later grow into an ongoing fascination with collecting bugs and insects – and he soon developed a deep-rooted love and respect for the outdoor life, forming an unbreakable bond with his new home and the countryside that surrounded it. A major part of embracing this new 'outdoorsy lifestyle' involved taking part in some of the region's more traditional pastimes.

'Hunting is in my blood,' Chris told *Outdoor Life* magazine before recalling how his dad and uncles loved to hunt and fish most weekends in the woodlands surrounding the family's new home. It's hardly surprising that the young Chris would inherit his father's passion for the sport, although, regretfully, he didn't always have as much free time to join them as he'd have liked. In the same interview he confided, 'I didn't hunt as much as a teenager, though I longed to,' before explaining, 'Since I played football and every weekend in the fall consisted of a game or practice I was forced to listen to my friend's stories seething with jealousy.' Chris undoubtedly spent many an evening hanging onto his father and uncles' every word as they shared their adventure stories with anyone who would listen.

While he may not have been able to take part in every field trip, he still managed to learn how to handle a gun and track animals in the wild, as well as picking up the basics of skinning and butchering the spoils of the hunt. Chris bought his first shotgun when he was just twelve years old, using money he'd earned from babysitting. It was a single-shot breakaway and became the first of many guns that he would own over the years. Talking about his extensive gun collection recently to *GQ*, he admitted, 'It's really more just about collecting shit,' than a genuine obsession with owning large amounts of firearms for protection or in response to any perceived threat.

In time, hunting would become even more of a passion for Chris, when his commitment to the TV drama *Everwood* forced him to relocate from his LA home to one of America's most abundant hunting areas. *Everwood* was filmed in several locations in and around the Salt Lake City area – a region which boasts some of America's best hunting and fishing reserves – and it wasn't long before he was taking full advantage. 'I became passionate about big game hunting when I moved to Utah,' he explained to *Outdoor Life*, 'I lived there for four years, had the time and money to really get into it and became absolutely obsessed.'

Later, on his return to LA, Chris admitted that his hobby raised eyebrows among his newer friends, 'There aren't a ton of hunters in Hollywood.' Chris still adamantly sticks to his guns (literally) when defending his unusual hobby. He said that, 'The people I've talked to about it are actually fascinated with the subject,' before adding, 'I think I've changed a few minds regarding the sport.' When faced with the fairly typical retort, 'As long as you eat all the meat,' he is refreshingly blunt. 'I have to be honest with them,' he admitted, 'My passion for hunting is not simply the result of a need to feed myself,' before joking, 'there's grocery stores for that!' In one of his first appearances on Conan O'Brien's late-night chat show, Chris told stories of his early hunting experiences, even admitting to killing and eating squirrel meat. The interview footage went viral online and he later told *Outdoor Life*, 'I love telling people that story! It freaks them out. Especially here in Hollywood!' before admitting that squirrels might be considered a delicacy in comparison to some of his self-caught meals. 'I've definitely eaten more exotic meat than squirrel. Stories of possum are coming to mind,' he said before ending the interview by sharing a few of his cooking tips – 'I brined them for a few days, then pan-fried them with spices.'

As a teenager, Chris's growing interest in nature and animals was not merely reserved for killing them. As he grew older, he kept numerous pets, most of which could be thought of as fairly exotic. By the time he was interviewed for the *Seventeen* website in 2004, he had accumulated quite a menagerie, which included 'A pet lizard named Puff, five goldfish (Pinky, Brain, Jowels, Pearl and Sandy), an Oscar fish named Chef, two Pacus, an albino frog named Whitey, a bonsai tree, four Venus Flytraps, a fruit fly farm and sea monkeys.'

As a kid what experience he did have of hunting led, in turn, to him gaining quite a reputation as a junior taxidermist.

He learned how to treat and preserve animal skins and even attempted to work on some of his larger kills, with varying degrees of success. In 2012 he told *Outdoor Life*, 'The last thing I did was a coyote. It didn't turn out great, and I felt I wasted the pelt,' before admitting, 'Since then, I've taken all my trophies to a pro.'

While Chris's confidence in his own abilities may have dwindled over time, his love of the art of taxidermy only blossomed. Later he became a collector, filling most of his future homes with numerous weird and wonderful stuffed animals. Luckily, it was a hobby he shared with his future wife, Anna Faris, and they would eventually put their individual collections together to form an extensive – and ever so slightly macabre – menagerie. It's easy to see how the process of discovering his new home greatly affected the young Chris. His many adventures, exploring the local countryside, developing his outdoor skills and taking up new hobbies were planting the seeds of a lifestyle that would stay with him for the rest of his life. But, unfortunately, it wasn't all fun and games for the youngest members of the Pratt family. Realistically, there was a more pressing need for the family to give up their nomadic lifestyle – the children desperately needed a more permanent base to continue their schooling.

On arriving in Lake Stevens, Chris was about to enter second grade and it's easy to imagine how his experiences over the previous few years had sharpened his skills in terms of learning how to fit in and make new friends as quickly as possible: not knowing how long he was going to be in any one place definitely added urgency to breaking the ice and making 'fast friends'. Consequently, it had also given him a self-sufficient streak; a confidence and contentment with his own company, which undoubtedly must have set him apart from many of his peers. His easy-going nature allowed him to integrate comfortably with the many different cliques at school – the jocks, the geeks and everything in between – but his self-assurance meant he rarely looked to others for validation or sought approval from friends, meaning he never developed a desperate need to fit in with any one particular group. He was thought of as humble and outgoing by his classmates and was popular for all the right reasons. Thus, Chris became one of a rare breed who became universally accepted by his fellow students – a position that saw him repeatedly voted 'class clown'. Subsequently, towards the end of his school days, he was honoured to be chosen by his fellow Lake Stevens High School classmates to speak on their behalf at the 'Class of '97' Graduation – apparently, after his suitably heartfelt and moving speech, there wasn't a dry eye in the auditorium.

As Chris entered his early teens, he began to excel in various school-sports activities, initially juggling baseball, football and track-and-field, and eventually becoming the captain of the school's wrestling team. 'I played every sport growing up,' Chris told *The Big Lead* website. 'I was definitely an athlete.' He played Little League baseball until his freshman year in high school (aged fourteen/fifteen) but was forced to make a tough choice when he realised track-and-field and baseball were played in the same season at his high school. He recalled, 'I elected to do track because I was a shot put/discus thrower.' Around the same time, he started to take an interest in competitive wrestling, a sport that was virtually hotwired into the DNA of Lake Stevens' high-school athletes. 'Wrestling there is like high school football in Midland, Texas,' he told *The Big Lead*. 'Kids start wrestling at four or five years old,' before admitting to the *Seattle Times*, 'Wrestling really changed my life for the better.'

Chris was taken under the wing of Brent Barnes, a high-school wrestling instructor who was a four-time state champion in his own right. Barnes would eventually coach Chris for four years, taking him all the way to the state championships. Over the course of his senior years, Chris became a vital ingredient in the Lake Stevens High School wrestling team and was fondly remembered by his mentor as 'dedicated, creative and eclectic.' Barnes was adamant that hard work and dedication to the sport were often more important than brute strength or pure athleticism when it came to winning trophies, telling the *Seattle Times*, 'It's such an intense sport. There are probably more tears involved than there are in any other sport,' before adding, 'It's very personal.' As a senior Chris placed fifth at the State championships in 1997 and fond memories of his time on the wrestling team lingered long after he left high school.

As he began to find fame through his work on *Parks and Recreation*, Chris showed his support (and supplied the narration) for an *MTV* documentary film called *On the Mat*. Charting the ups and downs of a group of wrestlers (and Coach Barnes) from Lake Stevens High School as they progressed towards the state championships, Chris's involvement in the film meant a lot to the current crop of athletes, as well as to his former coach. It prompted Barnes to sing Chris's praises to the *Lake Stevens Herald*. 'He's never forgotten where he came from,' before adding, 'He's a pretty special person ... he's the type of person who gives back.'

The film played at the Tribeca Film Festival in 2012, eventually winning the 'Best Online Feature' award.

Years after their time training and attending competitions together, Barnes pointed out that it had been obvious to him that Chris was destined for future success. 'I think for any of us who watched him grow up, we're not surprised by who he is and what he's become.' Barnes cited Chris's likeability and his ability to make the whole team laugh: qualities seemingly unrelated to the sport, which were equally important to his success as a competitor as his physical stature or his actual skills on the wrestling mat. He also recalled Chris's flawless Jim Carrey impersonation and how, even then, he was surprisingly quick-witted and always ready with an unexpected joke or lightning-fast comeback. He told the *Herald*, 'He can ad-lib ... he's always been funny and friendly.' For Barnes, much of the success Chris would achieve in later life was simply the result of everyone else being allowed to see a version of the Chris he'd known as a teenager, only this time it was amplified and projected onto a much bigger canvas. Barnes told *Heraldnet. com*, 'He's taken that personality of his and worked hard to turn it into a craft he can share with people.'

Despite his obvious abilities as an all-round sportsman, it would seem the teenage Chris was most at home on the football field. His father had been a star player on his high-school football team back in the day and was keen to see his son follow in his footsteps, enthusiastically coaching him in the game from an early age. At just over 6ft tall, with a solid, 'corn-fed' physique, Chris cut an imposing figure as he entered his mid-teens, something which didn't go unnoticed by the school's football coach, Ken Collins. Drafted into the team (The Lake Stevens Vikings), he played fullback and inside linebacker, and proved to be an important element in the team's success.

A childhood injury to his thighbone had left Chris with one leg slightly shorter than the other, meaning he had difficulty kicking his game up into second gear. He told *The Big Lead*, 'I would get the ball and in the open field I would fall down.' Chris admitted he was comparatively slow and clumsy on the field but was never afraid to get stuck into the rougher aspects of the game.

But, yet again, it would seem it was his ability to entertain that set him apart from the rest of his teammates. 'I have a zillion Chris stories,' Collins told the *Lake Stevens Herald*, adding, 'He was just so funny.'

It would seem, however, that not everyone saw the funny side of Chris's high spirits and 'have-a-go' attitude. He soon found himself cut from the track-and-field team following an incident that involved him accepting a dare to run across the school running track in the nude. Evidently, his desire to entertain and make people laugh was not only interfering with his sports activities, it was fuelling his growing interests in acting and performing in front of an audience.

More often than not, during breaks from schoolwork, Chris could be found at the back of the classroom or in a corner of the school cafeteria performing his own hilarious versions of his favourite *Saturday Night Live* sketches, or perfecting his long list of impersonations. He was becoming increasingly involved in school shows, taking the stage at assemblies, and he even began performing as part of a comedy/acting group, staging shows and sketch reviews at a local dinner theatre. Here, the paying audience were not only expecting to receive a decent meal but also to be entertained by a show, which was included in the price. This experience would prove to be an invaluable training ground for Chris's improvisational skills, sharpening his quick responses to unexpected situations, as the actors were invariably forced to fight for attention from an audience considerably more interested in what was on their plates than what was on the stage in front of them.

Chris seemed to have it all. He was an outgoing, well-liked, hard-working student, with undeniable prowess in several sports and a growing interest in acting. However, while it appeared that he had plenty options open to him in terms of pursuing further education, in reality, he didn't seem to be giving much thought to life after high school at all. While a sports scholarship at one of America's choice universities looked well within his grasp – or even signing up for a drama course in New York or LA that might have sent him down an obvious path – Chris appeared to have no firm plans for his future. He told *Entertainment Weekly* about a conversation he had with wrestling coach Brent Barnes some time before graduation: 'I came into his office and he said, "Chris, what do you want to do with yourself?" I was like, "I don't know, but I know I'll be famous and I know I'll make a shit-ton of money."' He went on to explain, 'I had no idea how. I'd done nothing proactive. It was as dumb as someone saying, "I'll be an astronaut. I'm sure I'll stumble into an astronaut suit and end up in space one day."'

While it was to be a few years before his somewhat optimistic predictions would come true (and, in a sense, he would even eventually make it into space), he did, indeed, 'stumble into' making his next move. At seventeen, deciding he wanted to stay close to home, Chris half-heartedly accepted a place at a local community college, studying acting straight after high school. Although it is unclear why he didn't attempt to spread his wings a little further – it seems unlikely that he thought he would receive the sort of training he needed in the Lake Stevens area in place of one of the US's more arty hotspots in New York, Los Angeles or even the relatively nearby Seattle – it's hardly surprising to learn that he didn't even make it to the end of the first semester, dropping out with no real back-up plan. Like his father before him, he seemed unable to zero in on any one particular line of work. Nothing seemed to hold his attention and, for a while at least, it looked like his many talents and the potential he'd shown during high school would go to waste. And while he may have lacked the 'chasing dreams' wanderlust that had prompted his father to roam the country for years, the result was more or less the same. Still living at home with his parents in Lake Stevens, he began a period of drifting from job to job.

Like his acting peer (and future co-star) Channing Tatum, Chris found part-time work as a stripper – although it is unclear if he still harbours enough fond memories of this experience to spark any real ambitions to appear in the forthcoming *Magic Mike* sequel. He eventually began to earn enough money to survive, going door-to-door selling books containing discount coupons. While it was the very definition of a 'dead-end' job, he definitely had the necessary charm to succeed, even winning an all-expenses-paid trip to Jamaica after showing an early aptitude. 'I think I was rookie salesman of the year,' he told the *Empire* podcast. 'I broke some rookie records.' In a scenario befitting a classic Andy Dwyer epic failure, Chris described an incident during a celebratory dinner with his workmates on the trip, where he somehow managed to spill a whole tray of drinks over one of his female colleagues. Thankfully, though, it wasn't just future acting choices he picked up during this period; he also acquired some handy self-preservation techniques, many of which would prove very useful in his future career. He told the *Huffington Post*, 'You learn to deal with rejection by being indifferent to the results,' adding, 'I learned this from door-to-door sales and every shitty job I've done ... you have to protect yourself from heartbreak.' It certainly helped him develop a thicker skin and gave him the ability to shake off disappointments: a much-needed skill for any Hollywood newcomer during the years of fruitless auditioning that usually precede landing a dream role.

As Chris turned nineteen, his time in Lake Stevens was coming to an end. A 'too good to refuse' offer to take his first steps out into a much bigger world and 'retire' from the world of door-to-door sales was just around the corner. But he would never forget the warm welcome extended to his entire family by the Lake Stevens community as a whole; acceptance that had allowed the Pratt family to finally put down some permanent roots after years of drifting from town to town. His father, Dan, remained a Lake Stevens resident until his death in 2014 and Kathy, his mother, still holds a job at the town's Safeway supermarket. Chris would make no attempt to shake off those roots either, often returning to Lake Stevens for short visits with his own extended family of nieces and nephews, organising hunting trips with his old school buddies and even attending his 'Class of '97', ten-year high-school reunion in 2007.

Chris's childhood – living among uncomplicated, honest, hard-working people – helped instil in him a down-to-earth quality, a 'good ol' boy' charm and, perhaps most of all, an overriding talent for never taking anything in life too seriously. As a teenager he seemed to lack any burning ambition, in terms of forging a particular career for himself, but he left Lake Stevens with confidence to spare and a belief that the only way you really achieve anything meaningful in life is through hard work. It was these qualities that would be witnessed in much of his acting work over the next decade, sowing the seeds for many of his most memorable characters and performances. While the most obviously recognisable link to his own small-town upbringing can be found in *Parks and Recreation*'s dim-witted but lovable Andy Dwyer – the quintessential underachiever, born and bred in Pawnee and satisfied to live there for the rest of his life – there are other elements of Chris's character in most of the roles he later played, whether it be *Delivery Man*'s Brett (a new dad struggling to cope with the pressures of parenthood) or *Moneyball*'s Scott Hatteberg (a real-life baseball player who was given a second chance to shine when many thought his professional career was over). All these characters share some of Chris's own spirit, enriched with a touch of his natural charm and good humour. Indeed it was his ability to channel much of what he'd learned growing up in Lake Stevens into his work as an actor – qualities that also helped form his general outlook on life – that would eventually set him apart from virtually everyone else in Hollywood.

CHAPTER TWO

SURF'S UP

'I'm like a mama bear, so proud of him, the cub.
He is amazing and so sweet and good. He's a shiny soul,
and I'm so lucky to have met him.'
RAE DAWN CHONG, DESCRIBING HER 'BABY BEAR'
PROTÉGÉ, CHRIS PRATT – *STAR MAGAZINE*

Teenage slacker. College dropout. Dead-end job. Lack of ambition. A bit on the heavy side. Has own guitar.

While this may sound like a brief (and wholly accurate) character summary for Andy Dwyer, Chris's character on *Parks and Recreation*, it is also a fairly accurate description of the man himself around the time of his nineteenth birthday. Stopping just short of living in an abandoned construction pit, Chris's lifestyle at the time would have acted as the perfect back-story for Andy's character if he'd ever felt the need to 'go full method' for the role. It would appear that much of the potential he had shown during his high-school years had quickly evaporated after graduation and his life had more or less slowed to a monotonous crawl before he'd even left his teens. It's hardly a unique story – 'star high-school football player fails to recapture his youthful glories in the real world of professional sport' or 'talented actor abandons a promising career after countless rejections' – but the truth was surprising and a little more disappointing than simply failing to meet his obvious potential. It seemed that he hadn't even tried to make his mark in any of the fields he'd shown an interest or aptitude in. There were no hard-luck stories of retirement through injury or reluctantly giving up his dream after endless unsuccessful auditions. It appeared as though he simply hadn't developed the necessary drive or desire to pursue a career in anything at all during his first few years as a high-school graduate. Instead, ditching his dead-end job as a discount-coupon salesman, he accepted an invitation from an old Lake Stevens buddy. With little to lose, he took a one-way trip to Hawaii.

He later described the feeling of accepting the offer as being like winning the lottery or, more accurately, comparing it to someone 'buying him a winning lottery ticket', given that he didn't even pay for the flight himself. With no money of his own to spare, it was his friend Zeb who stumped up the cash. Zeb was determined it was the right thing for his best friend to do and the pair became room-mates for the next couple of years. Chris later described the period to the *Complex* website as 'the greatest time of my life ... we were truly free,' before admitting that he was prone to exaggerating the pair's living arrangements to their friends back home. 'We told friends we had a beach house,' he said, before revealing the truth: 'In a way we were homeless.' The pair had ended up living out of an old camper van, which just happened to have characters from the *Scooby-Doo* cartoon series painted on its side and, when the weather permitted (which was most of the time), they lived in a tent they had erected on the beach. Chris looks back on the whole experience with great fondness and typical good humour, however. 'We were able to transcend the difficulty of home ownership. There was no liability, no overhead,' he said, before weighing up the pros and cons. 'There were fleas and mice that also lived in our van and we didn't have anywhere to go to the bathroom, [but] getting three [beers] for $6 was a positive.'

In August 2014, only a couple of weeks after *Guardians of the Galaxy* had smashed US box-office records, he posted a photograph of himself on Facebook standing next to his old van with the caption, 'Can't believe I found this picture!!! That is the van I lived in!!!' The image went viral and acted as a fairly inspiring reminder that anything is possible and that the old-fashioned 'American Dream' is, perhaps, very much alive and well in the twenty-first century. Living from day to day in his beat-up van, with his long, matted, sun-bleached hair, Chris was the living embodiment of the term 'beach-bum'. Describing the Maui beach he'd made his home, he told the *Independent* newspaper, 'It's a pretty awesome place to be homeless,' before putting his apparent destitution into context. 'It would be different if I lived on the streets of Chicago and ate garbage from a dumpster.' The truth was that both he and Zeb were finding jobs wherever they could and usually earning just enough to survive. 'We just drank and smoked weed and worked minimum hours, fifteen to twenty hours per week,' Chris explained. 'Just enough to cover gas, food and fishing supplies.' He summed it all up as a 'charming time.' While it's obvious the boys were 'living the dream' in many respects, their lifestyle did have its dangers. Chris would recall, in an interview with the *Daily Mirror*, how a simple fishing trip turned into a frightening, near-death experience. 'I was fishing on this rock point called Three Sisters. It's really, really turbulent and dangerous water – shark infested. It's all sharp lava rock that rises and falls ten feet with every bit of tide, it's so deep and so powerful.' Suddenly aware that he'd strayed farther from the safety of the shore than expected, he was soon engulfed by a series of fast-moving and overpowering waves. He continued, 'I felt the weight of the water start pulling me in. I was wearing flip-flops and I just dropped everything, went down and grabbed the lava rock.' He then recalled how he'd somehow managed to maintain a grip on the jagged rock and made his escape before the next set of waves. 'I somehow climbed up the wall. I lost my shoes, my rod, but I was very lucky,' he said, before concluding, 'That's the closest I've come to death ... one of those moments [when] you think you might not make it out.'

By the time the boys had been living their own brand of 'the good life' in Maui for a couple of years, Chris was earning his 'gas and beer money' by picking up shifts as a waiter at the resort's Bubba Gump Shrimp Company restaurant. It seemed that he had the perfect temperament and qualifications for this type of work, where a minimum-wage salary could be bolstered by picking up extra tips, and he was obviously in his element entertaining the customers and turning on the charm, when required. As the name suggests, the popular restaurant chain specialised in fresh seafood and shrimp dishes, as well as offering a range of southern and Cajun cuisine. The award-winning brand has a strong link with the movie industry, having been co-created by Paramount Pictures as a tie-in for their 1994 film, *Forrest Gump*. Taking its name from the fictional restaurant chain created in the movie by Tom Hanks's titular character, it wasn't unusual to see famous movie stars among its clientele, especially in a popular holiday destination (and much-used film location) like Hawaii. On what must have seemed like a normal evening's service, Chris was about to make the most important connection of his professional life and one that would forever change his career path.

On this particular evening, actress and budding film director Rae Dawn Chong was having dinner with a friend in the restaurant. As the daughter of Tommy Chong, one half of the notorious stoner comedy duo Cheech and Chong, Rae Dawn was almost pre-destined to follow in her father's footsteps and make her living within the entertainment industry. While it's undeniable that her parental connections might have opened some doors for her at the start of her career, it would seem that she found success as an actress on her own terms. After a couple of guest spots on popular television shows, she was soon making her mark on the big screen. Thanks to her Afro-Canadian/Chinese heritage, she was a strikingly beautiful young woman, her uniquely exotic look making her instantly memorable to casting directors faced with a sea of girls who looked exactly like the girl they had seen just five minutes before. She picked up high-profile roles in several well-received films, including a small part in Steven Spielberg's multi-Oscar-nominated *The Color Purple*, before finding her niche as the female love interest in countless action movies throughout the mid-1980s and 1990s. One of those films was 1985's *Commando,* in which Rae Dawn was cast opposite Arnold Schwarzenegger in his first lead role following his break-out turn in James Cameron's *The Terminator* the year before. The film was a box-office hit, but over the years found an even bigger audience as a home-video cult classic. As it turned out, Chris was also a huge fan of *Commando*, a film he swears he's watched 'about 4,000 times'. When he recognised *the* Rae Dawn Chong sitting in the restaurant, he wasn't about to pass up the chance to talk to one of the stars of his favourite movie and, besides, there might just be a decent tip in it. In the *New York Times* he recalled approaching Rae Dawn's table and saying, 'Hey, you're a movie star!' before introducing himself as a die-hard fan of *Commando*. A good fifteen years after *Commando*'s release – and with a CV now littered with countless low-budget and straight-to-video action movies – Rae Dawn was probably overjoyed to be remembered for something slightly more worthwhile. She later told *Star Magazine*, 'Chris came over and pitched himself to me, claiming he was an actor too.' The director recalls being instantly charmed by him; impressed by his ability to make people laugh. She stated, 'He was funny, quick, big-hearted and gorgeous.'

As luck would have it, Rae Dawn was having a quick break in Hawaii before starting her next job. She recalled, 'As it turned out, we were [still] casting a movie I was going to direct

in LA and I needed someone to star as the "hunk" in my film.'
She gave Chris a copy of the script, telling him to prepare for
a read-through, before setting up a makeshift audition for the
following week. The film in question was a horror comedy
going by the name of *Cursed Part 3*. And although the part
earmarked for him wasn't huge, he figured it was still a part in a
real movie. Chris read and reread the script at least a half dozen
times before the meeting and he later deadpanned to the *New
York Times*, 'I thought it was the best thing I ever read,' before
adding with a smile, 'It probably was the best thing I ever read.
I hadn't read a whole lot of anything up to that point.'

Script quality aside, he planned to grab the opportunity
he'd been given and run with it. Talking to *Star Magazine*, Rae
Dawn confirmed his commitment to the part: 'Chris showed
up early and was totally prepared.' She added, 'He blew
everyone away!' However, his elation at getting the part was
short-lived, as he soon learned the film was scheduled to start
shooting in LA within a matter of days. Living hand-to-mouth
and with no spare cash saved for luxuries such as air travel, it
looked as though his dream would be grounded before it had
even left the runway. Luckily for him, however, Rae Dawn
made sure his travelling expenses were included in the deal.
And so a matter of days after winning the role, with his flight
paid for by the film's producers, Chris was on his way to LA
to begin shooting his first job as a professional actor.

While the lucky break and the experience of making a
proper movie were invaluable, the finished product was
probably best forgotten. Intended to be a full-length feature,
the movie ended up as a short film consisting of twenty

minutes of unfinished and almost completely incoherent rough footage – low on horror and even lower on comedy. Horror-review website *Blackhorrormovies.com* describes the film as 'pretty bad' before trying to give a brief summary of the plot: 'Not surprisingly, something lurks among the trees, although we never get to see what it is, and it never kills anyone (at least, not in this director's reel).' It went on to state, 'With the low, low production value, *Cursed Part 3* has the feel of a corporate training video.' Surprisingly, they did have one positive thing to add, damning the cast with faint praise by saying, 'Normally with a project this cheap, I'd say that the acting is terrible, but it's actually not bad here.' While this might be Chris's first positive acting review – albeit one which probably doesn't sit at the top of his current CV – he was his own worst critic, admitting to the *Complex* website, 'If you watch the movie, I'm fucking awful. The movie's terrible and I'm especially terrible,' before confessing, 'My friends have told me it's the worst movie they've ever seen.'

Despite *Cursed Part 3* being the end result of his first professional acting job, Chris's attitude towards the industry had been transformed by the experience of just being on a real movie set. Making the film ignited a spark – suddenly he knew he'd found his passion. With little hesitation, he had committed to making his living as a full-time actor. He later described the moment of realisation to the *New York Times*, saying it was 'like one of the famous Hitchcock push-ins.' As he began to reject his 'easy-come, easy-go' lifestyle and everything in his previously shambolic post-high-school life suddenly pulled into focus, he admitted, 'My world changed. I knew it right at that moment.' While *Cursed Part 3* hadn't exactly got him a seat at the table for the 2001 Academy Awards (although it must have been in the running to pick up a Razzie or two), it served as a means to an end. Chris told *Complex*, 'I have no regrets about getting my start in [*Cursed Part 3*]. I have the opposite of regrets, whatever that word is.' He pointed out how the job taught him the necessary basics of his new profession – 'I learned how to hit a mark' – and went on to explain, 'I went from living in a van to having a car and a reel and my foot in the door in Hollywood.' In real terms, it had allowed him to relocate to LA and he was now undoubtedly in the best possible place to begin the next chapter of his life.

In July 2014, only a couple of days prior to the release of *Guardians of the Galaxy*, Chris looked back at his decision to move to LA almost fifteen years previously and how his ambitions changed almost immediately once he got there. He told Kaleem Aftab, a reporter from the *Independent* newspaper, 'Originally the dream was to pay my bills doing nothing other than acting.' Later, he revealed how ambition and an unexpected need to succeed took hold almost immediately once he was on the Hollywood treadmill. It reawakened the competitiveness he'd experienced as a high-school sportsman and his career aspirations began to change as a result. It seemed that this side of his character was still feeding his desire to succeed, as he admitted, 'I got there, but the dream is constantly evolving.'

As the work started to trickle in, he grew more confident in his abilities and began seeking opportunities to stretch himself as an actor, actively pursuing a wider variety of roles.

He continued, 'My dream was to do roles that are more than just the bad guy, or the douche. Then it was to do sidekick roles, then comedy. Now it's like I've crossed over this line where I actually say no to stuff.' He recognised that it was a far cry from his less than auspicious first steps into the acting profession, putting him in an enviable position. 'I could never have fathomed that,' he confessed. 'Before I would have done commercials for herpes medication if you wanted me to... gladly.' He added, 'Just as long as I didn't have to wait tables again.' While a chance meeting had given him his first break – which had then helped him realise that acting might just be the perfect way never to have to don an apron or dish out menus ever again – it was no guarantee of success in a notoriously cut-throat industry where close to 90 per cent of professional actors are said to be 'between jobs' at any one time.

Like every young actor trying to make a mark for himself in Hollywood, Chris had to play the game. His modest fee from *Cursed Part 3* had given him enough spare cash to get himself set up in LA so he found himself somewhere to live and used the rest to pay for his first set of professional headshots – the photographs actors use as a calling card to send to agents and casting directors when auditioning for jobs. In his early twenties, Chris was considerably luckier than most. He was very handsome, maintaining the scruffy, sun-bleached hair from his days in Hawaii, and at 6ft 2in, with an athletic build, he was definitely someone who would be topping a lot of callback lists. Sometimes 'the look' was enough. He never failed to make a good first impression and, as an added bonus, you always got something extra. Chris was the guy who could always make you laugh and he knew how to make people like him – it's always good to remember that, in Hollywood, a little charm can go a long way!

Unlike most new arrivals, he was already equipped with a fairly thick skin. His early experiences as a door-to-door salesman had more than prepared him for the endless cycle of hopeful auditioning, which more often than not was followed by crushing rejections. Somehow, he remained optimistic. For nearly two years he survived doing the kind of 'under the radar' acting jobs that kept him busy and put food on the table but which, ultimately, gave him very little traction as far as forging a successful career went. He soon realised that maintaining a positive attitude was probably the only power any actor has while trying to break into the industry. During those first couple of years, any illusion of directly influencing your own future is little more than a fantasy.

He told *Yahoo Entertainment*, 'You can't really plan it,' before stressing, 'Anyone who claims that they had a hand in planning their career is probably lying a little bit.' Sometimes it can be a seemingly random series of events that puts a specific actor in a certain role at just the right time but, even then, dumb luck seems to always play its part. He went on to explain, 'I think a big part of what we do comes down to good fortune... knowing what movie to say no to,' before admitting, 'For the majority of your career, you are not willing to say no to anything because you want to work. And especially when you first start out, you will take anything.'

Everyone has their share of false starts and Chris was no exception. In 2001 he landed a key role in *The X-Team*, a pilot for a proposed series on America's ABC television network. The show was conceived as an action-adventure series, tapping into a growing market for extreme sports – such as snowboarding, B.A.S.E. jumping and free climbing. The main plot focused on the adventures of a secret, elite Black Ops team, consisting of Gen X, extreme sports athletes. Hoping to attract the late teen/early twenties demographic, who were becoming increasingly important to advertisers, ABC decided not to cut any corners, opting to shoot the majority of the show's pilot episode on location in New Zealand.

While everyone involved in making *The X-Team* seemed to be having the time of their lives, the end result was decidedly underwhelming. Ultimately, ABC decided to pass on picking up the show as a series and eventually re-edited the pilot as a stand-alone, made-for-TV movie, airing it under its new title, *The Extreme Team*, in 2003. Chris realised that, even if it hadn't quite set him up financially the way he'd hoped, the job had paid well and it was all money in the bank. He told *Yahoo*, 'It was not enough money to buy me fourteen years but it bought me enough time to slowly, over fourteen years, develop a career and make enough to survive.' He had quickly identified that the trick was to keep earning and keep learning. Chris, like every other shrewd young actor in his position, intending to build a lasting career, realised he needed to pick up as many acting tricks as possible and learn something on every single job. It didn't matter if it was a quality HBO series, a low-budget TV movie or a Hollywood blockbuster, every day on set should be seen as a learning experience. While *The X-Team* series not making it to air must have been a huge disappointment at the time, he was philosophical about the job later, stating, 'That was my first movie [when] I was able to collect a paycheck and stop being a waiter,' and added triumphantly, 'I haven't had to do anything but be an actor since then.'

What came next would change his professional life forever and, in turn, it would have some fairly dramatic repercussions for his private life too. Accepting a role in a pilot, which was then picked up and turned into a series, meant that he would eventually have to relocate, uprooting his entire life from his base camp in LA to move almost a thousand kilometres to Salt Lake City in Utah. In the process, he would meet the girl who would give him some highly invaluable first-hand experience of life as one half of a celebrity couple. Chris was about to get his first major TV role as Harold 'Bright' Abbott in the WB series *Everwood*.

CHAPTER THREE

INTO THE
WOODS

*'If there's all these college guys who are like totally hitting
on high school girls, then there's probably a whole surplus of
neglected college girls who want to hit on high school guys.'*
WISHFUL THINKING FROM CHRIS PRATT AS
BRIGHT ABBOTT – *EVERWOOD*

Long before he became synonymous with almost single handedly rehabilitating the television super-hero genre through his role as co-creator and executive producer on the hit series *Arrow* and *The Flash*, Greg Berlanti had discovered a love of storytelling at an early age. As a child, growing up in the Rye area of New York, his idol was *Muppets* creator Jim Henson. Showing remarkable entrepreneurial skill for someone so young, Berlanti began designing and building puppets of his own and he soon had his own business venture performing at kids' birthday parties in the neighbourhoods surrounding his childhood home. Apart from learning a lot about characterisation and performance from Henson and his extraordinary team of puppeteers, Berlanti also picked up a few tips about building an entertainment empire of his own. He told the *Why We Write* website, 'I would sit and design a story based on the little facts of the birthday boy or girl's life,' before admitting, 'If you're curious what the rock bottom of the middle school caste system is, it's "The Kids Who Play with Puppets".'

In order to improve his social standing among his peers and, as he puts it, 'because I liked the idea of having sex in this lifetime,' he quickly dropped the puppets. He replaced them with real-life actors, turning his attention to playwriting while studying at Northwestern University, before moving on to write screenplays and, eventually, scripts for television. Very quickly in his TV career, he made a name for himself as someone who knew how to write convincingly about everyday life and down-to-earth people. His gift was finding compelling drama in the ordinary; the day-to-day problems which affect most people at some point during their lives, from the ups and downs involved in keeping a relationship on track or the smallest moral dilemmas we all face on a daily basis, to the more dramatic, life-altering consequences surrounding issues such as divorce, illness and bereavement. He had a knack of creating well-rounded, believable characters and he didn't shy away from exploring the more complex emotions involved in dealing with some of life's more challenging moments.

Berlanti cut his television scripting teeth writing for teen drama *Dawson's Creek* back in the late 1990s. After meeting Julie Plec – the future co-creator of *The Vampire Diaries* – at Northwestern, their friendship led to a casual introduction to Kevin Williamson, *Dawson's Creek*'s creator and show runner. Williamson was so impressed with the spec scripts

Berlanti had accumulated over the years that he handpicked the relative novice to join his writing staff as the show entered its second season. Broadcast on Warner Brothers' teen- and young-adult-targeting WB Network, the show had become synonymous with tackling 'hot potato' topics such as pre-marital sex, contraception and homosexuality. What had initially appeared to be a fairly straightforward, family orientated show – following four friends as they enter their freshman year of high school in the fictional seaside town of Capeside, Massachusetts – had quickly developed into something much more compelling.

For many, it represented a decidedly more unsettling vision of modern America, unafraid to highlight taboo issues that affected most teenagers in the US at that time. The show attracted more than its fair share of controversy in its first season, with many critics questioning whether the decidedly adult tone and subject matter was appropriate for a 'family network'. Berlanti took much of this criticism with a pinch of salt. He stuck to the show's basic principles of delivering a smart, sophisticated and, above all, entertaining teen drama that didn't talk down to its younger viewers, while still resonating with the adult audience who may have chosen to watch alongside them.

As Williamson moved on to pastures new at the end of season two, Berlanti inherited the show runner's position almost by default, having written almost half of the previous season's episodes. Feeling ill-prepared, he feared the worst. He told *Entertainment Weekly*, 'I thought, "This is disastrous, and it's going to end very badly."' But despite his initial trepidations, his relative inexperience and the seemingly random nature of his promotion, Berlanti rose to the challenge, taking the reins and guiding the show to even greater acclaim. At the tender age of twenty-six, he was only a few years older than the actors portraying the kids on the show and he later attributed much of his success – as well as his affinity with the characters and their situations – to this kinship. He told *Entertainment Weekly*, 'We were all very young and growing up together at the same time.'

While never becoming a huge ratings success, *Dawson's Creek* had developed its own distinctive voice. Its unique brand of angst-ridden, teen drama built a loyal but relatively small hardcore following during the six-season run. On cancellation in 2003, *Dawson's Creek* had secured its place as a much-cherished cult classic, as well as becoming one of the most influential and much-imitated shows on television – it's hard to imagine the likes of *Gossip Girl*, *The O.C.* or *The Gilmore Girls* existing without *Dawson's Creek*. Ultimately, the show had gained respect for never being ashamed to make its audience laugh one moment and cry the next. Many fans and critics alike considered the greatest strength to be its steadfast refusal to compromise in storytelling, never flinching when shining a light onto contentious issues or exploring troublesome subjects previously ignored by most mainstream, family-orientated dramas.

Berlanti's early reputation was built more or less entirely on his contribution to *Dawson's Creek*'s success. He subsequently forged a long and fruitful working relationship with the executives at The WB Network, who rewarded him with the opportunity to create his own show, building from the ground up and airing it on their network. While The WB was often seen as an 'underdog' broadcaster, routinely dismissed by critics and the other networks for its reliance on youth-orientated content, Berlanti told the *Television Without Pity* website, 'The WB was great, because the executives that were running it at the time said, "Look, we know we can't make shows for as much as bigger networks, but we can give [writers like] Joss Whedon or Kevin Williamson or J.J. Abrams a chance to say what they want to say."' It was in this atmosphere, where untested writers were given their first opportunities to shine, or 'out of the box' thinkers were given free reign to create shows that didn't necessarily fit any pre-existing television mould, where Berlanti planted the seeds that would grow into his first series as sole creator: *Everwood*.

Berlanti's first task was deciding exactly what shape his new show would take, telling *Television Without Pity*, 'The executives [at The WB] were really encouraging to just say what was personal to me and figure out a way to say it.' Looking back, he realised the shows he'd loved to watch most when he was growing up were 'family shows', something suitable for parents to sit down and watch with their kids. He cited *Northern Exposure* and *All In The Family* as favourites but found particular inspiration in *Family* – a drama centred on a normal American family, which aired in the US on ABC between 1976 and 1980 – and *Family Ties* – the Michael J. Fox half-hour comedy/drama that had turned the young actor into a household name during the show's seven-year run on NBC between 1982 and 1989. Explaining the starting point for virtually every new television show, Berlanti told the

Chicago Tribune, 'There's so much great TV out there, you [have to] think about, "What's not being done?"' He added, 'When we started [thinking about *Everwood*] there weren't a lot of shows like *Family*, where a ten-year-old could watch it and a sixty-year-old.' He continued, 'Shows like *Family Ties*, I would laugh at it and my dad would laugh at it. We were just trying to do that with an hour-long [show].'

The plan was to create a series that would appeal to a broad family audience but one which wasn't afraid to deal with the real-life problems that were too often ignored by most network-television drama. Berlanti went on to explain, 'The whole genesis of *Everwood* was, "Why is it that I can turn on the news every night and watch all these issues being talked about, and then I get to my TV shows and, unless it involves murder and/or people investigating a murder, it's not there?"' before concluding, 'The people [who run most TV networks] are scared.' As a fairly new channel eager to continue making its mark and with much less to lose than the more established networks, it's hardly surprising that he was given the full backing of The WB and, as the show began to take shape, his thoughts switched to the show's main premise.

Berlanti later told *Television Without Pity*, 'I felt in relationship dramas, male characters had been given the short shrift,' adding, 'I had personally never really seen [anything] on a drama like my relationship with my father, which was combative, but slowly got better as we became more and more sort of best friends.' With this in mind, he decided the show would primarily follow a male protagonist, telling the story of a recently widowed man trying to rebuild his troubled relationship with his children. Considering the scale of the undertaking and his relative inexperience in building a show from scratch, for Berlanti, the road to *Everwood*'s pilot episode was surprisingly straightforward. 'It was blessed from the beginning,' he told the *Chicago Tribune*, 'I wrote that script quicker than I wrote anything else. I remember meeting every one of those actors, they all seemed preordained,' before concluding, 'I'll never have an experience like this again.'

The pilot episode takes the audience to the titular Everwood, a fictional small town that flourishes in relative seclusion against the backdrop of the beautiful Colorado landscape. We are introduced to Andy Brown, a neurosurgeon who, prompted by the recent death of his wife in a car accident, has decided to give up his successful career in New York and relocate to Everwood. He uproots his two children – nine-year-old Delia and fifteen-year-old Ephram – choosing the town as their new family home largely due to his late wife's long-cherished memories of the idyllic Colorado countryside. The pilot – and much of the first season – centred on Andy's grieving for the loss of his wife and the children's struggle to come to terms with the death of their mother. This was set against the whole family's efforts to gain acceptance from the town's more established residents, which proved particularly difficult when Andy decided to set up his own practice, causing conflict with Dr Harold Abbott, Everwood's other physician. The audience was subsequently introduced to the Abbott family, Harold's wife and town Mayor, Rose, and their teenage children, Amy and Harold Brighton (aka Bright). The main drama, played out over the series' entire run, largely focused on these two families and their intertwined (and often unresolved) relationships with each other, as well as the impact they had on the lives of the other Everwood residents.

Veteran US television actor Treat Williams was on board to play Andy Brown, while Gregory Smith, who already had a decade's worth of experience as a child actor, played Ephram. Relative newcomer Vivien Cardone took the role of Delia, completing the onscreen Brown family. While the cast of almost a dozen main characters and series regulars came together fairly quickly, one role was proving especially difficult to fill. With the actors playing Dr Harold Abbott and his daughter, Amy, already cast – Tom Amandes and Emily VanCamp, respectively – Berlanti and his team were struggling to find the right person to bring the family's eldest son, Bright Abbott, to life.

In the pilot script Bright was written as a complex and often emotionally guarded individual. At the beginning of the season he has a dark secret, having lied about his involvement in the car accident which left his best friend in a coma, but he was also expected to add a great deal of comic relief to the show's more serious storylines. Berlanti would later admit that, like many of his *Everwood* creations, Bright Abbott contained elements of his own personality and general characteristics. He confessed to *Television Without Pity*, 'Bright was the kind of cad in me ... he had that element of charm, the guy who can talk his way out of anything.' It proved to be a tricky balancing act. Creating a character that had obviously made some bad choices in life but one also sympathetic enough for audiences to root for as the show progressed was not an easy compromise to achieve. As the last series regular to be cast, Berlanti's search for Bright came down to the wire but, with his perfect ensemble almost in place, he refused to compromise on finding that all-important final piece of the puzzle. Thankfully, he was about to meet a relatively untested young actor by the name of Chris Pratt.

As a last-minute addition to the casting call, Chris had only been given *Everwood*'s pilot script on arrival at the studio, just moments before his actual audition. Berlanti told the *Hit Fix* website, '[Chris] just landed from the airport and didn't have the lines memorized... in fact, he'd just looked at them minutes before.' But despite this apparent disadvantage, he was undeniably impressed. 'Chris walked in and had the part from the start.' Typically, he had no intention of letting such a small matter – not knowing any of the dialogue from the script he was due to audition with – destroy his confidence, trusting that the force of his personality would be enough to swing it his way. 'He tossed the pages in the air and started riffing on the scene and had us all in hysterics,' recalled Berlanti, before adding, 'I thought... right now, it's just a few lines, but he was the kind of actor you could have built a whole show around.' Bright's progress was never intended to be a main focus for the show but, over time, the combination of Chris's personality and the writer's growing affection for the character saw his main story arc become one of the most relatable and compelling for many of *Everwood*'s most devoted fans.

With Chris signing on to portray Bright, the entire cast and production team headed north. They would be in-transit for the duration of the pilot's shooting schedule, moving from

Los Angeles to locations in Denver, Colorado and across the border into Canada. Reduced production costs had prompted many US television shows and movies to use the area as a base. Thus, the breathtaking scenery of Canmore and Calgary served as suitable stand-in locations for *Everwood*'s intended Colorado backdrop.

With post-production completed on the pilot episode, it was now in the hands of The WB executives as to whether *Everwood* made it to the screen and was then picked up as a full series. It seemed that they were suitably excited by what Berlanti and his team delivered and the show received an initial order for a further twelve episodes to air alongside the pilot. As a fully-fledged series, *Everwood* now needed a more permanent home and, preferably, somewhere a little closer to Warner Brothers' established West Coast base of operations. Suitable locations were scouted in nearby Utah. Being separated from California by only one state (Nevada) and sharing much of the impressive landscape and natural features of neighbouring Colorado, it proved to be the perfect compromise. Soon the area surrounding Salt Lake City would become home to most of the cast and crew during filming. Many of the cast even chose to relocate there completely, staying on during the show's annual hiatus periods – usually a three-month break between filming blocks of episodes. Chris was one such convert to the Utah lifestyle. Life in the relative calm and isolation of the area must have been a welcome break from the noise and hustle of LA and in many ways it was fairly reminiscent of Lake Stevens, his childhood home. Situated in a similarly unspoilt landscape, relocation allowed him to reconnect with many of the outdoor hobbies he'd enjoyed during his formative years.

While Chris was undoubtedly taking full advantage of his time away from the *Everwood* set, he wasn't forgetting what he was there for. As a relatively untrained actor, he had plenty to learn and he took every opportunity to soak up each new experience on set. Soon he was picking up basic tricks and techniques, learning how to hold his own among the other actors or step back and let the focus go elsewhere within a scene. He was fast becoming an integral part of the impressive ensemble cast and the work he was doing on the show saw him reach new heights as a performer. Key to the success of any long-running series is creating the type of relatable, well-rounded characters an audience wants to spend a lot of time with. Characters change over time and the real trick is allowing those characters to evolve naturally, form realistic relationships and interact in a believable manner in whatever dramatic situation they find they are placed in. It's a difficult trick to master but it seemed like the entire *Everwood* team were on a creative high.

The writers poured everything they had into the initial batch of scripts before turning them over to a team of similarly driven directors and actors, who were desperate to live up to the outstanding work they saw on the page. The storylines featured in the first season walked a thin line, often switching between scenes of serious, emotional drama and more light-hearted moments. It was achieving this balance of drama and comedy that would set *Everwood* apart from its competition and it seemed that no one understood this more than Chris.

As filming continued, he began to find his groove. He was enjoying the ensemble nature of the show, feeding off some very experienced and talented actors, as well as forming a tight gang with the younger members of the cast. Greg Berlanti, talking to *Hit Fix*, recalled how exhilarating it was to watch him in action. 'After a few episodes I realised he was even more special than we thought,' he explained, 'We never knew what kind of dailies we were gonna get back and it became exciting because we would send dramatic scenes and he'd find comedy ... and in the comedic ones he would find moments of drama.' Berlanti concluded, 'I thought he was kind of like an acting Buddha... always in the present moment and always reacting so honestly and truthfully.'

With such limited experience in front of the camera, it was remarkable that Chris could deliver such perfectly pitched performances so early on in his career. It's easy to assume he wasn't acting at all. Maybe he was just 'being himself'. But it's naïve – and a real disservice to his skills as an actor – to dismiss his talents so readily. Arguably, his key strength as a performer, even at this early stage, was his ability to find his own truth in every character or scene he played. Whether it involved simply injecting his characters with recognisable elements of his own personality – traces of his unique sense of humour or his impeccable comic timing – or working at the darker end of the spectrum – tapping into his real fears and emotions – he was willing to stretch himself and was slowly gaining confidence on the job.

For him it was a nurturing and inspiring place to learn and experiment as an actor and it would seem Berlanti was integral to creating this uniquely safe and creative environment. Even this early on in his career, the director was not afraid to go head-to-head with studio executives if he felt he needed to veto a decision or protect his vision. This strength of purpose rubbed off on the cast and crew, giving them confidence, helping them believe they were part of something worthwhile to raise their game accordingly.

Chris later told *Entertainment Weekly*, '[Berlanti was] capable of showing real heart without being melodramatic. A family drama like *Everwood* could be corny – the young love, loss and regret, that's all very soap opera – but he was able to do it with pure class and quality.' He added, 'He had a creative control over the show, and you could really feel his presence.' On the flip side, with a show runner like Berlanti in charge, maintaining an ever-watchful eye on his team of writers and protective of his overall vision, it is apparent that the actors had very little control over mapping their characters' storylines or eventual fate. In an interview with the *Los Angeles Times*, Chris's co-star, Emily VanCamp, admitted, 'You never know what they're going to throw at you until you get the script,' before adding with a laugh, 'that's what's scary.' While being completely at the mercy of the *Everwood* writing staff might be a frightening prospect for many of the actors, they could be assured the show's entire creative team had the utmost respect for the cast they'd put in place so meticulously only a short time before. While direct collaboration with the actors may not have occurred during the early plotting stages, the writers increasingly began to understand exactly what the actors were capable of. In Chris's case, it seemed that they thought he was more or less willing and able to do anything. Berlanti was quick to confirm the collaborative relationship between the actors and the show's team of writers, while simultaneously praising his whole cast, telling *Hitfix*, 'They were, and Chris is the perfect example of it, the kind of actors that made every line better.'

The *Everwood* pilot was broadcast on the WB network on Monday, 16 September 2002. While its ratings were not huge – the first season averaged out at a solid, but unremarkable, 4.8 million – the general consensus among critics was tentatively positive, with most forgiving the fledgling show's shortcomings and allowing it the chance to find its voice. Ken Tucker at *Entertainment Weekly* said the show was 'as all-American as all get-out', before adding, '*Everwood* is a new example of a way to create so-called family programming that's not excessively sappy or smotheringly moralistic.' He went on to praise its writer and creator, saying, 'Greg Berlanti lovingly crafts so many coincidences that pretty soon you either buy into *Everwood*'s world or get off its wavelength pretty quickly. Me, I found its intricate symmetries engaging and clever.' He concluded, '*Everwood* ain't brain surgery, but that's also what helps make it an easygoing charmer.' Less favourable was the review in *USA Today*, where Robert Bianco said, '[*Everwood*] never knows when the corn syrup is thick enough,' before going on to add that the show was nothing more than a melting pot of well-worn television clichés.

Very quickly after the pilot aired, The WB announced it was giving *Everwood* a 'full-season pickup'. This meant they intended to order another nine episodes on top of the thirteen already in production and it became the first of 2002's new shows to get a 'back nine'. Berlanti's response was understandably ecstatic, 'It's phenomenal ... We've had the time of our lives. Everyone's going to be thrilled to keep working. Now we can continue to breathe life into these characters for the rest of the year.'

As the season progressed, Chris (as Bright) was picking up more and more scenes. Berlanti and the writers were taking note of his unique ability to find comedy in almost every situation, allowing them the opportunity to seamlessly inject humour alongside the show's more dramatic moments. It soon transpired that it wasn't only the *Everwood* cast and crew who had noticed the fledgling actor beginning to take flight. Before long, he was being singled out by many reviewers as the primary reason to watch the show, with *Entertainment Weekly* becoming particularly enamoured by the character of Bright (and the actor who played him). Bright's musings on the world around him started to regularly pop up in the magazine's weekly 'Sound Bites' feature – where reviewers highlighted the best lines from the previous week's shows – delivering lines consistently funnier than most top-rated sitcoms at the time, whether it was Bright's singular view on the complexities of dating ('Man, this relationship stuff is like the hardest videogame in the world. As soon as I level up, there's a new robo-assassin waiting to take me out because I don't know the secret code.'), or his limited understanding of great literature ('You want to see *Pride & Prejudice*? What, is that about racism?').

Long before she received international acclaim for *Gone*

Girl, the bestselling novel and subsequent screenplay, as a staff writer for *Entertainment Weekly*, Gillian Flynn acknowledged Chris's contribution to *Everwood* in an article discussing underrated television actors who found a way to shine as supporting players amid talented ensemble casts. In the piece entitled 'Something Special', she said, 'Chris Pratt takes what could have been a stereotype – the dumb-jock, best buddy – and turns him into so much more than a sidekick, in part thanks to sheer, laidback charisma.' It was this kind of critical attention that allowed *Everwood* to stealthily snare its audience.

What quickly transpired was a feeling that the people who loved *Everwood* REALLY loved *Everwood*. Berlanti immediately noted the scale of the fans' interaction with the show, aware that every episode was being instantly recapped and reviewed online. He joked with the *Broadcast* website, 'When I started on *Dawson's Creek*, we'd get a box of fan letters once a month.' Under such scrutiny and with an unexpected level of input from the fans, *Everwood* became one of the first shows to interact with its online fan-base. Berlanti would actively engage with fan-sites and bloggers who posted episode recaps and soon the show had secured a small but very vocal, hardcore fan-base.

Never achieving major critical acclaim – nor the ratings that often accompany it – the show was never a priority for The WB and that, according to Berlanti, meant that the creative team were never put under any kind of close scrutiny by 'The Suits' at the network. 'My personal assessment of what happens in TV and film and the entertainment business in general is, the more money that gets poured into something, the more jobs that are created, the more people have opinions about creative stuff are around,' he told the *Chicago Tribune*, before stating, 'Really creative stuff happens two ways – people are prominent enough that they are left alone, or people had other things to do that month and you're under the radar.'

But maybe the position of flying 'under the radar' proved a double-edged sword for *Everwood*. While never rustling up the kind of critical noise which ensures viewer buzz, steady ratings or the potential for the kind of unwanted network attention which Berlanti was keen to avoid, the show also invariably failed to secure a free-pass when it came to deciding which shows would be picked up for the next season. Instead of unquestioned renewal each year, suddenly the show went under the microscope and it seemed everyone who was anyone at the network had an opinion about its future. Berlanti would brace himself for the end-of-season battle, open to criticism and permanently ready to fight for *Everwood*'s future. 'You always want to hear good notes,' he told the *Chicago Tribune*, adding, '[But] there's a difference between notes from people who enjoy the product, and notes from a fearful place of "Let's keep the numbers up this way."'

And so began a four-year rollercoaster ride for Chris and the rest of the cast and crew. Every year, the ratings averaged out around a respectable 4.5 million, never climbing any higher than the first season peak or hitting the kind of numbers enjoyed by the most popular dramas of that time – *E.R.*, *C.S.I.* and *The West Wing* – and every year, the show's future hung in the balance. Despite the uncertainty, Chris was undoubtedly having the time of his life, happy to count his blessings and keep on doing a job that didn't involve waiting tables.

While many of his fellow actors might have struggled with the precarious nature of the show's future, he had adopted a more easy-going, take-it-as-it-comes attitude towards life a long time ago. Having never really worried about the future before, he certainly wasn't going to start now. He decided to embrace his current circumstances and was determined to enjoy himself, no matter what happened in terms of *Everwood*'s survival. He reasoned that he'd make the best of things and, while living in Utah, made every effort to reconnect with his childhood passion for hunting, fishing and all things outdoorsy. He was making up for the many trips he'd been forced to miss due to his high-school football commitments and it soon became one of his favourite ways to unwind after a particularly hectic period of filming. 'Being outdoors, listening to the world wake up around me, I shed all the stress that comes with my job,' he explained to *Outdoor Life*, before adding, 'Whatever stress the regular world creates for any outdoorsman can be washed away for a while ... Some people fast, some people go on a cruise or visit a day spa. I get out in the woods with a rifle or a bow. That's my release.'

It seemed that *Everwood* had not only given him a new home in the heart of one of the best hunting regions in America, it had provided him with the regular work and steady income necessary to fully indulge his passion for the first time. He admitted, '[I] had the time and money to really get into it and became absolutely obsessed ... I have a secret spot in Utah that is my favourite place to hunt. It borders a [wildlife conservation area] to the north and a county that prohibits hunting to the south. It's protected, private, beautiful and abundant.' He added, 'I love long-distance shooting and I'm not sure there's anything as exciting as calling in predators.'

Over the course of the next few years, he would spend many long days on hunting and fishing trips, regularly inviting a few of the guys he grew up with in Lake Stevens to join him but, more often than not, he would use the time to disappear on his own. 'One of my favourite parts of hunting is getting away from it all,' he admitted, before adding, 'These days there's a lot more to get away from. That's probably why I cherish it so much.' He had regular work, decent money and all the perks that go along with becoming a recognisable face on a popular television show and, as he was about to reveal to the world, he had met a gorgeous new girlfriend too. The only real problem being... she was his sister!

Emily VanCamp may only have been Chris's on-screen sister but it was still a tricky situation for the couple. It's hardly surprising when gossip filters out from a TV or movie set, suggesting two of the stars have started dating or formed some sort of romantic relationship. It's a tradition that stretches back as far as the film industry itself – one which saw Elizabeth Taylor and Richard Burton meet and fall in love on the set of *Cleopatra* in the early 1960s and, more recently, Angelina Jolie and Brad Pitt became Hollywood's current power-couple while shooting *Mr. & Mrs. Smith* in 2005. The whole experience of filming is invariably intense and removed from 'real life', with the cast often forced to spend weeks on location with only each other for company. The situation is only magnified during the making of a long-running television series, when actors might spend as much as nine months of the year together, year after year. While neither Chris nor Emily had specifically been told they couldn't date another cast member, they were both aware it was something that might be frowned upon. Chris told Michael Ausiello, in an interview for *TV Guide*, that he was aware people might expect them to be nervous about entering into a relationship with a co-worker but the couple were adamant they knew what they were doing. 'We weren't apprehensive at all,' he admitted, 'we said, "Fuck it. Let's just go for it, because it's important to us."'

For the first six months of their relationship, they tried to keep it a secret from anyone who wasn't a close friend or relative, unsure what the reaction might be from the rest of the cast or, indeed, the show's producers and creative team. Chris confirmed, '[We were] trying to hide our relationship from the set ... We were trying to stay secretive and didn't want it to get out there ... I don't know why, and looking back on it, it was foolish.' Over time, the pair started to get more serious and decided to be more open about their status as a couple. Chris described it as a massive release, admitting it was almost an act of defiance, telling Michael Ausiello, 'Eventually it just felt very good to kind of just come out with [it],' before adding, '[We said], "Ah, fuck it. We're together. We love each other, and if you don't like it, you can kiss our ass – our collective brother and sister kissin' ass."'

Once everyone on set was aware of their status as a couple, they could relax, vowing never to let their relationship interfere with their work commitments. As Chris would later tell *TV Guide*, 'Once we get on set, we really just kind of became our characters and left our relationship behind,' before confessing, 'We would sneak a kiss here and there, but we would try and stay as professional as possible so no one would get uncomfortable. We certainly never bring any arguments to the set or anything like that.' While the *Everwood* team took the news in their stride, a few fans found it harder to accept, as Chris recalled: 'Every once in a while we get that one person that's like, "That's really creepy. You just kissed your sister."' Chris was typically laid-back about the whole thing, saying with a smile, 'It never really weirded us out... because, you know, it's all fiction.'

Former show runner Berlanti had moved on to oversee the production of other shows during *Everwood*'s third and fourth seasons, handing the reins to regular writer Rina Mimoun. Under her supervision, *Everwood* began to evolve and many fans noted that the show was trying to spice up its storylines, most likely to widen its appeal and attract viewers from some of The WB's youth-targeting shows, such as *Gilmore Girls*, *Smallville* and *Supernatural*. Perhaps fearful of cancellation as *Everwood* entered its fourth season, the creative team started to ramp up the melodrama, showing little regard for the characters, which had been so richly drawn over the previous three years. It was clear that *Everwood* was changing its direction.

Chris and Emily discussed the show's evolution in an interview with the *Los Angeles Times*, with Chris keen to acknowledge the high benchmark the show had set for itself. 'The pilot was just awesome, just perfect,' he said, 'There was this thirty-episode arc in [Greg Berlanti's] head that was his vision. If you see the first couple of seasons on DVD, you can really see how awesome that was.' He added, reflecting on the apparent shift in direction, 'The strength of the show [has been] that it's something that's a little atypical of The WB, which is why we have fans outside the typical demographic recognise us,' finally concluding, 'I think we're becoming a little more close to what [The WB's] core audience is used to, and it's definitely a change from what it was in the beginning.' Emily made it clear that, despite the apparent shift in tone, evidently suggested by the network executives and producers, the entire *Everwood* cast was pulling in the same direction: a direction which felt more true to the original spirit. 'There's an integrity that we all really try to maintain on the show,' she said. 'That's something that's really important to us.'

Some of these changes were unanimously rejected by members of the cast, who over the years had become a very tight-knit and single-minded group. Often they would stand as a united front to veto certain storylines if they felt they were not in keeping with their characters or the spirit of the show. It seemed that some of the female cast members had a particular fight on their hands. In the same *Los Angeles Times* interview, Emily explained how she and certain other girls in the cast were 'constantly fighting to not take our clothes off.' She added, 'It's like this ongoing battle,' and concluded, 'It's all about maintaining that integrity, that's what holds it all together, I think, [but] obviously, that stuff sells.' Chris agreed that, too often, it felt like the producers were chasing a different audience. 'Sometimes they forget we're not like a mountainous O.C.,' he said, before adding in his typically deadpan manner, 'I'm always fighting to take my clothes off.'

Things only got worse for *Everwood*, as midway through season four the show lost its usual Monday-night timeslot. Instead, it moved into a much tougher Thursday-night line-up, where it struggled for viewers when playing directly against the number-one-rated drama series *C.S.I.* and popular reality show, *The Apprentice*. Every year the show had prepared for the worst, never knowing whether the current season would be its last, making sure every season finale tied up the majority of loose ends and made sense as a series finale if the call for renewal didn't come.

Behind the scenes a decision had been made to close the entire WB network once it had merged with the CBS-owned UPN (United Paramount Network). This would make way for a brand-new channel – The CW – to launch a few days later. While Berlanti was sure the show would prove to be an integral part of the new network, he was realistic enough to accept its possible cancellation. He told the *Chicago Tribune*, 'I don't know that I would blame anyone at the CW network ... I think they are trying to do their best.' Instead, he laid the blame squarely at the feet of the former executives of The WB, stating, '[They haven't] gotten behind the show when they needed to. With the exception of the first year when we got terrific promotion and a terrific launch, it's never gotten the kind of push [that it should have].' In the end, a few WB shows, including the tonally similar *Seventh Heaven*, were thrown a lifeline and picked up to air on The CW but *Everwood* was not so lucky. As season four moved towards its conclusion, it became apparent *Everwood* was coming to an end.

For Berlanti, it was a particularly bitter blow. Aware that the show had strayed too far from its original manifesto, he had planned to return to *Everwood* as show runner for season five. He claimed, 'That may have been in part because I saw the writing on the wall.' Philosophical and eager to dissipate some of the outrage from fans the cancellation had ignited, Berlanti said he had 'no hostility towards the CW at all for not picking up *Everwood*.' He stated, 'Our show was not cancelled because another show was picked up,' adding, '*Everwood* was just cancelled and that's that, and it didn't have anything to do with *Seventh Heaven*.'

It was a sad time for everyone involved but particularly bittersweet for Chris. He had undoubtedly grown attached to the place he'd made his home for the last four years. 'I really started to enjoy living in Utah,' he told *TV Guide*. 'It has everything that I like to do there: fishing and hunting and camping and hiking and skiing.' He went on to admit, 'I kind of fell in love with Utah, but also fell in love with my girlfriend, so it's a trade-off,' before adding, 'I get to take her with me to Los Angeles.'

Contemplating his time on the show, he was determined to look on the bright side, arguing that it had had a pretty good run and that the entire cast and crew could be justifiably proud of what they'd achieved. 'I think everybody feels pretty good about it,' he stated. 'The fact that we were able to go as long as we did, it's such a positive thing and it's hard to look back on it with any negativity.' In the end, he was nothing if not pragmatic, adding, 'It's just television. Shows get cancelled and people move on and you hopefully can see that the glass is half-full and be like, "Wow, that was a great experience."' While leaving *Everwood* behind was both a physical and emotional upheaval for him, it wasn't long before he landed his next acting job, fresh on arrival back in Los Angeles. He was about to join another ensemble cast but the experience would prove to be dramatically different to his time spent on set in Utah.

Josh Schwartz had created *The O.C.* in 2003 in response to the growing demand for youth-orientated drama and female-targeted programming, which had experienced a massive boost, thanks to the success of such shows as *Sex and the City* and *Gilmore Girls*. Airing on The Fox Network, it had been a surprise hit during its debut season. It quickly became something of a pop-culture phenomenon, picking up solid ratings, as well as enjoying a decent critical reception. But as the show entered its fourth season, things were beginning to get a little stale in the fictional town of Newport Beach. As ratings fell steadily from year to year, it was obvious the viewers were losing interest and when Fox only ordered sixteen episodes (as opposed to the previous season's twenty-five), it was clear that the network was also losing faith. While much of the cast and crew were resigned to the show being cancelled, Schwartz was determined to give it one final creative push, hoping to recapture some of the excitement and humour of its debut season.

Schwartz had become a big fan of Chris's work on *Everwood* and, when he realised the show was coming to an end and the young actor would soon be available, he created the character of Che especially for him. He told *Hit Fix*, 'We were looking to inject some real humour back into the show,' before acknowledging that Chris was a crucial component in his plan to revive it: '[He] was one of the funniest guys around.' What was intended to be a six-episode story arc was eventually extended as Schwartz and the writing team fell under Chris's spell. 'He was super charming and so fun to watch,' Schwartz admitted, 'We kept coming up with reasons to keep him on the show because he was so good. All the other actors really loved him too.'

Chris's appearance on *The O.C.* was undeniably a breath of fresh air but he himself found the experience less than satisfying. He told the *Big Lead* website, '[After *Everwood* was cancelled] I was just happy to be working,' before explaining, 'But [the rest of the O.C. cast] was very much in the situation where no one really wanted to be on the show anymore and everyone was tired of telling the same stories and playing the same character.' He tried his best to give them a new outlook on their situation, gained from his own recent experiences on *Everwood*, recalling, 'I came in and tried to add some perspective – "Hey guys, this ends and then it sucks, enjoy it while you can."' While many hardcore fans appreciated the efforts being made to bring their much-loved show back from the brink – and some critics even commented on the creative revival – it was too little, too late. In January 2007, just as *Buddytv.com* reported their fears of the show's imminent demise, saying, '*The O.C.* is winding down, in all likelihood, and it's a shame. The show is hitting its creative stride just now, in its fourth season, and no one cares,' Fox announced that it would not be picked up for a fifth season.

Although Chris's time on *The O.C.* was brief – in the end, his character appeared in only nine of the sixteen episodes – it made a lasting impression on the actor. It made him realise just how fortunate he'd been to have a special show like *Everwood* as his incredible – and it now seemed thoroughly unique – introduction to television acting. In an interview with *Big Lead*, he contemplated the precarious nature of the acting profession, encouraging more actors to follow his own long-held philosophy on the subject, to spend less time worrying about career progression and enjoy the moment. 'There's no [point] looking past what you're in. A lot of people say, "I got this, but what's next?" and they focus on that so much,' he stated, before concluding, 'You definitely have to enjoy it while you can. No ride lasts forever.'

With the end of his time on *The O.C.*, Chris bade a fond farewell to the world of television drama. While he would return to the small screen a few years later as a member of the *Parks and Recreation* cast, bringing Andy Dwyer to life in a comedic role that would colour much of the rest of his career, his focus had turned towards making his mark on the big screen in a fiercely competitive business. Like most inexperienced actors, he would be forced to compete with scores of others for the chance to even audition for a hotly contested role. He would face off against hundreds of young actors, many with exactly the same look and a matching set of skills. Faced with such competition, it's smart to know exactly who you are as an actor, to hone your skills and fully exploit anything that makes you unique. All Chris had to do now was figure out who he was, and what type of actor he really wanted to be.

CHAPTER FOUR

GETTING THE JOB DONE

'I just want to make sure that I stay
working hard. I think I will. I hope I will.'
CHRIS PRATT, ON BEING AN ACTOR
FOR HIRE – GQ

By the time Chris had returned to LA in 2006, he had gained plenty of on-the-job experience but had had very little formal training. He had drifted into most of the acting jobs he'd landed so far, never having set his mind on snagging a particular role or having had to fight to keep on working. In the end, it was this more instinctive, and some might say haphazard, approach to his acting career which saw his CV begin to fill up with a wide variety of roles and take on the somewhat schizophrenic appearance it has today.

While being tied to a long-running television show may limit the amount of extracurricular projects an actor can pursue, in 2004 he managed to secure a supporting role in the film *Strangers with Candy*, completing filming during an extended break in his *Everwood* shooting schedule. The movie was a big-screen adaptation of the comedy series of the same name, which aired for three seasons on *Comedy Central* between 1999 and 2000. The TV show had featured future *Daily Show* and *Colbert Report* stalwart Stephen Colbert, Amy Sedaris (comedienne and sister of bestselling author and humorist David), alongside actor/writer Paul Dinello. They'd all had a hand in the show's creation, alongside improv specialist Mitch Rouse, and while the show enjoyed an auspicious beginning, it had failed to grow beyond the cult status that was practically hotwired into its DNA.

The series told the story of Jerri Blank (played by Amy Sedaris), a runaway rich girl turned 'junkie whore', who describes herself in each of the opening titles as 'a boozer, a user and a loser.' After several long spells in prison, she decides to reform and re-enter her life at the point she left it – returning to her old high school as a forty-six-year-old freshman. Each of the thirty episodes acted as a spoof morality tale (verging on immorality tale), inspired by a series of 'scare you straight' type public-information films aimed at high-school students and frequently shown in the US during the 1970s and 1980s. The film was a loose prequel to the series, following the same premise, with Sedaris, Colbert and Dinello reprising their roles as Jerri Blank and school-teachers Charles Noblet and Geoffrey Jellineck, respectively. With his teen-idol good looks and shaggy blond hair, Chris was perfect casting for the high-school football star Brason, who was soon to become the inappropriate object of desire for Sedaris's 'banged up too long', over-sexed heroine.

While it's a familiar 'High School Jock' role for Chris – which, at first glance, may not seem a million miles away from his *Everwood* character – the backdrop couldn't be more different. Although both series aimed to highlight everyday issues and moral problems, their approaches were decidedly different. While no one in *Everwood* ever came to the conclusion that 'violence really isn't the only way to resolve a conflict but it's the only way to win it', or ruled that being bulimic was a 'great way to get attention', it could be said the characters within the world of *Strangers with Candy* had a somewhat unique moral code and a slightly skewed outlook on life.

It remains unclear why, almost four years after the series ended its run on *Comedy Central*, the creative talent involved with making the original show felt the moment was right to unleash a *Strangers with Candy* movie on the unsuspecting world. The concept of creating outrageous comic caricatures like Jerri Blank and placing them among a (relatively) normal cast of supporting characters would prove hugely influential to the likes of Sacha Baron Cohen – whose comic alter-egos Ali G, Borat and Bruno existed in a recognisably familiar world – or in similarly absurd and cult-ish comedy shows such as *Arrested Development*. In real terms, while *Strangers* undoubtedly had its admirers, it never really translated beyond its relatively small cult audience. Luckily, that small but ardent fan-base included some very notable actors and comedians. This, coupled with the highly respected credentials of the film's co-creators, managed to attract a strong – and sometimes unexpected – supporting cast. Filling small but pivotal roles, the cast included Allison

Janney (during her *West Wing* heyday), respected British actor Ian Holm, Hollywood power-couple Sarah Jessica Parker and Matthew Broderick, as well as the late Philip Seymour Hoffman, delivering a broadly comedic turn in the same year he would pick up the 'Actor in a Leading Role' Oscar for his career-defining performance in *Capote*.

While it was obvious no one would be picking up an Oscar for their work on *Strangers with Candy*, the film succeeds as a riotous comedy spoof. Largely bypassing the gross-out humour that, in the era of The Wayans and Farrelly brothers, had become synonymous with the genre, *Strangers* manages to deliver enough genuinely funny moments, sharply satirising its intended targets and pushing some of its actors to the furthest extremes of caricature in their performances. Chris, however, plays it straight. And amid the madness and deliberately OTT performances from the main cast is all the funnier for it. Showing an early flair for the deadpan delivery he would later master as Andy Dwyer in *Parks and Recreation*, he even manages to maintain a straight face during a song-and-dance number, dressed from head to toe in a skin-tight, silver and black catsuit.

If the arrival of a *Strangers with Candy* movie seemed tardy on its completion in 2004, the selling of distribution rights and legal clearance wrangles only served to delay the film's release even longer. It was two years later, in June 2006, when it finally hit theatres in New York. Shortly afterwards, it had a limited run, screening at around a hundred cinemas across the US. From an estimated $3.5 million budget, the film earned around $2 million. This considerable loss may be largely responsible for shutting down Amy Sedaris's movie career and sending her back to television, where she appeared on shows such as *Raising Hope* and *30 Rock* and still has a recurring guest-star role on CBS's *The Good Wife*.

Aside from making one other TV movie – *Path of Destruction* – in 2005, Chris seemed content to avoid taking on any extra work during his *Everwood* hiatus periods. When shooting stopped for three months or so between seasons, he was most likely be found enjoying everything the Utah countryside had to offer, on camping expeditions with girlfriend Emily, or hunting with a bunch of his old Lake Stevens pals. This seemingly idyllic lifestyle would soon come to an end with *Everwood*'s cancellation in 2006, forcing him to contemplate a return to the decidedly less relaxing hustle of LA and the realisation that he was more or less back where he'd started in 2000. In the short time he had before leaving Utah, he managed to rustle up a small part in the movie *Wieners*, which was shooting on locations surrounding Salt Lake City. Although the finished product failed to live up to the early promise shown in the script, ending up as little more than a series of slapstick gags and sexual innuendos, it did give him the chance to hang out on location with the film's star, *Saturday Night Live* veteran Kenan Thompson.

On arrival back in LA, Chris's short stint on *The O.C.* may have helped him acclimatise and readjust but the next year or so was something of an eye-opener. His seemingly charmed life as a much-loved character on a long-running television show was over and he was forced to deal with some of the harsher realities of life as a struggling young actor.

To add to his troubles, his relationship with Emily would grind to a halt at the end of 2006, after nearly two years of fairly intense dating. Chris had just visited her on the New Mexico set of her first post-*Everwood* movie, *Carriers*, and things had seemed fine. In an interview with *TV Guide*'s Michael Auisello, conducted while driving around the location, he was asked if there were wedding bells in the future. He joked, 'I think Emily and I are very much in love and often people who are very much in love get married,' then added, 'But we're both still young so who knows.' However, it would seem that marriage was not on the cards after all and soon after Emily's return from New Mexico, the couple split. It seemed like outside the protective bubble of living and working together on *Everwood*'s Utah set, the couple had struggled to juggle their increasingly busy careers and conflicting travel schedules and had trouble keeping their relationship on track.

Emily would go on to forge an even stronger working relationship with Greg Berlanti, joining the cast of *Brothers & Sisters*, his first project under his new deal with Touchstone and the ABC Network, before taking the lead in ABC's *Revenge*, which finished airing its fourth season in May 2015. She further explored her penchant for dating onscreen co-stars, again hooking up with the actor who played her onscreen brother in *Brothers & Sisters*, Dave Annable, before a brief fling with Brit actor Joseph Morgan, her co-star in the TV mini-series adaptation of *Ben-Hur*. Emily then met her current boyfriend, Josh Bowman, on the set of *Revenge*, where he plays Daniel Grayson, her on/off love interest on the show.

Alone and back in LA, Chris now faced the daunting prospect of re-entering the demoralising cycle of attending countless auditions and learning how to deal with the inevitable rejection which followed. While the rejection itself was something he had come to terms with long ago, he became increasingly infuriated by the majority of casting agents' and directors' inabilities to see past his physical appearance and the work he'd done previously. Their willingness to pigeon-hole him as 'The Football Player', 'The High School Jock' or 'The Frat Boy' saw him cast in several comedies but overlooked for more serious and dramatic roles. While he was happy these roles were taking full advantage of his undoubtedly sharp comic abilities, Chris couldn't ignore the nagging feeling that he was capable of more. He was a confident young man and a certainty about the level of gravitas he could deliver had begun to filter through into his acting choices. Perhaps if he was guilty of anything at this point, it was trying to run before he could walk.

Soon he found a coping strategy to deal with any potential disappointment. Vowing not to get too stressed about the prospect of winning any particular part, he described his thought process to the *Huffington Post*. 'You don't want to get too excited as an actor,' he stated, 'because it's happened before where I'm auditioning for something and I go in and I kill it and I know it's mine. And I get excited and I start imagining what it's going to be like to be on set and to be doing this thing.' He then revealed the disappointment and typical internal dialogue that took place in his head on his eventual rejection. 'They're like, "Oh, they went in a different direction." And I'm like, "You have to be kidding me! Everything was so lined up for this to be mine." And I'm heartbroken.'

Most actors are, understandably, wary about revealing the parts they didn't get. This might simply be to appear respectful to those who ended up playing those roles or to downplay their own personal failure, but during this period, Chris admits he auditioned for two of the most iconic characters in recent movie history – Captain James T. Kirk in J. J. Abrams' *Star Trek* reboot and Jake Sully in James Cameron's groundbreaking 3D epic, *Avatar*. His failure to land either of these roles would surely have been a bitter blow to him at the time and one that highlighted the problem he faced on a worryingly regular basis.

Obviously, both films went on to be hugely popular, with the successful relaunch of the *Star Trek* franchise acting as undeniable proof that Disney had found a safe pair of hands to take up the reins on their proposed *Star Wars* sequels and, half a decade after its release, *Avatar* still holds its position as the highest-grossing movie of all time. In turn, these films would help launch long and successful careers for both Chris Pine and Sam Worthington respectively, but, in retrospect, and in light of Chris's recent success, it's easy to imagine either of these films with a 'Starring Chris Pratt' credit. Chris had lost out on both occasions to similarly untested young actors – Pine and Worthington were far from the household names they are today – leading him to believe the problem was rooted in something other than his apparent inexperience. He concluded that it had a lot more to do with the blinkered perception of himself as 'an actor who only does comedy' and the fear that an audience would not accept him in a primarily dramatic role.

Chris recalled the *Avatar* audition as a particularly crushing experience and one that would help shape the course of his future acting choices. 'They said they want somebody that has "that thing", that "It factor",' he told *Entertainment Weekly*. 'I walked into that room knowing that I did not have "that thing" and I walked out thinking I would never have "that thing", probably.' These days it seems that he is practically overflowing with 'that thing' and has 'It factor' to spare. Perhaps, at this early stage in his career, his relative inexperience and lack of any discernible acting ambitions – outside earning enough money to pay the bills – signalled a lack of hunger to succeed or gave him less of an edge when it came to auditioning for more 'heavyweight' roles. Whatever the reason, it triggered a fairly dramatic rethink in terms of the type of roles he was actively pursuing. He explained further to *Entertainment Weekly*, 'I figured, I'll find a way to make money and if that means I'm playing character roles, that's terrific. People have to work.' With typical candour he then added, 'I just don't want it to be at a fucking restaurant.'

Thus, Chris seems to have taken a step back. He decided to largely forgo auditioning for the flashier lead parts, opting instead to appear in a series of secondary and supporting roles. While some of these would place him back in the Frat Boy/Football Jock territory he'd initially struggled to escape, it seemed there was logical reasoning behind this decision. If casting agents and directors insisted on typecasting him in these parts, he was determined he would make them as, if not more, engaging than the characters further up the cast list. As he had done with Bright in *Everwood* and Che in *The O.C.*, Chris would make sure his own personality shone through during every second he was on screen. He would make every line count and steal virtually every scene he was given in every film.

With his next project, *Take Me Home Tonight*, Chris moved even closer to finding the type of actor he wanted to be and, along the way, he met the girl of his dreams, the future Mrs Pratt and mother of his first child: all wrapped up in the neat package of movie star Anna Faris.

CHAPTER FIVE

KIDS IN AMERICA

*'I knew I wanted to marry her pretty soon after I met her.
It took a while for me to admit it, because it would have
been crazy to be like, "I want to marry you" the first
day I met her. But I could have!'*
CHRIS PRATT, ON EXPERIENCING LOVE AT FIRST SIGHT
WITH ANNA FARIS – *CELEBRITY CAFE*

Take Me Home Tonight was conceived as an affectionate love letter to the 1980s. An attempt to capture the spirit of the era in the same way John Hughes had done with the likes of *The Breakfast Club* and *Pretty in Pink*, while also mirroring the somewhat more realistic portrait employed in Cameron Crowe's *Say Anything...* With this combination, the filmmakers hoped to celebrate rather than ridicule the period and earn the same positive response, critically and commercially, that Crowe's film had enjoyed on its initial release in 1988. Topher Grace, the former *That '70s Show* actor and one of his old high-school friends, Gordon Kaywin, conceived the story – loosely based on their own experiences after high school – as a comedy-drama that focused on the events of one night in the late 1980s. Grace told *Collider*, 'We wanted to make sure we didn't make fun of anything. We didn't have those giant brick cell phones and say, "How crazy is... this!?" Because no one in the eighties said, "How crazy is Michael Jackson with one glove? What's that all about?"' As Grace and Kaywin's idea began to take shape, they noted that previous generations all had a treasured film, which looked back a couple of decades and reflected something more than simple nostalgia back at the audience. But they couldn't think of one for their generation. Surely the time was right for a movie set in the 1980s, which might resonate with the younger cinema audience but would also ring true for those who actually grew up in the decade?

Grace recalled, 'We thought, "They haven't done that movie for this generation of moviegoers." They did one in the 70s about the 50s, *American Graffiti*. They did one in the 90s about the 70s, Richard Linklater's *Dazed and Confused*.' He added, 'I think people think *American Graffiti* came out in the 50s. I think a lot of people think *Dazed and Confused* came out in the 70s.' Why not produce a movie that felt like it was actually made in the 1980s, rather than one swamped in revisionist nostalgia or a parody that merely served to mock the clichés of the period? This basic idea was handed to screenwriting couple Jackie and Jeff Filgo, with whom Grace had previously worked on *That '70s Show*. The script they delivered plays with many of the John Hughes/1980s movie-genre conventions, never straying too far from the traditional themes of unrequited love, coming-of-age lessons and outsider angst. But its strength lay in its ability to turn most of those clichés on their head, or pull the rug from under them just at the moment when the audience think they know what's about to happen. What it delivered was a raunchy comedy, with a twist of romance and a dash of wish fulfilment, which wasn't afraid to pull a few punches.

Grace hoped to build a truly memorable ensemble cast from a group of his contemporaries. Thus, he took the lead role of Matt Franklin – a former high-school loser and now MIT graduate, who kills time at his dead-end job at the local video store fantasising about his former high-school crush, Tori Frederking – the Prom Queen he was never brave enough to ask on a date, played by Australian newcomer Teresa Palmer. The role of his best friend, Barry, went to the Tony Award-winning stage actor Dan Fogler, with the rest of the cast rounded out by stand-up comedian Demetri Martin as an ex-school friend of Matt's, Anna Faris as Matt's sister Wendy, with Chris taking the role of her douche boyfriend, Kyle. Grace told *Redblog*, 'You read those books about *Saturday Night Live* in the 70s, where someone's in a bar and Belushi's hanging out, then Bill Murray comes in and Gilda Radner shows up. I'd think, "Man, I wish I'd lived in that moment."' He elaborated on that idea, telling *Vulture*, 'I wanted to work with and find a new Brat Pack. I love that I've worked with big movie stars. It is the best way to learn how to be an actor. But I also really wanted to work with my peer group while it was in bloom.'

The idea of trying to capture that type of lightning in a bottle – catching a like-minded group of young actors just on the verge of stardom – is surely every casting director's dream, but equally important to Grace was the thought of building a group of believable friends with real onscreen chemistry. 'We fashioned this movie after *Dazed and Confused*,' he confessed to *Redblog*, '[That movie] has Ben Affleck and Matthew McConaughey and Parker Posey, and you know they were all hanging out somewhere together. I felt that way on our film hanging out with Dan, Demetri, Anna and Chris.'

The cast assembled in late 2006, while shooting took place in early 2007, with several locations in Phoenix, Arizona standing in for the Los Angeles and Beverly Hills setting. Grace was right and the cast bonded quickly, bringing a positive and creative atmosphere to the set. Joining an ensemble cast such as this was hardly anything new for Chris and it was an environment in which he thrived. He had instantly bonded with his *Everwood* cast-mates and effortlessly infiltrated the tight-knit cliques at *The O.C.*, and it would seem he had learned that the real trick was to just be his good-natured, easy-going self around the set. His infectious personality and uncanny ability to see the funny side of everything helped the cast gel quickly. Grace confirmed that there was a particularly relaxed and collaborative atmosphere on set, telling *Collider*, 'Everyone learned from everyone ... I think you make each other better by sharing some of your secrets with each other about acting and everyone made everyone stronger in this.'

Anna Faris was already a successful actress when she signed on for *Take Me Home Tonight*. She'd been the breakout star from *Scary Movie*, the horror parody that grossed over $250 million dollars in 2000, and she would stick with the franchise through three equally successful sequels. By 2006 she'd taken the lead in several other comedies, as well as giving notable dramatic performances in *Lost in Translation* and *Brokeback Mountain*. Chris had already formed a fairly good first impression of Anna and was obviously excited to meet her, telling the *Daily Mirror* in 2014, 'I really fancied her in *Scary Movie* – she's hilarious in that.' Playing a newly engaged couple in the film, the pair shared most of their screen-time together and it would appear from the onscreen chemistry that they hit it off immediately. Although Anna was already married at the time, to actor Ben Indra, it's obvious the pair had made an instant connection. After three years of marriage, Anna's career was taking off, just as her husband's was beginning to flounder. She told *Marie Claire*, 'That kind of destroyed my marriage,' before adding, 'The divide became too great.' By the time shooting had wrapped on *Take Me Home Tonight*, she was already in the process of separating from Indra and she filed for divorce in early 2007.

While it would appear that Chris and Anna's relationship remained strictly professional and that they didn't actually get together while making *Take Me Home Tonight*, there is little doubt that the time they spent together on set helped form a solid foundation onto which their future relationship was built. Anna was definitely not looking to jump straight back into a serious relationship. While she insists she actually went a bit wild straight after her divorce, the full extent of her rebellion seems to have involved getting a post-divorce boob job and drinking a little too much every now and then. Rather than a symptom of her going off the rails, she simply reasoned, 'Why not?' and considered it a celebration of her newfound independence – both financially and in terms of her relationship status.

Apparently there was something in the air on the *Take Me Home Tonight* set and the obvious chemistry between the main cast on screen transferred to some lasting off-screen friendships. It was in this arena, if not in any other, that the film could be seen as a complete success. Several years later, Grace would tell *Collider*, 'We all still hang out ... that's why you want to do one of these,' before elaborating, '[To] not only work with people who are great – you can tell they are on the way to stardom and greatness – but also you want to know them personally.'

While it seems that everyone involved in the project was working towards the same goal – creating a film immersed in the same world as John Hughes' biggest successes, albeit with a slightly more adult twist – ultimately, the movie misses most of its intended targets, never quite managing to hit its narrative stride or create a truly engaging group of characters. Powered by the same type of wish fulfilment that saw Ferris Bueller steal the car, crash the parade and lead a rousing chorus of *Twist and Shout*, while inevitably winning the girl of his dreams, *Take Me Home Tonight* could be seen as a reality check; the wake-up call that should probably have followed that particular 'Day Off'. But while the character of Matt Franklin has a certain underdog charm, he's no Ferris Bueller, and Grace lacks much of the 'lovable rogue' quality that Matthew Broderick exuded in the role that made him a star. In the few scenes when the obvious camaraderie among the key cast members is reflected in the action taking place on screen, the film is momentarily elevated to something more interesting than just another 'One Wild Night Can Change Everything', coming-of-age story. However, finding a consistent tone proves elusive as *Take Me Home Tonight* juggles post-teen angst and bawdy laughs with a more nuanced approach to the period setting. It was this attention to detail and determination to paint an accurate picture of the time that would prove to be problematic for the filmmakers when the time came to screen the movie for preview audiences and the financial backers, Universal Pictures.

'It tested really well,' Grace explained to *MTV*. 'It's an audience film. It's not drama but there was a real hesitation because there is so much cocaine in it and our feeling at the time was, "You can't do a movie about Prohibition without alcohol and you really can't do a movie about partying in the eighties, at the age these kids are, without showing cocaine."' But the executives at Universal had doubts about showing so much casual drug use in what was predominately a youth-targeted comedy. Universal were (and still are) a huge multinational, multimedia organisation with a lot to lose if the film triggered a backlash and their initial reaction was, 'We don't know if this is right for us.'

Grace was sympathetic towards the company's doubts, telling *Redblog*, 'I get it. They're owned by a big corporation and a bunch of kids doing coke in a movie is kind of a tough thing to swallow.' In a different kind of film, things might have gone another way but no one wanted the project to be hindered with the dreaded R (Restricted) rating, ruling out a large proportion of the movie's potential audience and box-office poison for what was otherwise a fairly light-hearted, feel-good comedy. Attempts were made to salvage it, including discussions about removing the majority of scenes involving drug use from the film. While this might have soothed Universal, the filmmakers worried that they would be being dishonest, throwing away a vital element of truthful grit and effectively neutering the project. Without the grain of uncomfortable reality, it lacked substance and lost most of its edge.

With no compromise reached, *Take Me Home Tonight* was sidelined by Universal. While this delay wasn't necessarily unusual, things went from bad to worse when Sony Pictures released the similarly themed *Superbad* in the summer of 2007. With a present-day setting and an arguably higher-profile ensemble cast – Jonah Hill, Seth Rogen, Michael Cera and Emma Stone – *Superbad* was a much easier concept to sell to an audience. A straightforward 'R'-rated comedy, it revelled in its unashamedly adult content and, unlike *Take Me Home Tonight*, was unhampered by any desire to remain grounded in reality or pay homage to a genre that probably meant very little to anyone under the age of thirty.

As a consequence, *Take Me Home Tonight* remained 'on the shelf' for nearly four years, only securing a release in 2011 when another production company, Relativity Media, acquired the film from Universal for $10 million. During the long period of limbo, veteran film producers Ron Howard and Brian Grazer had come onboard, guiding the filmmakers and helping them turn the movie into a viable commercial project. Howard and Grazer acted as the perfect intermediaries; their company, Imagine Entertainment, already had a long and extremely successful co-production history with Universal and they were determined to help the filmmakers realise their original vision for the film and ensure *Take Me Home Tonight* reached American theatres intact. As Grace would later tell *Vulture,* when the time came to finally promote the movie, 'What [Howard and Grazer] said is, the movie is not going to become dated – it's already entirely dated. So let's find the studio that is going to embrace this for exactly what it is.' A deal was struck with Relativity Media and at the beginning of 2011, preparations were well underway for the release of the film.

Grace was nervous about which version would see the light of day, expressing his concerns to *Collider*: 'Normally, when something's held, it's cut and you're at the fifth version of a cut of someone's idea.' Ultimately, his fears proved unfounded and Relativity's CEO, Ryan Kavanaugh, proved to be a valuable ally. 'He understood that you can't make a movie like *Dazed and Confused* if it doesn't have pot in it. You just can't; it doesn't ring true. It's not the real thing we talk about,' Grace explained to *MTV*, before adding, 'He and his team embraced it and that's the film we got to see.' It had been an extremely rocky road and, with so much time having passed, it would have been understandable if the majority of the filmmakers and cast had moved on and were unable (or unwilling) to come back and help promote the film. For Grace, it was a no-brainer: 'We're so happy with the film. It's creatively what we wanted and it's exactly the opposite of the normal situation where stuff gets cut. [For this movie,] it was the opposite: We got to put stuff back in.'

Having survived in its original cut, the US release date was set for 4 March 2011. Despite being armed with a perfectly pitched marketing campaign – including a promo video for Atomic Tom's cover of The Human League's 'Don't You Want Me' from the original soundtrack, which saw Grace reunite with Teresa Palmer, Dan Fogler and Anna Faris to re-enact scenes from dozens of iconic 1980s movies, as well as giving him an opportunity to air his uncanny Michael J. Fox impersonation – *Take Me Home Tonight* sank without a trace at the US box office. Pulling in a fairly meagre $3.5 million dollars in its opening weekend, the film's total box-office gross was just shy of $7 million dollars. Set against a budget of $19 million, it was seen as a commercial disaster. Critically, the movie didn't fare much better, with the *Daily Mail* describing it as a 'Laugh-free U.S. comedy', before branding it, 'relentlessly unappealing' and the *New York Post* reviewer dismissing it as 'a tediously unfunny comedy'. Elsewhere, there was a glimmer of hope as Mary Pols at *Time Magazine* called the film 'an amiable diversion, kept afloat by some comic moments of the raunchy, silly variety,' and the *Minneapolis Star Tribune* seemed to get the point entirely, giving it a three out of four-star review and stating, '*Take Me Home Tonight* is a time capsule from the heyday of John Hughes and Cameron Crowe, a time when comedies allowed their characters to be human as well as humorous.' At least a couple of critics, if not the cinema audiences of America, had grasped the original intentions.

Despite many of the key players returning for interviews and publicity, a few of the main cast, including Chris, were unable to get on board for the eventual release. In reality, a lot had happened to the *Take Me Home Tonight* cast since the film had wrapped in early 2007. Grace's idea of a new 'Brat Pack' wasn't too far off the mark, with virtually everyone involved in the project moving up a few steps on the Hollywood pecking order. Grace had featured in *Valentine's Day* and *Spider-Man 3*, while Teresa Palmer had starred opposite Adam Sandler and Nicolas Cage, in *Bedtime Stories* and *The Sorcerer's Apprentice* respectively, and taken a lead role in the big-screen adaptation of the young-adult novel, *I Am Number Four*. Demetri Martin had become one of America's best stand-up comedians, producing several critically acclaimed TV specials, and Dan Fogler had become one of the most prolific voiceover artists in Hollywood, having contributed to *Horton Hears a Who!* and *Kung Fu Panda*, as well as starring in several well-received independent films. But perhaps the biggest change in circumstances between where they started out in 2007 and where they were in 2011 was for Chris Pratt and Anna Faris. Not only had both seen their professional careers reach new heights but they were now a married couple, having got engaged two years earlier, finally getting around to tying the knot in the summer of 2009.

CHAPTER SIX

WAITING FOR A GIRL LIKE YOU

'She's not just hired to play the hot girl ... I mean obviously she's a hottie, but she gets to put herself in these roles that typically only guys play.'
CHRIS PRATT, ON WHAT SETS ANNA FARIS APART FROM HER CONTEMPORARIES – *ENTERTAINMENT WEEKLY*

Back in 2007, while there had been an obvious instant and mutual attraction between Chris and Anna, their actual romance was an unconventional, slow-burner affair. With Anna in the process of separating from her husband – which, from the outside at least, appeared to be fairly complicated and protracted – they had become friends rather than lovers and had grown closer over a relatively long period of time.

Chris had become very close to Anna during the filming of *Take Me Home Tonight*. He had obviously been a shoulder to cry on and a great source of comfort for her during a very difficult time and, most importantly, he knew how to make her laugh. The couple's friendship continued to blossom during the six months or so immediately after filming, with Anna going as far as describing herself as Chris's 'wing-man'. But with his status as 'the former star of *Everwood*', she recalled that he really didn't need her help when it came to meeting women. They were so incredibly relaxed in each other's company that Chris admitted he would leave his porn magazines out in the open when Anna came to visit and that they would also discuss, often in great detail, his sexual encounters as a young, single guy living in LA. It would seem as though Chris's thought process was, 'She's not interested in settling down again, so there is no point trying to make a move on her, right?' This unconventional start to their relationship has all the hallmarks of a classic romantic comedy plot and the eventual outcome of 'When Chris Met Anna' goes a long way towards proving the theory that men and woman really do struggle to be 'just friends' for any length of time. As Harry – Billy Crystal's character in *When Harry Met Sally* – so rightly asserted, 'The sex part always gets in the way.'

Things began to change as soon as Anna decided she wanted to file for divorce. She had become the main breadwinner during her marriage to Ben Indra and, as such, had elected to pay her ex the sum of $900,000, as well as handing over property and a share of her acting royalties, as part of the settlement. While this payout may not have been too much of a financial blow for Anna – she had, after all, just landed her first proper lead role, as Shelley Darlington in *The House Bunny* – she must have felt that her newfound (and expensive) freedom was something to be savoured. Her independence was hard-fought and she decided to enjoy single life to the full. Admittedly, this rebellious streak was short-lived but she embraced the wild-child divorcee lifestyle whole-heartedly. Anna told *Entertainment Weekly*, 'I wore this grubby Garfield T-shirt and these baggy jeans all the time. Personal hygiene? Nah.' She continued, 'I was drunk all the time ... Next thing you know, I'm living in an apartment with potato chips and mustard and tons of beer.' Anna would hit the bars with or without her girlfriends and, unsuccessfully, tried to pick up guys. She recalled, 'Maybe I was giving off a weirdly aggressive vibe, which was why I couldn't get anyone to have sex with me.' If a guy said no, she'd simply ask him what his friends were like. Anna admits, 'It was a selfish time in my life,' but remembers being somewhat conflicted, adding that she also felt 'strangely liberated' and 'weirdly empowered'.

Chris's friendship was largely responsible for bringing Anna out of her post-divorce spiral and their relationship changed as soon as she called to tell him she was finally going to divorce her husband. At that very moment, Chris knew he would marry Anna sooner or later. When the couple did eventually start dating in early 2008, it seemed they were fated to be together. They were shocked to find out they had grown up in neighbouring towns in Washington State, living less than twenty minutes away from each other throughout most of their teenage years. Both were undeniably 'outdoorsy' types, enjoying long hiking treks, sleeping outdoors on camping trips and sharing a deep-rooted love of animals and natural history. In an interview with the *New Yorker*, Anna describes being shown around Chris's apartment for the first time, bursting into tears of joy after discovering a giant African stick insect framed on the wall – she, too, was an avid collector of preserved bugs – and once this unusual connection was made, it would seem there was no looking back.

From the outside, there's no denying that Chris and Anna appear to have been virtually made for each other, almost freakishly compatible and well-matched in terms of temperament and outlook on life, as well as in their shared career. Their palpable relief at each having found their respective 'other half' is refreshing and almost uniquely pure at a time when it's all too easy to be cynical about real romance in Hollywood. During their early courtship, the couple were largely untroubled by the glare of intrusive media speculation but, as their relationship developed and their status as one of Hollywood's 'Golden Couples' grew, they have been surprisingly uninhibited and candid when it comes to looking back. In later years, they would freely discuss their initial attraction, the unlikely equilibrium of their relationship and the difficulties involved in maintaining a relationship when working in the movie industry. They would also spend a fair amount of time complimenting the other's talents and many good points.

In 2011 Chris told *Interview*, 'I'm truly pinching myself,' before gushing, 'I'm like, "Oh my God, my wife is really cool, really hot, and really funny, oh my God." What happened?' and then asking, presumably with a smile, 'I just want to know what terrible things happened in my previous life that gave me the fortune to have this happen.' In another interview, with *GQ* magazine in the following year, he was seemingly no further forward in figuring out the secret of his good luck, proclaiming, 'I married way out of my pay grade. I have no idea how that happened,' before saying, 'I'm not going to question it too much. I don't know what it is, man. I guess chicks dig love handles or something.'

It would seem the couple's relationship was built on a lot more than Anna's love for men of the slightly more rotund variety. It's easy to see that they shared something much more profound, built on a mutual respect and a deep-rooted understanding of the other's strengths and weaknesses. Chris had eventually moved into the home Anna once shared with Ben Indra – a relatively modest 1950s ranch-style house in the Nichols Canyon area of the Hollywood Hills. It was reported Anna and her ex-husband had previously attempted to sell the property, putting the single storey, three-bedroom house on the market for close to $2 million during their separation. But in the end, Anna had acquired the house as part of the divorce settlement and decided to stay put. Of course, when you describe a house in the Hollywood Hills as 'relatively modest', you have to take into account the many other, far more elaborate houses in the surrounding area and, while Chris and Anna's new home was far from being a mansion, it was hardly a two-up, two-down either.

Situated in a quiet and secluded cul-de-sac, it was as private as any home could be on the 'Hollywood Star Map' tourist circuit and it wasn't long before they turned their first home together as a couple into a bug collector's paradise. Chris told the *Daily Mirror*, 'We have a lot of fossils, dead bugs, preserved animals, taxidermy, things like that,' before confirming that combining his stockpile of treasures with

Anna's similarly exotic menagerie had its drawbacks, stating, 'Our house is going to look like the Natural History Museum.' He went on to describe their new home's décor: 'The bugs are in glass frames, they're beautiful. She had a collection, I had a collection, we merged them on this one wall and I was like, "Wow, that looks really great."' Surely this is proof enough, if any further proof were needed, that Chris had found his perfect match in Anna.

The couple counted Jonah Hill as one of their closest neighbours and the young actor – and Chris's future *Moneyball* co-star – soon became a part of their social circle. Disinterested in the typical Hollywood party scene, Chris and Anna were determined their home would become a peaceful hideaway, a respite from the chaos and intrusion that seemed inevitable within their profession. Most of their social life as a couple was fairly domesticated, centred around entertaining friends and family at home and generally doing simple, homebody-type things, like cooking for each other and watching movies together.

The pair's early courtship appears to have flown under the radar of most celebrity-gossip websites and magazines; something which could be attributed to the couple's lifestyle, rather than a lack of interest in reporting their personal lives. But by any standards, they were not the typical Hollywood couple. Firstly, during much of their courtship, Chris wasn't nearly as famous as Anna. He had obviously been in a successful TV show and a few movies but he was hardly a household name. Anna was a much bigger star but, in real terms, even she had found fame in a relatively niche market and it would be a while before the more intrusive paparazzi-style reporters would be particularly interested in their comings and goings. Secondly, Chris and Anna had little interest in keeping themselves in the public eye. They were rarely seen leaving fashionable restaurants together or taunting paparazzi after late-night party sessions in the city. In fact, save for the necessary 'on the red carpet' shots or posing together at movie premières, they were rarely photographed together at all. In a move that might seem rather unique amid the typically publicity-hungry Hollywood set, Chris and Anna tried to live their private life, almost exclusively, in private.

Their engagement and subsequent marriage, however, was unavoidably played out in a slightly more public arena. After almost a year together, Chris decided to ask Anna to marry him. He recalled his proposal in an interview with *Entertainment Weekly*. 'I asked her, "Well, if a guy wanted to marry you, what would he do?" And she said, "Oh, if you asked me, I would say yes." And so then that kind of took the pressure off.' Almost immediately he bought a ring but waited until Anna's birthday later in the year to actually pop the question. On a romantic getaway to the place they had both grown up, in the Pacific Northwest, at a deserted restaurant in Roche Harbor, Chris took out the ring and said, 'Remember...'

These events went largely unreported by the media at the time and it was only a few months later, in February of the following year, that details of the couple's relationship started to appear in the press. By early 2009 both actors had continued to build steadily on their early successes. By climbing the celebrity pecking order as their respective careers moved on to the next level, they inevitably became more of a target for celebrity-gossip sites and the media in general. While both Anna and Chris had found sufficient interesting and profitable work, it was Anna who had truly risen to the Hollywood 'A' list. After her lead turn in *The House Bunny* had turned the movie into a genuine box-office hit, making an estimated $70 million worldwide and hitting the number-one spot in the UK and US box-office charts on its opening weekend, her career was on a roll. She subsequently carved out a fruitful, if sometimes unsatisfying, niche for herself, playing 'the dumb blonde who might not be quite as dumb as you think' in a range of big-budget comedies, such *as Observe and Report*, with Seth Rogen, and *My Super Ex-Girlfriend*, alongside Luke Wilson and Uma Thurman. She countered the disappointment she often felt about her 'Dumb Blonde' persona by choosing to appear in a few movies with a slightly more 'indie' sensibility, such as 2007's *Mama's Boy* and *Smiley Face*.

Chris, on the other hand, while maybe not achieving quite the same level of recognition as Anna, had seen his stock as a film actor raised substantially by supporting roles in a couple of high-profile movies and in joining the cast of a new television sitcom for NBC, with the promise of a six-episode, recurring guest-star role. It was this slight imbalance in their fortunes that saw their engagement announced along the lines of, '*The House Bunny* star Anna Farris is engaged to former *Everwood* actor, Chris Pratt'. While far from being a problem for the couple, the distinction between being recognised as a 'star' or simply being an 'actor' seemed to have been at the heart of Chris's career choices for some time and was shaping his CV accordingly. Since he moved to Los Angeles and his subsequent decision to stop chasing the type of leading-man roles he was frequently getting frustratingly close to but never quite reaching, he had dedicated himself to becoming as good as he could be in whatever role he was given. Thus, by the time the couple were preparing for their imminent wedding in mid-2009, he had accumulated a few interesting, if not exactly career-defining, supporting roles over the previous couple of years.

Back in 2007 he was lucky enough to be cast opposite James McAvoy and Angelina Jolie in the big-screen adaptation of J. G. Jones and Mark Millar's cult graphic-novel series *Wanted*. With a relatively big budget and plans to film in several locations around the world, this was a real change of pace for Chris. While initial shooting took place a little closer to home, in Chicago, the production then became a truly globe-trotting affair, with most of the cast and crew travelling onwards to Europe for several weeks of principle photography. While this was undoubtedly the chance of a lifetime for Chris, appearing alongside one of the biggest stars on the planet in a big-budget action movie, his appearance in the film was limited to a few scenes and amounted to little more than a cameo in the final cut. But as his new approach to work prescribed, he made every second of screen time count.

Chris played Barry, the co-worker/friend of the main character, James McAvoy's Wesley Gibson. Wesley is a desk-jockey loser whose life is turned upside down when a rogue agent, Fox (played by Angelina Jolie), from a secret society, The Fraternity, is sent to inform him of his predetermined destiny to be trained as a member of her covert team of assassins. In a voiceover early in the film, Wesley describes Barry as a 'sack of shit' and we discover very quickly that he's not exaggerating. Constantly buzzed on energy drinks, Barry is an obnoxious creep, who also just happens to be sleeping with Wesley's girlfriend. Most of Chris's scenes take place during the first half of the movie, setting up McAvoy's character as a put-upon loser and showing Barry to be just one of Wesley's many minor irritants and tormentors.

Creating Barry wasn't necessarily too much of a challenge for Chris – he was merely an extreme version of the beer-swilling jocks, douche bags and bullies he'd been playing for the last few years – but as a wholly humorous character, it gave him free rein to flex his comedy muscles. One scene shows Barry somehow managing to persuade Wesley to buy him a pack of condoms after he discovers he's misplaced his wallet. The fact that Barry had left his wallet at Wesley's apartment while he was having sex with Wesley's girlfriend – and we are in no doubt about what those new condoms are for – was all part of Barry's 'charm'.

Directed by Timur Bekmambetov, *Wanted* was the Russian filmmaker's first English-language production, following the international breakthrough of *Night Watch* in 2004 and its 2006 sequel, *Day Watch*. Both films enjoyed enormous critical and commercial success in Bekmambetov's native country, with *Night Watch* eventually out-grossing the first *Lord of the Rings* movie in Russian cinemas. A subsequent international distribution deal saw the film's worldwide box-office takings reach $32 million, which was unprecedented considering this was a subtitled fantasy-adventure movie shot in Russian. At its inception *Wanted* must have seemed like an unlikely summer blockbuster. An obscure comic-book series adapted into a $75 million Hollywood action movie – and by a relatively unknown Russian director. On top of all that, it starred an untested 'action star' whose only previous lead roles had been in a handful of decidedly less adrenalin-fuelled literary adaptations, such as *Atonement*, *The Chronicles of Narnia* and *Starter for 10*. Coming a couple of years before the release of *Salt*, the action movie that sealed Angelina Jolie's standing as a bankable lead, even her presence and past experience as an action hero wasn't enough to give the film that all-important 'must see' status. Back then, Jolie's reputation rested on two *Lara Croft* movies, both of which had been dealt a fairly harsh critical reception, and her performance as half of the titular *Mr. & Mrs. Smith* – a decent movie but one which had tarnished her reputation a little, given that the only prize she picked up for her performance in that film was Brad Pitt, who was someone else's husband at the time!

Wanted went on to become one of the surprise hits of the year, grossing in excess of $340 million at the worldwide box-office and finishing at number sixteen on *IMDB*'s year-end popularity chart. Ironically, it lagged quite a few places behind the film that held the number-five position on the very same chart – a little, female-led comedy called *The House Bunny* – but it was an important breakthrough for Chris. *Wanted* was undoubtedly the biggest, most high-profile release he had been involved with so far and this huge bump in exposure seemed to be opening all the right doors in Hollywood.

In early 2008, Chris joined the cast of *Jennifer's Body*, a spoof horror-comedy written by Diablo Cody and starring Megan Fox and Amanda Seyfried. Fresh from winning a 'Best Screenplay' Oscar for her teen-pregnancy comedy *Juno*, Cody was definitely attempting something new. Putting a feminist twist on the predominately male-dominated horror genre, with aspirations of delivering a smart and ironic comedy, *Jennifer's Body* was certainly a brave – if largely unsuccessful – experiment.

Where Chris fitted into all this was, perhaps, a little more straightforward. He was cast in a small role as a local trainee police officer, but yet again, he was being asked to deliver little more than the typical Frat Boy/Jock character he had perfected over the previous few years. Unfortunately, while the script has much of Cody's usual flare and quick-witted bite, the film itself fails to deliver enough satisfactory scares to be considered a decent horror movie and isn't quite funny enough to make it fly purely as a comedy. Panned by critics and virtually ignored by cinema audiences, it was considered a minor flop at the US box office, taking a measly $6.8 million on the opening weekend. It did, however, drum up an international box-office total that was almost double the original budget and successfully bucked the genre trend by attracting an audience of predominately young woman, with girls under twenty-five accounting for 51 per cent of the audience. While the film itself had done little for Chris, he could only hope the majority of that audience would follow him onto his next project, the female-targeting comedy *Bride Wars*.

To say the plot of this movie is flimsy and trite is hardly the point – two lifelong best friends end up as sworn enemies when they find out their dream weddings are scheduled to take place at the same venue, on the same day – it is, after all, a piece of frothy entertainment, but *Bride Wars* stands as one of the best (worst) examples of a worrying trend that had started to consume many non-'R'-rated comedies in the late 2000s – comedies which were more or less completely devoid of comedy.

Starring Kate Hudson and Anne Hathaway as the titular feuding brides, Chris was hired to play Fletcher, the fiancé of Hathaway's character, Emma. Fletcher seems like an average, slightly put-upon guy, doing his best to survive the 'tons of crazy' falling down around him in the run-up to his wedding day. Chris gives Fletcher an easy-going charm and a sweet, almost bashful sexiness. Once again, these are arguably qualities which could easily be attributed to the actor himself and proof indeed that his attempts to find elements of his own personality in every character he played were paying off. Each of his scenes, most of which he shares with Hathaway, feel almost improvised, appearing decidedly more naturalistic than the rest of the movie. One sequence, which sees him riffing on which *American Idol* judge Emma should aspire to be, feels particularly loose and unscripted, giving him a rare moment to shine and show off his natural comedic timing. While Fletcher is a slight departure from the long list of sports-obsessed, football-shirt-wearing, beer-swilling jerks that were beginning to litter his CV, he quickly reverts to type and, by dumping Emma on their wedding day, by the end of the movie Fletcher is revealed to be a controlling and insensitive creep.

Shooting took place through the summer months of 2008

– with the film using several of New York's key landmarks as a backdrop – as well as several additional days' filming in Massachusetts, split between locations in Boston and Salem. There is no denying that the movie makes the best of some of the most beautiful cityscapes in the world but, tonally, it can't quite find its groove and ends up undecided as to what it wants to be. Veering wildly from over-the-top physical comedy to saccharine-sweet sentimentality, all accompanied by a constant soundtrack of shrieking and unnecessarily vicious bitchiness, *Bride Wars* is a mess.

On its release in January 2009, *Bride Wars* received mainly negative reviews and accumulated a 10 per cent approval rating on the Rotten Tomatoes website. The *New York Times* described it as 'dopey if largely painless', before ending with, 'Die, Bridezilla, die!' *USA Today* branded the film 'absurdly sexist and mired in retro stereotypes,' while in the UK, BBC Radio 5 Live's Mark Kermode vowed to give up his job as a film critic entirely if *Bride Wars* didn't make it onto his '10 Worst Films of the Year' list. In his first *Kermode Uncut* blog post of 2010, the critic revealed that *Bride Wars* had, indeed, made his 'Bottom 10', placing at number eight, just ahead of some of 2009's biggest cinematic miss-fires, including *Marley & Me*, *Terminator: Salvation* and *Couples Retreat*.

But the film's critical mauling wasn't all doom and gloom for Chris. Despite being almost universally panned by critics, *Bride Wars* went on to become a genuine box-office hit. Pulling in more than $115 million worldwide, the movie fell just short of the US Top 50 'Highest Grossing Films of 2009' and even snagged Anne Hathaway a People's Choice Award for 'Best

Comedy Movie Actress'. Ultimately, a lot of people saw the film and Chris's profile received another welcome boost. More importantly, it was a turning point in his development as a supporting actor.

An element of his acting technique which was rapidly coming to the fore during this phase of his career, is probably best exemplified by the performance he gives in *Bride Wars*. Aside from the rapid and unlikely descent his character makes into total-douche territory towards the movie's final scenes, the overriding feeling you get while watching it is that Chris is more or less playing a slightly heightened version of himself. Amid the improbable chaos going on around him, every second on screen he seems to be projecting something wholly real and believable, somehow finding a relatable truth within his character. It was this trick of always trying to find something of his own personality or to put a recognisable piece of his own character into any given role that was beginning to bear fruit and set him apart from his contemporaries. Chris's contribution to *Bride Wars* could easily be considered one of its few highlights and while this might be considered a back-handed compliment, it wasn't a bad position for any young actor to be in. Being the best thing in a bad movie was definitely a whole lot better than being the worst thing in a good one. Unfortunately, none of this applies to the next project he signed up for.

Arriving in US cinemas in October 2009, *Deep in the Valley* would be Chris's last film to hit US theatres before the much-delayed release of *Take Me Home Tonight*. And although it was his first lead role in a full-on comedy, when it is revealed that the movie was retitled *American Hot Babes* for the UK market, expectations should be kept justifiably low. Chris was cast as Lester Watts, a slacker who earns extra cash from his liquor-store job by selling alcohol and cigarettes to under-agers, siphoning off his ill-gotten gains to feed his porn obsession. While all this sounds like fairly typical douche-bag casting for Chris, the film takes this persona to new lows. As the plot develops, Lester and his best friend Carl (played by Brendan Hines) are somehow transported, via a vintage porn-viewing booth, into an alternate universe where everyone thinks and acts as if they are starring in a porn movie. Sounds great so far? It really isn't.

With an eye on the lucrative gross-out comedy market, which had delivered huge box-office success over the previous decade for the likes of the Farrelly brothers and Adam Sandler, it's possible the script was aiming to give the likes of *Bill & Ted's Excellent Adventure* or *Weird Science* an 'R'-rated twist. Unfortunately, *Deep in the Valley* has none of the charm or goofy inventiveness that turned those movies into cult classics and rarely lifts itself above an endless parade of bodily-function jokes and juvenile smut. Within the confines of this wafer-thin plot, Chris's character's ultimate goal is to try and have sex with as many girls as possible but his desperation and haplessness jinx every opportunity he gets, landing him in countless situations where he never quite manages to get past first base with any of the sex-crazed girls. Ultimately, the only physical contact he gets amounts to little more than a series of kicks to the crotch. Chris does his best with the material he's been given but there's little scope for him to add much of his usual charm or wit. Elsewhere, the decision to use stunt casting to fill several roles with glamour models and, let's just say less-qualified actresses, has the main actors fighting a losing battle. With appearances from Denise Richards – a former Bond Girl and an ex-Mrs Charlie Sheen – as well as a brief cameo from Kim Kardashian, the film really doesn't stand a chance.

Putting *Deep in the Valley* aside – please, *please* put it aside – Chris was beginning to find his niche. By playing a slightly exaggerated version of himself – as the lovable rogue or charming best friend – it gave him the perfect platform for his own special brand of free-wheeling performance. While it may seem like he was 'just playing himself', almost fooling us with a form of 'non-acting', he was actually making something very difficult look easy. Falling somewhere between improvised comedy and playing things naturalistically, but with just the right amount of dramatic undertone, Chris was hitting the sweet spot that makes the most successful supporting actors stand out in every role they take. Think Joan Cusack in *Working Girl*, *Broadcast News* or *Addams Family Values*, Rupert Everett in *My Best Friend's Wedding* or Jack Black in virtually everything he did prior to 2003's *School of Rock*. These are the type of roles that get character actors noticed and, quite often, as in Joan Cusack's case, get them nominated for Oscars, or at least get their names at the top of a few more casting lists. Chris seemed to be finally finding his way as a more nuanced performer, moving in a direction that could easily see him fulfil his true potential as a gifted and versatile character actor. It's ironic then that, between the release of *Jennifer's Body* in September 2009 and

Take Me Home Tonight's eventual release in March 2011, he didn't appear in any movies at all. It seemed that real life had become the priority for Chris and Anna at that moment in time. Ultimately, their respective career choices towards the end of 2008 and into the beginning of 2009 suggest they had decided to concentrate on something much more important: each other.

From the outside, their relationship seems surprisingly normal. Everything about them appears considerably more stable and balanced than that of the average 'Hollywood Couple' and their marriage has the air of a perfectly worked out, equal partnership. Their obvious compatibility plays an important part in the perception of them as the ideal team. 'We laugh a lot,' Chris told the *Daily Mirror*. 'On a daily basis, she will say something that no one else could ever think of saying. She cracks me up.' But their strength comes from something altogether more unusual. Working within the same profession can be tricky for any couple and both having a successful acting career can be doubly hazardous. As Anna had already found out in her previous marriage, an inequality in terms of fame and success can easily lead to jealousy and bitterness, which can undermine any relationship but Chris and Anna had vowed to remain supportive towards each other, viewing the ups and downs of their respective acting careers as all part of the industry they were in.

'It's good that both Anna and I are in this business,' Chris told *Complex*. 'There's a mutual understanding that travelling for a job is part of the machine and the mutual respect for the priority that our work has to take, sometimes even over our relationship. We're not gonna pile any guilt onto that situation.' He attributes much of this easy collaboration to Anna's straightforward and unpretentious outlook on life in general. 'One thing I've found that's really helpful in our relationship is that [Anna's] very normal,' he told *A.V. Club*, 'She doesn't act like a big star or a comic icon or anything like that. She's really down-to-earth and sweet.' Anna was similarly complimentary about her husband, telling *People*, 'It's easy to assume he is sort of a golden retriever of a man, but he's really smart,' before adding, 'He is an incredible husband. He doesn't let fame seduce him. He's still the same dude.' The pair had worked out a system to ensure neither one felt neglected or 'left out'. Chris explained to *Complex*, 'You gotta check in. You can't just trust that everything's gonna be fine. You gotta make visits. You gotta be romantic still. You gotta make sure that your relationship is a major priority as well.'

This ability to keep each other grounded, neither of them allowing the other's success to upset the balance of their relationship, helped them retain perspective during Chris's period of transition from comedy and supporting roles to more dramatic performances and, eventually, to the leading man he is today. It would seem as though he relied on and respected Anna's professional judgement and they were constantly discussing their respective career choices. He told *A.V. Club*, 'We do talk about comedy, about movies, about our careers and possible projects, but it's not in this sort of "Oh, OK, Mr. Hollywood, let's talk about movies" kind of way. It's really nice to have someone who's intelligent and articulate to talk to about what you're doing, because it's a big part of who we both are.' He summed up Anna's contribution to ironing out any potential worries about where his career was going by saying, 'Oh, my God, it's so perfect being with someone who knows exactly what I want to do.'

This certainty and synchronicity was only growing stronger between Chris and Anna and, after months of happily wearing wedding rings they'd bought for each other, they decided it was about time they considered making it official. Although this vague notion was very much at the forefront of their minds, neither made any real move towards making the shared notion a reality.

While most celebrity weddings take months, if not years, to organise and the most basic of ceremonies requires a degree of pre-planning, it would seem that Chris and Anna had other plans, or rather they didn't really have a plan at all.

While the couple were enjoying a hard-earned vacation on the Indonesian island of Bali, both had fallen ill, suffering with severe food poisoning. Anna described the dire circumstances they found themselves in to the *Irish Independent*. '[It was] the really rough kind, you know, sharing the toilet.' While desperately trying to find something appropriately bland and comforting to eat, she made a startling discovery. 'I was looking for chicken broth on the room-service menu and saw the hotel also did weddings,' she recalled. 'While still feverish, Chris said, "Let's do it."' So the couple hastily contacted the hotel management and made arrangements to get married right away. Anna elaborated, 'So the staff found us some traditional Balinese clothes and a local priest,' adding in her typically self-deprecating style, 'We had no idea what was going on but we came back married.'

While the idea and ceremony may have been entirely spontaneous, there's little doubt that the couple knew exactly what they were doing. By 'running away' to get married, Chris and Anna had managed to avoid most of the media circus they deemed intrusive and unnecessary but which seemed to increasingly go hand in hand with their emerging celebrity couple status. So instead of a multi-million dollar event, with hundreds of guests (which no doubt would have included quite a few famous faces), they were married at a simple ceremony on a beach in Bali on 9 July 2009. It's testament to the couple's decision to remain fiercely protective of their privacy – and typical of their attempts to try and avoid the obvious pitfalls and clichés associated with 'The Hollywood Celebrity Wedding' – that there were no celebrity-gossip magazines present at the ceremony, no exclusive photographs sold to the highest bidder. It was a full month after the event, in August 2009, that *People* magazine printed a statement from Anna's agent announcing a few basic details of the couple's wedding. With that, Chris and Anna settled into the next phase of their new life together. It would be several months before either of them took any major film roles and both seemed equally content to put their movie careers on hold for the time being and concentrate on enjoying their newlywed status. Anna did a couple of less taxing voiceover roles while Chris took a moment to ponder his next move.

Despite now beginning to attract the type of small-but-interesting movie roles he preferred, Chris decided to go back to his roots and chose instead to return to television. At the start of 2009, shortly after completing work on *Deep in the*

Valley, he had been offered a small 'guest star' role in a new sitcom at US television network NBC. His character was linked to one of the show's main plotlines but was supposed to only last for the first six episodes, when he would then be written out. It looked as though Chris had taken the job merely as a stopgap in order to pull back from the broader comedy roles he was being offered and give himself some time to work out what he wanted to do next. It's ironic then that this job, more than any other, would become a real career-defining role for him, acting as the springboard that launched him onto the next level in terms of developing his acting skills and kick-starting the most rewarding chapter of his career. He was heading for Pawnee, a small (and wholly fictional) town in Indiana, and waiting for him there was a life-changing role in *Parks and Recreation*. Chris was about to make the acquaintance of Mr Andy Dwyer.

CHAPTER SEVEN

PAWNEE: FIRST IN FRIENDSHIP, FOURTH IN OBESITY

'By day, Andy Dwyer, shoeshinist. By different time of day, Andy Radical, possum tackler. By night... no job. Do whatever I want.'

CHRIS PRATT AS ANDY DWYER – *PARKS AND RECREATION* (EPISODE 24; *'THE POSSUM'*)

In January 2015, as part of the build-up to *Parks and Recreation*'s return for its seventh and final season, members of the main cast were set a challenge to sum up the show's entire run in just thirty seconds. Like several of her fellow cast members, Amy Poehler uses the time to describe the story arc of her own character, Leslie Knope, while Nick Offerman seems to merely remember his residency, as Ron Swanson, as one seven-year-long breakfast buffet. Aziz Ansari (Tom Haverford) and Aubrey Plaza (April Ludgate) have forgotten entirely which show they've been starring in and give pretty good descriptions of *Pimp My Ride* and *Battlestar Galactica*, respectively. Only Chris Pratt seems to have been really paying attention. Foregoing the opportunity to focus entirely on his own character, Andy Dwyer, he does a fairly good job of capturing the spirit and sweetness that permeates the show.

He says, 'Parks and Recreation is a thoughtful, optimistic, progressive comedy, set in the period of the early 2000s in the fictional town of Pawnee, Indiana. It represents the musings of an elite, intellectual group of writers led by Mike Schur and features the "Who's Who" of actors in comedy, not only in the core cast, but in its exceptional group of guest stars over seven glorious seasons.'

While this briefest of descriptions ignores most of the main plot details and skips the story arcs of its characters in favour of paying tribute to the many talented people who brought the show to life, it's a pretty good place to start.

Parks and Recreation was the brainchild of two very experienced comedy writer-producers, Greg Daniels and Mike Schur. Daniels' first real job was a three-week try-out as a staff writer for Saturday Night Live (SNL), which turned into a very successful three-year stint. He later made his name as part of The Simpsons' staff, joining at the beginning of the show's fifth season before moving on to another long-running animated comedy, King of the Hill. Daniels' real 'big break' came when he successfully adapted The Office, the BBC sitcom co-created and written by Ricky Gervais and Stephen Merchant. He steered the fledgling show through a turbulent birthing process, eventually turning it into a long-running hit for US TV network NBC.

Mike Schur was another SNL graduate. Although his six-year tenure didn't cross with Daniels', the pair teamed up to work on *The Office*. While he was there, Schur acted as producer, as well as writing several episodes, and even appeared in the show as a recurring character – Dwight Schrute's cousin Mose. In 2007, the newly appointed co-chairman of NBC's entertainment division, Ben Silverman, approached Daniels and Schur with the idea of writing another show for the network. He suggested an *Office* spin-off, to cash in on the success of that show and expand on the world they'd already created. After months of throwing ideas back and forth, the pair failed to find a suitable idea for a spin-off. Instead, they decided to create a brand-new show, focusing on the lives of small-town bureaucrats working in a local government office. With a vague idea for a premise and the knowledge that their show wouldn't necessarily need to feature any cast members from *The Office*, Daniels and Schur went in search of someone to play their (as yet undecided) lead character. After some speedy negotiations, Amy Poehler, another *SNL* graduate, agreed to take the lead role and soon the project began to solidify around her.

Between joining *SNL* in 2001 and her departure in 2008, Poehler had become one of the most popular cast members in the show's esteemed history. She had shown considerable skills as a comedian, as well as being a versatile and engaging character actor. Schur admitted as soon as she was on board 'all other ideas dropped away' and described her in an *Entertainment Weekly* interview as having 'so many colours and she's funny in all of them,' before adding, 'In the acting world it's called range – in the comedy world it's called delightful smorgasbord.' Amy had been looking for a project to launch her post-*SNL* career and *Parks and Recreation* – and in particular, the character of Leslie Knope – seemed the perfect fit.

Poehler fell in love with Leslie's optimism and dogged determination, telling *Entertainment Weekly*, '[Leslie's] not savvy at all, but she's smart, she's capable, she works hard. I want her so badly to succeed. I just want to pick her up like a little baby and tell her how to flirt with guys.' While the writers had settled on the idea of a low-level, female bureaucrat struggling to make her mark in local politics and cutting through copious amounts of sexism and government red tape, they also wanted to focus heavily on a central female relationship. Thus, Poehler's character, Leslie, would find an ally in Ann Perkins, a nurse who gives Leslie the idea for a project and would later offer tireless support in her political causes and, eventually, become her closest friend. Daniels and Schur already had one former *Office* cast-member in mind for this role: Rashida Jones, who had played Jim Halpert's girlfriend, Karen Filippelli, during the show's first few seasons. Jones, the daughter of legendary record producer and musician Quincy, was a very accomplished and versatile actor and her pairing with Poehler seemed to open up endless possibilities and offered even greater inspiration for the show's writing team. The only other cast member attached to the project at this point was Aziz Ansari, a talented stand-up with a flair for improvised comedy, who had been hired to play Tom Haverford, one of Leslie's co-workers.

Despite the uncertainty surrounding the finer details of the project in these early stages of development – and Daniels and Schur insisting the show would have its own identity from the outset – there was still much speculation in the media about whether it would, in fact, be an expansion of the world, situations and characters featured in *The Office*. While this proved to be untrue, the show – still only referred to as *Untitled Amy Poehler Project* – would mirror the same mock-documentary feel as *The Office*, including characters sometimes acknowledging the unseen camera crew, or directly talking to camera for intercut reaction shots and interviews.

The pilot episode, written by Daniels and Schur, was finished by mid-2008 and submitted to NBC for approval. On reading the script – and knowing that Amy Poehler was onboard as its star – NBC immediately commissioned a six-episode first season. As Poehler was pregnant with her first child when she agreed to take the role, filming of the pilot was delayed and the unusual decision was made to postpone the entire production until after she had given birth. This meant the crew had very little time to complete production if they wanted to meet the proposed early-April transmission date. It also meant they'd have to go straight into production on the rest of the season's episodes almost immediately. Schur told *NJ.com*, 'We had to work around Amy's pregnancy, but only because we got Amy to be in the show,' before adding, 'I'll take that trade-off any time.' This period of limbo allowed Daniels and Schur more time to find the rest of their main cast and crew, as well as giving them a chance to fine-tune their first batch of scripts. Schur, discussing the show's prolonged birth, admitted, 'We certainly had our share of obstacles, but they were good obstacles, if that's possible,' eventually concluding,

'In this day and age, I think every new show has a mountain to climb, and I'd never complain about the details of ours.'

Soon other key cast members were announced. These included Nick Offerman as Leslie's boss, Ron Swanson, Paul Schneider as city planner Mark Brendanawicz and Aubrey Plaza as the office's ultra-sarcastic and tirelessly indifferent intern, April Ludgate. Several smaller recurring character roles were created, including office workers Jerry Gergich and Donna Meagle – played by Jim O'Heir and Retta, respectively – as well as a proposed 'guest star' spot for the actor playing Ann Perkins' slacker boyfriend, Andy Dwyer.

When he was asked to audition for the role of Andy, Chris assumed it would be just a few weeks' work. In the script, the character seemed to have a natural exit point at the end of the six-episode story arc. Happy to take the job, he saw it as little more than a good opportunity to hang out at home in LA with some of the industry's most talented actors and comedians. 'I had a pretty good idea that by the end of the run, Rashida's character would break up with him,' he told the *A.V. Club*, 'so I thought I could just have fun with it, and that would be that. There were no guarantees.' Schur and the rest of the production team, however, had other ideas. More or less as soon as Chris had nailed his audition and had signed on as Andy, the writers started to reconsider. 'We originally conceived of Andy as a character who would fade away,' Schur told *NJ.com*, 'But Chris was so great we had to make him full-time – and we decided that right after we cast him,' concluding, 'It seemed like a waste to have him around for such a short time.'

When Andy is introduced in the pilot episode both his legs are broken and completely encased in plaster. It is revealed that he sustained his injuries after falling into an abandoned construction pit, which is located behind the house he shares with Ann. Over the course of the first few episodes, we see him take full advantage of his incapacitated state, running Ann ragged, being waited on hand and foot and generally behaving like an inconsiderate jerk. At first glance, Andy is a fairly dislikeable character but somehow Chris manages to win the audience over almost immediately.

In an interview with *Entertainment Weekly*, he described Andy as 'mentally stupid, but he's also emotionally stupid,' adding, 'IQ is just a number, and his is really low.' He went on to say, '[Andy's] a big child, mentally, but also in spirit and naiveté,' before speculating, 'That quality allows you to excuse him for some of his other behaviour.' He theorized further, in an *A.V. Club* interview, suggesting that Andy's appeal lay in the fact that he was basically helpless, saying, 'It's easy to forgive that kind of behaviour in someone when they're so emotionally vulnerable. What I draw on is that childlike innocence.' He added, 'Everything he does, he does because he's in love, and that's an admirable quality, so it makes his antics more forgivable,' before concluding, 'He can be dumb and foolish and laughable, but I try to focus in every scene on the fact that he's got a big heart.'

Chris also implied Andy's dishevelled and 'doughy' physical appearance made him somewhat less threatening. He told *A.V. Club*, 'I think if Andy were super-fit and buff, people would really hate his guts,' before adding, 'He thinks he's really handsome, but he's just this dude with a double chin and a belly, who sits around and drinks beer and eats pizza and doesn't really work toward anything.' Chris might have realised very quickly that carrying a few extra pounds was beneficial to Andy's likeability but it took a while for him to get used to it in real life. 'When the first couple of episodes came out, I looked at them and thought, "Oh, my God, Chris! Dude, hit the gym already!"' But his opinion soon changed when he saw how the audience reacted to Andy. 'I heard people laughing, and all of a sudden, I thought, this is kinda cool,' he added, 'It's almost like it's the first time I'm playing a man and not a boy.' He speculated that it was this unlikely mix of selfishness, charm and lack of ambition that seemed to drive Andy for much of the first season, telling *Interview* magazine, 'Andy is one of those kind of guys where, throughout the course of his life, the bar has been set pretty low. He doesn't put a lot of pressure on himself, and there's not a lot of pressure on him to succeed, other than being happy and playing his music.' Talking to *A.V. Club*, Chris went on to recall how his co-star, Nick Offerman, described Andy during the early stages of the character's development, 'Andy is living the American dream – the new American dream, which is do as little as possible and get as much in return as possible.'

As the series progressed, Andy became more driven. At first, it was simply his desire to make it up to Ann but later he endeavoured to make everyone around him happy. He sought acceptance by helping them do what they needed to do in whatever way he could and always with an endearing, childlike need to please others and have them love him back.

Chris told *Interview*, 'I think that what's driving Andy is that he really means well, and he wants to do well and be a good person. He's not necessarily always capable of that, but I think he does mean well and he does want to grow, so naturally he will grow.' In an *Entertainment Weekly* interview, show runner Mike Schur agreed, 'He's literally going to pull himself up from his bootstraps. And if the show lasts into the tenth season, he'll be elected mayor of Pawnee. He just will, because everyone who meets him loves him.'

It's easy to assume that Schur is, in fact, talking about Chris as much as he's describing the character of Andy. And while many might assume that the actor and Andy are more or less the same person, Chris himself finds the comparison baffling, if not a little insulting. He told *Glamour* magazine, 'It's funny because I meet people in real life and they tell me that I am Andy. I'm like, "What? This guy is a homeless person, and lives in a pit in the backyard of somebody's house,"' before adding, 'Give me some credit. I'm a married father with responsibilities!'

In fact Andy's evolution, even over the course of just a few episodes, was enormous. What had been initially planned as a secondary character, signed for only six episodes, had graduated to becoming an integral member of the cast and a vital component in the show's overall alchemy. This was fairly typical of how the creative team worked and, as Chris would later tell *A.V. Club*, 'A lot of what they planned gets thrown out the window when it becomes clear how things are developing. We're obviously working from a plan, but they're very willing to just throw everything out there, see what's working, and see who has chemistry.'

Production on *Parks and Recreation* finally got underway in mid-February 2009 after a last-minute name switch. The show's initial title, *Public Service*, was abandoned amid fears it might be seen as scoffing. As NBC Entertainment co-chairman Ben Silverman told the *New York Times*, 'We don't want to seem mean about it,' before quipping, 'Can't make fun of public service!' While the shooting delays to accommodate Poehler's pregnancy had put certain pressures on the creative team, it seemed to have little effect on the atmosphere that prevailed on-set during filming.

Although the cast were encouraged to add elements to their characters and were given a lot of freedom as to how they approached their performance during those early stages, *Parks and Recreation* was actually a very tightly scripted show, with a talented and experienced team of writers working behind the scenes. While improvisation from this particular group of actors would eventually be encouraged – and became a key element in the general tone – it was the scripts that were undoubtedly the backbone (and much of the flesh) of the show's funniest moments during that first season.

'I wouldn't say it's an improv show at all,' Chris confessed to *A.V. Club*. 'The majority of the jokes we're laughing at are the result of this brilliant think-tank of writers we have.' He would go on to describe the working methods, which were introduced from the outset and would later become increasingly important as the show progressed: 'We can do ten takes that are directly from the script, and still have time to do ten takes that go off-book, and allow it to evolve into something new.' He added, 'We have ample time to screw around with it.'

A key element that allowed this degree of experimentation was the choice to shoot with digital cameras. These were not only a lot more versatile, easier to set up and move around, they were also far more economical than shooting on film and allowed the actors greater freedom to tackle each scene with a multitude of ideas. 'With the multi-camera digital setup you're getting both sides of the scene at the same time,' Chris explained, 'That's how you end up with the occasional improv line, or a really good reaction shot that can make a scene work better.'

Very soon after meeting the rest of the cast and crew, Chris realised he had found the perfect showcase for his previously underexploited talents. Here, on the *Parks and Recreation* set, among a group of like-minded and equally fearless actors, finally he was beginning to find his acting mojo. 'I've always tried to find a funny angle on things, and 99 per cent of the time, it just doesn't work,' he explained in an *A.V. Club* interview, recalling his frustration at sometimes being pulled away from comedy towards a more grounded and emotional performance in the past, 'I always thought when I was doing more melodramatic stuff, like *Everwood*, that the directors were constantly reeling me in and stopping me being funny.' The freedom he was being given within his role as Andy was something of a revelation to him and he was determined to fully exploit it, saying, 'I've finally stumbled on a show that really caters to those strengths, and I'm happy about it.' Later, he would highlight the boundless creative energy pulling the team together in those early days, remembering it as a force that pushed the production forward and had everyone striving to fully realise the potential of the show – 'With a cast like this you see a lot of freestyling, a lot of improvisation, and they really swing with it,' he explained. 'I think everyone's going to get their moments and find their groove, it's just a matter of letting it work itself out.'

Chris had always been a very quick-witted actor. He was constantly able to throw funny lines into a scene, or twist what he'd been given into something even funnier, and he believed it was a skill he'd nurtured over a long period of time. 'I think the key to improv is life experience and having used comedy as a defence mechanism,' he told *Complex*. 'Whether it was to get out of fights or tough situations, combating bullies or whatever.' But he also admits to having a fairly unique approach to this type of off-the-cuff comedy, acknowledging any deviation within a scene must remain at least partly rooted to the script and that it never hurts to do a little preparation when you're trying to be spontaneous. 'I would say that 30 per cent of it is writing combined with lying,' he declared before explaining his secret. 'A couple of nights before you've got a scene, looking at the scene and writing yourself 10 extra jokes, and then, on the day you film, saying these jokes as if you just came up with them.'

Aside from sharpening his skills as a more nuanced comedy actor, Chris was being given the chance to fully explore the more physical aspects of his performance and it seemed there wasn't anything he wouldn't do to get a laugh. He explained to *Vulture*, 'The only way physical comedy works is if you don't see it coming. And the harder the fall, the funnier it is.' He concluded, 'You have to take some shots, and I've walked away with some bumps and bruises.'

One stunt, which involved him diving over a car to catch a football, ended in disaster. 'So I ran as hard as I could into the car; the idea was to let the car take my legs out instead of jumping,' he recalled. 'My midsection – mainly my hip – took the impact. And I did something like $1,600 damages into a Dodge Charger.' He concluded, 'It also hurt my balls for a good thirty seconds.'

If there was something to fall over, or an unexpected dive to be taken, Andy was on the case and Chris was not afraid to push it to the limit in other areas. With no concessions to his own vanity, Chris (as Andy) would often be seen in various states of undress (pixelated for TV, of course), running down the street, naked on crutches or simply trying to surprise Ann by turning up naked at her house, only to be a little embarrassed when Leslie opens the door. On that particular occasion, Chris decided to abandon the usual skin-coloured harness used to cover an actor's modesty during nude scenes and gave Amy Poehler a full-frontal surprise. This fearless attitude and lack of preciousness, coupled with the desire to get some big laughs, would eventually see him asking to be put in even more ridiculous situations. 'I kept pushing the writers to put me on rollerblades,' he revealed, 'because I think any man over 250 pounds rollerblading is instant hilarity. There's nothing funnier than a giant, grown man rollerblading. So they started doing that and it got laughs.'

The writers' room was buzzing, with everyone feeding off the creativity and positivity coming off the set. And while the cast were inspiring the writers to keep adapting the work they were doing and driving the show forward, the public's initial reaction to what they were seeing was decidedly underwhelming, to say the least. The press had got hold of some early focus-group results for the pilot and it had not tested well. *Entertainment Weekly* reported that among the many more trivial (and expected) complaints were a few that seemed a little more troubling for everyone involved in making the show. Many said it was just too similar to *The Office* in terms of its tone and the audience were becoming over-familiar with comedy without a laugh track and the mock-documentary style. Others said the pacing was too slow and the main premise was 'confusing'. Some felt all the men appeared 'sleazy' and the show lacked any 'datable' male characters while – most worrying of all – it seemed the audience was not connecting with the show's main character, Leslie Knope.

Schur, speaking to *A.V. Club*, revealed that the test audience saw Leslie as primarily 'ditzy' and that her professional ambitions made her 'oblivious' to the feelings of her co-workers. 'That was never our intention,' he insisted. 'We always thought she was really smart and good at her job. We realized we had screwed it up a little.' This disconnect was something he and the other writers had never really considered and it meant the public's perception of the character as 'an uncaring dumb blonde' was substantially removed from the bright, hopeful, generous and unwaveringly determined 'can-doer' they and Amy Poehler believed they had created.

Silverman, who had been largely responsible for the

conception, was less apologetic and considerably more bullish in his defence of the show, telling *Entertainment Weekly*, 'All the research we do around initial rough cuts is negative,' before adding, 'If you had seen the initial research on all of our and our competitors' successful shows, it tends to be like that.' The leaked test-screening results had obviously put everyone on high alert before the show even aired and despite reassurances from Daniels and Schur that the pilot they intended to broadcast had been completely re-cut several times in the meantime, the series got off to a rocky start, both in terms of critical reception and ratings.

As far as promotion was concerned, NBC had thrown everything they had at *Parks and Recreation*. For several weeks up front of transmission, countless TV spots heralded 'The new sitcom starring Amy Poehler, from the people who bring you *The Office*' and it seemed that, when the pilot finally aired on 9 April 2009, expectations were unreasonably high. Unfortunately, the audience seemed a little jaded about the concept of another show that, on the surface, appeared to be a carbon copy of *The Office*, with *Entertainment Weekly*'s Ken Tucker speaking for many when he said *Parks and Recreation* was 'a little disappointing' when directly compared to its more established rival. He did, however, end his review by saying, 'But I enjoyed all the performances, the attitude, and the atmosphere that's being created by Poehler and her collaborators,' and summed up with, 'I'm rooting for it.'

In some respects, this was as good a review as Daniels and Schur needed. They had staked a lot on simply bringing Amy Poehler to television in her own sitcom and building the perfect cast around her. The other stuff – the writing, the tone, the pacing – they knew they could work on later. While some of the points raised by the early test results had been addressed, others were too major to tackle during the show's condensed production schedule and the final headlong rush to completion and transmission, but Schur was convinced everything was fixable. 'Normally you shoot a pilot, test it a million times, tinker with it, reshoot stuff. You have six months between when you shoot it and when it airs,' he told *A.V. Club*. 'We didn't have that. We shot the pilot, then a week later we shot episode two. We treated that whole six-episode season like a pilot.' He was quick to point out that most new shows go through a period of adjustment at the beginning – none more so than *The Office* – but he also cited long-running hits like *Cheers* and *Seinfeld* as having turbulent first seasons, explaining, 'The obvious analogy is that you don't read the first eight pages of a book and then talk about whether the book works or not,' adding, 'People want so desperately in this day and age to declare something "thumbs-up" or "thumbs-down" that they declare it immediately. For a character-based comedy, it's absurd. You don't even know who these people are yet.' He went on to stress that he felt all the right ingredients were in place but they just hadn't found the right recipe yet. 'All of comedy at some level is trial-and-error, whether it's a stand-up trying jokes or a comedy show trying stories ... Until you know who the characters are, you just won't find them that funny.'

According to the US Nielsen ratings, the pilot reached 6.77 million viewers – a figure that had fallen to 4.25 million during the six-episode run of the first season. While this was slightly disappointing for everyone involved – and a huge ratings juggernaut would have been very welcome at the struggling NBC – it was not the worst start for a brand-new show, especially one that was altogether more sophisticated and understated than many of its contemporaries. The show was definitely facing some challenging obstacles, 'swimming upstream' against a current of much brasher, more obvious comedy.

Discussing the first season's lukewarm reception, Chris told *Vulture* he felt a lot of it was due to today's audiences being bombarded with predominately one type of comedy, which skewed their expectations. He asserted, 'Most of the writers in TV are from LA or New York, and those are places where people are cynical and snarky.' He added, 'It's way easier to be funny when you're being cynical and snarky.' In comparison, he felt *Parks and Recreation*'s general tone flew in the face of current trends in television comedy writing, admitting their creative team had set themselves a considerable challenge in trying to represent a much less world-weary part of the globe and project a more optimistic and uplifting attitude towards life. 'The show really captures the essence of a small town,' he stated. 'They have big hearts ... It's a good place to ground comedy right now. It makes you feel good to watch that.' Thankfully, the executives at NBC agreed with him. Despite middling ratings for season one, they reaffirmed their initial faith in the creators by confirming they would be giving *Parks and Recreation* a second chance, ordering a full season and setting an air date for September 2009.

Daniels and Schur were undoubtedly grateful to be returning

and the hiatus between seasons gave them plenty of time to 'get under the bonnet' and fine-tune some of the show's initial bugs. While they felt they had already addressed some of the problems over the course of the first six episodes, they hoped the majority of the issues would be ironed out in the writers' room. Schur told *NJ.com*, 'We're always trying to improve ... we're our own harshest critics. If the show lasts for ten years, I'd hope we get better every episode up until the series finale.' He continued by explaining that, as the preparations for season two got underway and the first few scripts had started to arrive, several changes had occurred organically. He referred specifically to the realigning of Leslie's character, which had developed a more decisive and assertive side, as well as being more quick-witted and savvy. Acknowledging these small changes in her character, he said, 'We realized that Leslie can be a little bit cooler than we had originally thought. It was a hundred little things like that.' He then went on to explain that, by making Leslie more human and relatable, they had made her much less of a figure of ridicule to her colleagues, causing a shift in tone for the entire cast. He stated, 'It's probably just the result of the writers learning how to write for Leslie, and all the characters, really,' before adding, 'There are some nice moments in the first few episodes of this season where we see the other characters being more supportive of her.'

In retrospect, Schur was keen to admit that, while treating the entire first season as a pilot had caused some initial teething problems, he stood by their decision not to lose any time in getting the show to air. He attributed a huge part of the audience's uncertainty and negativity to the fact they were merely unfamiliar with the characters, stating, 'Overall, I think we did a pretty good job of establishing the world,' before adding, 'It's a character comedy, so the episodes are naturally going to get more interesting and fun the more people know the characters.'

For Chris, moving into season two saw him experiencing a considerably bigger seismic shift, both personally and professionally. Not only had he got married to Anna during the summer hiatus, his character on the show had been elevated from 'guest star' to a full-time member of the main cast. Shortly after his first audition, Schur had hinted that there was always the possibility he could become a cast regular and, true to his word, he and the other writers began altering Andy's basic character immediately after Chris was hired. Schur told *A.V. Club* their thought process was simply, 'This guy's too funny to not use.' Once Chris was actually on set and the writers could see exactly what he was capable of, they began to write more and more funny stuff for Andy to do. 'We slowly changed that character to one that's more loveable and sweet,' Schur said, adding, '[He's] a moron and doofus, but not a bad person.'

As Andy's character developed, so too did Chris's performance skills. Over the next few seasons, Schur noted his transformation as an actor, becoming a considerably more intuitive and confident performer. Commenting on how Chris would often arrive on set with minutes to spare, having only superficially glanced at the scenes he was filming but still being able to deliver, Schur told *GQ*, 'When the cameras start rolling, he will do something that is so different and unexpected that you'll be shocked and scared. By the time you're done with the scene, he will have done it eight different ways with eight great performances, and you'll have an embarrassment of riches.'

Aside from the obvious 'prattfalls' and some perilous moments on rollerblades, Chris himself felt inspired by the changes of tone within the writing. He began adding his own subtler shades of pathos and vulnerability to his performance. To accommodate his new status within the cast, the writers moved Andy's character into the *Parks and Recreation* offices, as the resident shoe-shine. This placed Andy right in the centre of the action and opened up his character to innumerable new situations. He was now perfectly placed to form his own relationships with the other characters (outside his previous association with Ann and Leslie) and to join in with a wider variety of storylines. While being a shoe-shine was hardly taxing work – in fact, there are many scenes where he is either asleep or deliberately turning away clients – this would be Andy's first real job and he threw himself into it with typical childlike enthusiasm. The real sweetener about Andy having a regular job was that it allowed him to concentrate more on his music career and soon the exploits of his band and their ever-changing name became a long-running gag on the show.

From the outset Andy being in a rock group had been a great source of comedy, culminating in their performance in 'Rock Show', the season-one finale. Here, their song, 'The Pit', perfectly showcased their unique ability to not only 'rock really hard' but also 'inform people about a small public works project'. Chris's love of music and playing guitar had been a constant from his teenage years and he had acquired adequate skills as a musician to convincingly front his onscreen band and even compose one of their more sensitive ballads, 'Ann' – sample lyrics: 'I look in the street. I look under the car. I look very far, for Ann. She's not in the trunk. She's not in the shed. She's not in my head, oh, Ann'.

The band, as described by Chris in an *A.V. Club* interview, has 'the big fake Hootie and the Blowfish crappy rock sound,' and Andy sings, 'sort of chewing the words', in an affected, sub-Eddie Vedder growl. Chris admitted, 'I'm not a great singer, but I can do those sorts of impressions, so I was trying to cut loose and give it that sound.' While the band is most often referred to as 'Mouse Rat', it is revealed they have also gigged under numerous other names. The best of these include Department of Homeland Obscurity, Scarecrow Boat, Teddy Bear Suicide, Puppy Pendulum, Just The Tip, Everything Rhymes with Orange, Nothing Rhymes with Orange and, during the shows where they play a fully instrumental set without Andy, Rat Mouse. All the full-band songs performed by Mouse Rat were written by composer Mark Rivers, who doubles as Mouse Rat's drummer, and while the numerous band names are bad, the song titles themselves are even worse. Throughout the course of the series we have heard such gems as 'Sex Hair', 'The Pit', 'Two Birds Holding Hands' and their undisputed masterpiece '5,000 Candles in the Wind' – written after Andy was asked to come up with a memorial song that was '5,000 times better than Elton John's "Candle in the Wind".' It also became a running gag that every single Mouse

Rat song would contain one of the following lyrics: 'Spread your wings and fly' or 'You deserve to be a champion'.

As the seasons progressed, Andy's character became more complex and three-dimensional and, subsequently, Chris was given more opportunities to shine (no pun intended!). After Andy's relationship with Ann apparently ended at the end of season one, the writers initially decided to prolong his agony by having him desperately try to win her back, only to see her start new relationships, first with town planner Mark Brendanawicz, and later with season-two incomer Chris Traeger (as played by Rob Lowe). Eventually, a tiny spark of sexual tension was introduced between Andy and the office intern, April Ludgate, a relationship which blossomed steadily over the course of seasons two and three and would later become one of the main cornerstones of the show.

Aubrey Plaza was a relatively inexperienced but very talented improv and sketch comedian when she was brought to the attention of Mike Schur, who wanted to hire her despite the fact there was no specific role for her in the initial *Parks and Recreation* concept. 'We wrote the part for Aubrey,' he explained to *A.V. Club*. 'Allison Jones, who is one of the people who cast the show, called me and said, "I just met the weirdest girl I've ever met in my life. You have to meet her and put her on the show."' A quick get-together was arranged with Schur and his co-writer, Greg Daniels, and the pair outlined their plans for a potential character to Plaza. Daniels recalled in *New York* magazine that, when told they were toying with giving Leslie a dumb-blonde assistant, Plaza's immediate response was to tell them, 'Your idea is stupid.' Having made a fairly unique first impression, she went on to offer a different spin, telling *Complex*, 'We started talking casually, and I threw out a couple of ideas. "Wouldn't it be funny if they had a college intern who didn't really want to be there and was only there for the college credit?"' The idea instantly sparked the creation of April Ludgate and the role was written entirely with Plaza in mind.

After landing the part, Plaza would joke, 'I found out later that they wrote me into the pilot, and even used my name. But then I had to audition for it ... they changed the character's name from Aubrey to April so I wouldn't think that it was written for me,' adding, 'I pretty much had it in the bag, but I didn't know it.'

It turned out to be something of a landmark few days for Plaza as, during the same week she was hired to play April, she was cast in two movies: Judd Apatow's *Funny People* and Edgar Wright's *Scott Pilgrim vs. the World*. In the same way that the writers had tweaked most of the main characters in the show, so April's persona rapidly evolved and was given new depths as the full extent of Plaza's talent emerged on set. Schur told *A.V. Club*, 'After we established [her central relationships], we realized she had more range and is a more interesting performer than someone who just rolls her eyes.'

The chemistry between Chris and Aubrey was obvious from the start. They share the same deadpan sense of humour and, as the relative novices in the group, naturally gravitated towards each other on set. However, it's highly unlikely that anyone could have predicted that lovable, flabby, layabout Andy – who attacks everything with puppy-like zeal – would have anything in common with eye-rolling, deadpan April – who crushes every idea with exasperated negativity and withering, pitch-black sarcasm – but in the hands of Chris Pratt and Aubrey Plaza, it somehow worked.

At first, Andy is reticent to get involved with April due to the age gap between them – he's twenty-nine and she's only twenty – but it seems it's more likely he is struggling with the simple arithmetic involved in Tom Haverford's relationship test, which states that it's OK – and totally not douche-like – to date a girl who is 'half your age plus seven years.' As all the obstacles preventing Andy and April getting together eventually start to fall away – she turns twenty-one and Ann settles into a long-term relationship with Chris – their tentative romance swiftly develops – Andy finally admits he likes April 'in a romantical kinda way' – and by the middle of season three there's an impromptu marriage proposal, a rapidly arranged wedding and the unlikely lovers become somehow believable – and completely relatable – newlyweds. The innocence and optimism these characters display in their haphazard approach to marriage is improbably infectious and wholly reflective of the entire show's 'The-Little-Town-That-Could' attitude. If there's one relationship on television that begs you to root for it, it's the one between Andy Dwyer and April Ludgate.

During the airing of season two, the show began attracting the type of cult status among its small viewership that so often leads to an eventual explosion and elevation to 'full-on pop culture phenomenon' and, more importantly – to the network at least – a sizeable hike in ratings. With Andy now

Above left: A young Chris Pratt alongside former girlfriend and *Everwood* co-star, Emily VanCamp.   ©*Barbara Binstein/Getty Images*

Above right: Always a family man, Chris attends the *Strangers with Candy* Sundance party with his mother, Kathy.   ©*Evan Agostini/Getty Images*

Below left: Boys just want to have fun: Chris and fellow actor Adam Brody at the launch of Turi Bar At The Rock 'The Vote' Bus Tour.   ©*Donato Sardella/Getty Images*

Below right: Chris arrives at the 2012 PaleyFest to participate in a panel about the hit show, *Parks and Recreation*.   ©*Michael Tran/Getty Images*

Above: Guardians of our galaxy? Chris Pratt with his co-stars (from left) Lee Pace, Zoe Saldana and Vin Diesel at a screening of *Guardians of the Galaxy* at The Cinema Society. ©*Andrew Toth/Getty Images*

Below left: Fantastic plastic: Chris poses with his on-screen persona, Emmet Brickowski, in *The LEGO Movie*. ©*Dave Kotinsky/Getty Images*

Below right: An award-winning actor, Chris accepts the Hollywood Blockbuster Award for *Guardians of the Galaxy*. ©*Kevin Winter/Getty Images*

Above: Chris and his actress wife, Anna Faris, cheering at a basketball game between the Los Angeles Clippers and the Los Angeles Lakers.

Below: Signing and selfie-ing with fans at the UK premiere of *Guardians of the Galaxy*.

Above left: C is for Chris: Chris is the winner of the Breakthrough Performer of the Year in 2014.

©*Michael Buckner/Getty Images*

Above right: Chris and Anna looking glamourous on the red carpet at the Academy Awards.

©*Steve Granitz/Getty Images*

Below: Taking his place at the podium, Chris joins *Parks and Recreation* co-star Adam Scott at Variety's 5th annual Power of Comedy.

©*Joe Scarnici/Getty Image*

supplying many of the show's most memorable moments, Chris was undoubtedly having the time of his professional life. But, as with virtually every US television show cursed with undeniably modest ratings, *Parks and Recreation* lived under the constant threat of cancellation, with the entire production completely at the mercy of the executives and moneymen at the network. Chris wasn't oblivious to the situation – he had been through the same thing repeatedly with *Everwood* and was smart enough to realise it was sometimes down to dumb luck whether a show survived from season to season. But it's easy to imagine his frustration, knowing he and the rest of the cast were doing an amazing job, delivering some exceptionally funny episodes and winning such amazing support from the fans watching the show. He told *A.V. Club*, 'You just have to keep on doing good work and hoping people will notice it. Our ratings haven't been great, but as the new episodes have come out, they're getting better. We're hoping that trend continues.' He concluded by saying, 'It's really just all speculation. You could be getting great numbers and still get told it's over.' But with all the main characters now gelling more effectively than ever and any initial glitches ironed out by the time Adam Scott and Rob Lowe had joined the cast towards the end of season two, NBC seemed happy to renew *Parks and Recreation* for another season, despite no dramatic increase in ratings.

In order to work around Amy Poehler's second pregnancy, the decision was made to continue shooting almost immediately after work on season two had officially wrapped and move straight into production for season three. After a three-week break – and with Poehler now six months pregnant – the entire cast and crew worked through the start of their expected hiatus period, writing and shooting six full episodes before finally shutting down in late spring/early summer. After working so hard to get ahead and make sure the first batch of episodes were ready to debut during the new television season in September, it was a surprise when NBC decided to leave *Parks and Recreation* off their fall 2010 schedule and push season three's air date back to January 2011. Much of the creative team were philosophical about the delayed transmission, including Mike Schur, who told *Entertainment Weekly*, 'We were very anxious to return, and it felt like something we didn't have a ton of control over, so our attitude was just: Put your head down, do your job, and make the shows as good as they can be.' While Poehler echoed Schur's frustration, she acknowledged there was a silver lining: the delay in broadcast meant the show was given a new, slightly later timeslot and would now air directly after new episodes of *The Office*. She said, 'It was frustrating to be shooting good shows and not have them be on, but I'm excited to have them be on in the space we've always wanted them to.'

Season three saw a particularly noticeable upswing in the show's critical reception, with *Entertainment Weekly* printing an article entitled 101 REASONS WE LOVE *PARKS AND RECREATION* and their chief television critic, Ken Tucker, naming the show the 'number-one TV Comedy' in his end-of-year review. This increasingly positive critical response was having a knock-on effect for much or the cast and, with *Parks and Recreation* now becoming a showcase for its principle players, their careers outside the confines of the series were flourishing. As the show and everyone involved in making it seemed to reach new creative heights during the third and fourth seasons, *Parks and Recreation* continued to struggle in terms of ratings. During an acknowledged creative peak in season three, the show lost almost 2.5 million viewers and had struggled to grow beyond an average of 5 million per season. Schur was adamant the team behind it were doing the best they could, pointing to the NBC network's disappointing performance in the market overall, as well as the difficulty in building a huge audience when the audience's attention is split over a million competing channels. He told *A.V. Club*, 'I would love it if our ratings went up and up, and we've done a pretty good job of making our show inviting and friendly, welcoming new viewers. Other than that, I'm not sure what else we can do. It's very disconcerting.' In reality, 'disconcerting' was putting it mildly and the show seemed to end every season under a cloud of uncertainty, never sure if it would be cancelled or renewed for another season.

Chris summed up the feelings of everyone involved in making the show, telling *Entertainment Weekly*, 'We feel like the *Bad News Bears*,' referring to the 1976 movie in which a group of misfits form a baseball team, take part in an ultra-competitive Little League competition and, despite being the obvious underdogs, end up winning against all the odds. He continued, 'Don't count us out. We'll eye-gouge. You're going to have to kill us dead!'

While the careers of its principle cast went from strength to strength, *Parks and Recreation* remained marooned near the bottom of the television-ratings league tables through its fourth and fifth seasons. With ratings hitting an all-time low at the end of season six, with the finale watched by fewer than 3 million viewers, NBC decided to pull the plug. As a concession to everyone involved in producing such a critically acclaimed and undoubtedly prestigious show, they ordered a shorter seventh season, announcing that these thirteen episodes would act as the series finale and would begin airing in January 2015.

For Chris his years on *Parks and Recreation* would be a transformative period in his life, both personally and professionally. Over the course of the show's seven-year run, he'd got married and had his first child and Anna and Jack were now an obvious priority. Going forward, Chris's immediate family took centre stage and, understandably, influenced the majority of the decisions he made about time spent away from home, either shooting locally or travelling abroad to far-flung locations. His career had started to flourish, largely thanks to the continued exposure *Parks and Recreation* had given him and no doubt helped by the engaging nature of his performance as Andy Dwyer. From very early in the show's run, the experience of playing Andy had started to influence his whole thought process in terms of what work he chose to do and where he imagined his future lay as an actor. He told the *Los Angeles Times*, 'You know, drinking and eating whatever I wanted and partying and having fun. I thought, this isn't a bad niche ... If I can get consistent work as this bumbling kind of fat guy who says funny things and falls down on rollerblades and gets really sweaty, why not?'

There were obvious similarities between Chris and his character Andy Dwyer, not least his appearance and good-humoured approach to life, but in helping to create such a well-loved and genuinely funny character, he had more than proven himself as a gifted comedy performer. Surrounded and inspired by other actors and comedians as skilled as the likes of Amy Poehler, Nick Offerman and Aubrey Plaza, he had developed growing confidence in his overall ability as an actor. Encouraged by his fellow cast members' versatility and numerous successful attempts to play drama as well as comedy, he set out to push himself – if he truly wanted to achieve his full potential, it was time to start stretching himself in more dramatic roles. Thus, while playing Andy had signposted an easy route to further success, he was not satisfied to simply roll over and have his career defined by Hollywood's notoriously narrow-minded approach to what kind of movies audiences wanted to see – sequels and remakes – and the type of actors they wanted to star in them – tried and tested box-office stars.

Chris's first year on *Parks and Recreation* had allowed him the time he needed to pull back a little from a possible career dead-end, playing countless frat-boy losers in an endless run of sub-standard comedies. Now he was ready to spread his wings a little and he reckoned there had to be some directors and casting agents out there willing to give him a chance. While Andy's journey over the course of seven seasons of *Parks and Recreation* closely mirrored Chris's own struggle to be taken seriously and find his place in the world, if you really wanted to see them, there were also obvious parallels to be drawn between his newly emerged attitude and the overall theme of the show itself. Chris himself acknowledged, in an interview with *Vulture*, that *Parks and Recreation* was 'grounded in optimism' and promoted an 'anything can happen if you put your mind to it' attitude – an attitude probably best exemplified by the show's principle character, Leslie Knope. There's no denying that Leslie's terrier-like determination to continually improve herself and her beloved town of Pawnee was both inspirational to the other characters in the series and equally relevant to Chris's own real-life mission to challenge himself. The idea that 'from small acorns, great oaks grow', which informed much of Leslie's character, could be directly applied to Chris and his resolve to further his acting career at this stage. Leslie's dogged self-belief and methodical approach to working within the restrictions of local government, pushing against the copious amounts of seemingly impenetrable red tape thrown in her path to thwart her every move, chime with Chris's own struggles to escape the long-established, blinkered Hollywood system, which seemed to want to limit his progression as a performer and side-lined him as little more than a comedy sidekick to their proven A-list stars. Informed by what he'd learned and armed with the same fighting spirit that had turned *Parks and Recreation*'s Lot 48 into Pawnee Commons, he embarked on the next phase of his career.

CHAPTER EIGHT

HOME RUN

'"Oh, yeah, I can do that." He looked at me like I was crazy.'
CHRIS PRATT, ON TELLING HIS AGENT HE COULD LOSE
FORTY-FIVE POUNDS IN THREE MONTHS TO PLAY SCOTT HATTEBERG
IN *MONEYBALL* – THE *SEATTLE TIMES*

Back in early 2010, with Chris's regular gig as Andy Dwyer seemingly assured for the time being, it would appear much of the pressure most actors feel – to keep working at all costs – had been lifted. Apparently, everyone in the Pratt household could afford to sit back, take a moment and be a little more discerning about the jobs they were accepting. Factoring in Anna's now substantial second income as a much-in-demand voiceover artist – she had already contributed to such hit movies as *Cloudy with a Chance of Meatballs* and the *Alvin and the Chipmunks* sequel (*The Squeakquel*, of course!) – it would seem the couple had reached an enviable turning point in their respective careers and neither of them now felt the need to do anything they didn't really want to do.

For Chris, this not only meant committing to fewer

projects outside his regular *Parks and Recreation* schedule – for the entirety of the series' seven-season run, he limited his extracurricular activity to one or two more movie projects per year – it gave him time to actively pursue a few more interesting supporting roles. Rejecting the pressure to chase after lead parts, he took inspiration from some of the more credible character actors who had managed to build a career in both comedy and drama. It was the multi-faceted careers of Bill Murray, Philip Seymour Hoffman and Sam Rockwell he wished to emulate, rather than those of Tom Cruise or Adam Sandler. By spending less time worrying about becoming a 'Movie Star', he was able to concentrate on making smarter choices, which in turn led to working with several of the world's most renowned filmmakers. While his career would take him on many unplanned and unexpected detours – and eventually deliver him right back to the place he was more or less determined to avoid – for the time being, he looked like he was in charge. Over the next few years, during his annual leave from Pawnee's Parks and Recreation Offices, his acting CV was enhanced by a fascinating, sometimes unexpected and undeniably eclectic list of supporting characters.

The story of *Moneyball*'s journey to the big screen was a complicated one, involving many false starts and a few questions being raised along the lines of, 'Why are we even considering turning a book about baseball statistics into a movie at all?' Based on Michael Lewis's 2003 bestseller of the same name – subtitled 'The Art of Winning An Unfair Game' – it was a non-fiction account of the Oakland Athletics baseball team's landmark 2002 season. That year saw the A's unexpectedly triumph over seemingly insurmountable odds, while also exposing fatal flaws in the basic foundations on which the entire professional baseball industry was built. The events covered by the plot of the subsequent movie adaptation, conceived as a classic underdog story, were indeed truly inspirational. The A's winning streak of victories was a modern-day David vs. Goliath battle, pitting a cash-starved team of skilled but sidelined players against baseball's blinkered player appraisal system, a practice which saw the game grow more reliant on multi-million-dollar signings and the concept that spending vast amounts of money on individual players was the only way to guarantee genuine talent on the field.

Lewis's book chronicled the Oakland A's use of a non-traditional system of player performance assessment under their general manager, Billy Beane. In the movie Beane (as played by Brad Pitt) is painfully aware that the Oakland Athletics are a 'small-market team' trying to compete against teams with 'deeper pockets'. At one point he goes as far as saying, 'There are rich teams and there are poor teams. Then there's fifty feet of crap and then there's us.' Financially handicapped by a limited budget and with very little spare cash to spend on acquiring the type of new players he needed to rebuild his team, Beane turned to an alternative method of player assessment: one founded on finding seemingly hidden value in players which other teams may have overlooked.

Sabermetrics was a system pioneered by Bill James, a baseball writer and statistician whose controversial theories had been dividing the leading lights of the game since the 1970s. Following his association with Paul DePodesta, a former Harvard graduate and baseball scout who had become one of sabermetrics's leading advocates, Beane was a recent convert to the system. Employing a fundamentally more scientific and statistical approach in determining a player's usefulness and ability to score runs, the sabermetric system eschews more traditional measurements of success – such as team batting averages – in favour of assessing the individual player's performance and specific contribution to winning each game. Beane was fighting against a system that attached real value to a player's appearance or how they conducted themselves in interviews away from the field. Where factors as arbitrary as deciding how attractive a player's girlfriend was could be used to demonstrate a player's confidence levels, which, in turn, could have an impact on their game. Beane faced an uphill battle. After he hired DePodesta as his assistant, the Oakland A's were soon pioneering proponents of the sabermetrics system. They used it to acquire a handful of seemingly past-their-prime players and, as Beane states in the film, 'create an island of misfit toys.' After a slow start and a string of bitter defeats, the players rallied. Soon, with their new signings gelling as part of a complete team, the Oakland A's embarked on an unprecedented hot streak, winning an unparalleled twenty consecutive games during the 2002 American League season – an unbroken record which still stands today.

Columbia Pictures had acquired the rights to the book as far back as 2004 and various screenwriters and directors circled the project over the next four or five years. Even in its earliest incarnation, the premise was intriguing enough to attract the attention of Brad Pitt, who signed on to play the A's general manager, Billy Beane. After several false starts, the project eventually landed in the hands of Steven Soderbergh, the acclaimed director who had successfully built a career that ranged from big studio films, such as the *Ocean's* trilogy and Oscar bait drama's *Traffic* and *Erin Brockovich*, to movies with a more indie or art-house sensibility, such as his breakthrough film, *Sex, Lies, and Videotape*, and later pet-projects *The Limey* and *The Good German*. With this pedigree and an association with Pitt extending back over the course of half a decade – taking in *Ocean's Eleven* and its subsequent sequels – Soderbergh seemed like a perfect fit. Unfortunately, his idea of blurring the lines between drama and documentary filmmaking, by using some of the actual baseball players to play the characters, made the executives at Columbia nervous. After several clashes with Soderbergh about the intended tone of the film and with only a matter of days before principle photography was due to start, Columbia pulled the plug.

With the project effectively 'on hold' for the foreseeable future, Soderbergh moved on and a new director, Bennett Miller, was hired. Back in 2005, he had been hot property in Hollywood, having just directed *Capote*. Miller's movie was the more successful of two competing Truman Capote biopics released that year, having left his rival, *Infamous*, trailing far behind at the box office and securing Philip Seymour Hoffman a 'Best Actor' Oscar for his portrayal of the titular lead character. Miller had so far failed to capitalise on his newfound status as a capable and credible filmmaker and, by 2009, it seemed that *Moneyball* would become the belated, much anticipated follow-up to his initial breakthrough success, as well as paving the way for a welcome re-teaming with Hoffman – who had signed on to play The A's manager, Art Howe.

Undoubtedly, this felt like another perfect fit. *Capote* had shown that Miller understood the delicate balance between factual accuracy and compelling drama and, for *Moneyball*, he knew he had an ace up his sleeve. Miller's secret weapon came in the shape of Aaron Sorkin. An industry veteran, Sorkin had amassed countless awards during his long and illustrious career in film and television and his standing in the industry had reached new heights as the visionary force behind the acclaimed TV series *The West Wing*. It was Sorkin's version of the script that would be Chris's first introduction to the *Moneyball* project.

With the nixing of Soderbergh's idea to have several characters in the film played by their real-life counterparts, the call had gone out to re-cast some of the key members of the Oakland A's team. Chris hadn't seen any script or read Lewis's book, relying on his agent to tell him the story that would later inspire the film. Initially, he was as confused as everyone else about how this particular source material would translate into a movie with a traditional narrative structure. Once he'd been informed that it was an Aaron Sorkin script, he was considerably less sceptical. Remembering his initial response to Sorkin's last big-screen project – an adaptation of *The Accidental Billionaires* by Ben Mezrich, which turned the story of Facebook founder Mark Zuckerberg into David Fincher's Oscar-nominated movie *The Social Network* – he realised there were parallels to be drawn. He told *Movieline*, 'I remember thinking, "How are they going to make this movie about *Facebook*?" And then I saw the movie and I thought, "Oh, wow. That's a character piece."' He was confident that Sorkin's involvement meant there must be a fascinating story to tell. 'The fact that Sorkin even came on board to write is a testament to how human the story is,' he reasoned, before adding, 'There is a real story in there about real humans. It's not just a baseball movie.'

He was convinced that this was an important project and one worth fighting for. It was just as well he was ready for battle because even getting a glimpse of the film's script wouldn't be easy. Chris told *Movieline*, 'It was one of those situations where the script was under lock and key, no one was allowed to read it,' before admitting, 'I got to read it shortly before auditioning. I had to sit there in the office and read the script and they wouldn't let anybody leave with it; it was very top secret.' He was blown away by what he read. 'It had some interesting stuff about statistics and about scouting,' he recalled. 'But it was really just a brilliant character piece.' He was auditioning for the part of Scott Hatteberg, a real-life player who had assumed his career was over prior to becoming a part of the A's winning team. Once he had read Hatteberg's part in the script, he knew this was exactly the type of role (and project) he'd been looking for. He said, 'I just thought, "That is just a perfect story. It's so interesting. It's a true human story... it's not a movie about baseball statistics."'

At last, this must have felt like the perfect opportunity for Chris to challenge people's expectations of him as an actor.

He'd dreamed of making the move from largely comedic roles to something with more of an emotional and dramatic edge and this script seemed to be his perfect way in. With Brad Pitt already on board, a director of Miller's calibre at the helm and the promise of an Aaron Sorkin script, word had quickly got out to every agent and actor in Hollywood. After years of false starts and dead-ends, there was now a tremendous amount of interest in the project and Chris was not the only one who really wanted this role. He had convinced himself that all he had to do was get through the first audition and he would prove there was a lot more to him than his previous film work might suggest. Unfortunately, his lack of experience as a dramatic actor seemed to be the least of his problems. He told *Movieline*, 'My first audition was with Bennett Miller and I thought it went well. I felt like we found some real moments,' but he went on to explain, 'When I left, my agent called me and said, "Chris, they really thought you were good, but they think you're too fat."'

It was quite a blow but rather than let it knock him down, typically, Chris took it as a positive piece of feedback. He decided not to see it as criticism but merely as another challenge. Chris would be the first to admit he'd gained a little weight over the last couple of years. Aside from purposefully 'bulking up' to play Andy Dwyer, his home life now seemed to revolve around entertaining at home, with plenty of good food and the odd beer or two, and he had been fairly open about Anna preferring him with 'a little meat on the bone'. With his agent's assurance that the role was still up for grabs, he vowed to lose the weight, stating that he was 'determined to become Scott Hatteberg whether they cast me or not.'

Chris's resolve saw him drop thirty pounds in under three months. The audition process continued and, after a couple of further readings – one with Brad Pitt and another with Miller – the Hatteberg role was still yet to be cast. Chris was now more or less down to the required weight, looking suitably trim and athletic, but Miller needed more. He wanted to convince baseball enthusiasts watching the movie, as well as the average cinema audience merely looking to be entertained, that what they were seeing were real baseball players, not just actors who looked the part. His principle objective was to deliver a realistic representation of the sport on screen and he insisted the baseball scenes in his movie would look and feel authentic. To that end, a large-scale physical audition was organised, with nearly 700 ex-players joining the actors in contention for the key roles. It felt more like an actual baseball try-out than an audition and Chris was suitably in awe. 'These guys were pros,' he said, beaming to *Movieline*, 'Literally ex-professional baseball players, both from minor and major league, but also foreign teams, ex-college guys,' before adding with a smile, 'They were real baseball players... These were guys with tattoos of baseball bats on their body.'

While Chris had played a little baseball at school, he'd dropped that particular sport fairly quickly to concentrate on football and wrestling and he was the first to admit he'd more or less stopped following the game in the late 1990s. But with a passing resemblance to the real Hatteberg and his obvious commitment to mastering a convincing baseball swing, it seemed the odds were definitely stacked in his favour. At the try-out audition Chad Kreuter – a former head coach who had been drafted in as a baseball advisor on the film – approached Chris and asked if he wanted to do some extra practice sessions to help him get closer to perfecting his game. Chris told *AskMen*, 'I think in that moment I kind of won the role, because he went back to Bennett and said, "You know, if I have time, I think I can work with this guy. I think I can make this guy look like a professional baseball player." And then we did a really intense training camp.'

Chris was now officially on board as Scott Hatteberg, one of the heroes of the Oakland A's 2002 season, and his main task was to successfully mirror the real Hatteberg's distinctive characteristics and style on the field. In 2001, as a player for the Boston Red Sox, Hatteberg suffered a ruptured nerve in his elbow. After extensive rehabilitation and a return to form as a batter, the injury had considerably reduced his abilities as a first baseman or catcher and effectively ended his career as an all-round baseball player. So, despite being a relatively young player, match-fit and in good physical shape, Hatteberg was soon transferred and ultimately cut loose by his new team. The apparent short-sightedness of his former team regarding his ability to score runs, which ultimately won games, made him one of the first players to be discovered and signed by Beane using the sabermetrics approach.

While Chris was confident that he already had the basics of a convincing baseball swing, his main problem was matching the real Hatteberg's left-handed batting style. With Kreuter's help, he was soon improving his technique and transforming his game, admitting to *Movieline*, 'I never batted left-handed as a kid playing Little League or pick-up games. I'm still probably more powerful and accurate right-handed ... but I think the mechanics of my left-handed swing are much better than my right-handed swing.'

The question of whether Chris should meet the real Scott Hatteberg during the shooting of the film was raised shortly after he'd officially been added to the cast list. Creating a character is one thing but coming face to face with the person you are supposed to be playing is something else completely. At first, he worried that meeting Hatteberg might contradict the characterisation he already had in mind, distracting him from the person he imagined while reading the script. Relating an early conversation he'd had with Miller, Chris told *Movieline*, 'I want it to be exactly how it's written in the screenplay because it's good and it made me cry. That's the story I want to tell ... We're making a movie based on a roadmap by Aaron Sorkin. I want to stay true to the screenplay.' He added, 'I thought, "My first instinct is very strong, and I don't want to start second guessing it."'

Miller was respectful of Chris's decision, allowing him to create his own version of the character but then, midway through the shoot and once the bulk of the dramatic scenes were complete, he took him aside. He insisted that meeting Hatteberg would not alter anything Chris was doing in his performance and could only help him with the more technical aspects of the baseball-related scenes. When Hatteberg eventually brought his family along for a set visit, it was the perfect, if slightly surreal, opportunity for Chris to meet the inspiration for his character and spend some time getting to know him. It turned out they had a lot more in common than either of them could have imagined.

Born and raised in neighbouring states, they were both keen outdoorsmen and shared the other's passion for hunting and fishing. On meeting Chris, Hatteberg was suitably impressed, telling *Moviefone*, 'The guy is probably the nicest guy around ... He has an infectious personality and is really upbeat,' before commenting on how he looked out on the field. 'He had my uniform on with my number and they were running around ... and he just nailed the movements ... It looks like he could have been a player.' Indeed Chris's portrayal was so uncanny that he even managed to fool the rest of the Hatteberg family, with Scott admitting that his kids had been a little freaked out seeing another version of their father out on the field. He said, 'I guess they were the greatest litmus test with how they would react and they were blown away at the mannerisms.'

Key to his overall performance was recreating believable relationships with the other players, on and off the field. Spending time with ex-pro players proved invaluable and he was quick to recognise their contribution. In an interview with *AskMen*, Chris said, 'There's a certain swagger ... there's a certain quality to people who are professional athletes,' before explaining further, 'They've been the best at what they do since they were children. They've grown up with the ability, with a gift.'

While the training was relentless and Chris's workout was harder than most, due to his need to improve his overall fitness levels and achieve the required weight loss, it helped forge a genuine team mentality among the entire cast – actors and non-actors alike. For Chris, this wasn't anything new but it was something he hadn't felt for a long time. 'I was an athlete growing up and I miss that,' he told *AskMen*. 'I was hanging out with dudes and making raunchy jokes and telling stories, trading details, you know?' He added wistfully, 'There's something I really miss about that.'

The bonds formed on the *Moneyball* baseball field endured long after the film was complete, resurfacing as the cast reunited at the red-carpet event for the movie's Toronto Film Festival premiere. Chris recalled, 'Brad and Angelina were there, Phil Hoffman walks by, and Stephen Bishop, my buddy on the project, ran across the carpet and gave me a big hug. And I got emotional – that was what it was about for me.'

Although some of the friendships and physical struggles he'd endured were all too real, it hadn't been easy for Chris to achieve such levels of intensity and credibility within every aspect of his performance. For the first time in his career, with Bennett Miller behind the camera, he was working with the type of director who would go to extreme measures to get the required performance. Chris recalled one incident, during a reconstruction of one of Hatteberg's first games with the Oakland A's, where he was obviously struggling to match the fitness levels of the pro players taking part in the movie. As Miller approached him in centre field, he recalled to *Movieline*, 'I was working my ass off; I was sweating, and he says, "Stop being such a fucking pussy" to me. I was volatile. It made me so mad.' He added, 'I think I even spat at his shoes.' On viewing the finished film, he noted that this scene, including shots of him furiously mumbling under his breath, had made it to the final cut. While Chris enjoyed a close and productive relationship with Miller throughout the shoot, counting the director among his best friends long after the film had wrapped, he realised there was more at stake than maintaining on-set harmony. 'This was the first time I'd ever worked with a director who sorta manipulated a performance out of me,' he confessed. 'I realized that was about the performance, it wasn't about camaraderie.'

Chris had already proved himself as an actor who knew how to use elements of his own personality like his quick-witted humour and charm to enliven virtually any part he chose to play but here, with every new skill he'd learned on the set of *Moneyball*, he was making a massive leap forward in terms of being taken seriously as an actor; someone capable of working at a more exposed emotional level and delivering believable, more nuanced characters. He was all too aware that his career was moving into uncharted waters. 'This was definitely a big step up for me in terms of the pedigree of the people I'm surrounded by,' he told *AskMen*. 'It's dramatic and very grounded and artful.'

Moneyball went on to pick up six Oscar nominations, including 'Best Film'. It was a sizeable box-office hit around the world, grossing more than $110 million on its release in 2011. And while he was on the extended Award Season tour, hitting the red carpet at the Oscars and giving countless interviews to promote the film, Chris began to realise this particular project would be a transformative experience in his career but he was fairly insistent that these were changes he'd been working towards for some time, and he'd viewed this type of role as a first step on an inevitable path. 'It was definitely different, but it feels really good,' he told *AskMen*. 'I've always wanted to do this. I've always thought that I could do something like this.' Finally he was on his way to becoming the actor he wanted to be and *Moneyball*'s success was about to kick-start a uniquely eclectic string of supporting roles for him and create a dramatic upswing in his stock as an all-round performer. And, as if to prove a point, around the same time he was showing off his newfound confidence as a 'straight' actor in *Moneyball*, Chris accepted a small role in another film: a full-on comedy called *What's Your Number?*

Starring and co-produced by his wife Anna Faris, *What's Your Number?* arrived during a mini-revolution in Hollywood. Following the global success of the *Sex and the City* movie in 2008, Hollywood film studios were slowly coming around to the concept that men were not the only ones who liked 'R'-rated comedies. Over $415 million at the global box office suggested women liked to see other women behaving badly on screen too. Always keen to capitalise on an under-exploited market, Hollywood began to embrace the idea that women could be just as funny as men. Soon, it was actresses like Anna Faris, who weren't afraid to be seen as raunchy or to push the boundaries of what was considered good taste for a woman to say or do in comedy, who began to reap the rewards. At the turn of 2011 there was suddenly a spate of 'female-driven' comedies, many employing enough of a frank or sexually explicit tone to merit an 'R' rating. Most eagerly anticipated was an all-female, ensemble-cast comedy called *Bridesmaids*.

When that particular film went on to become the 'sleeper' hit of the summer, eventually grossing almost $300 million worldwide, it looked like *What's Your Number?* might just be another huge box-office hit for Faris.

As the film's lead character, Ally Darling, Anna decides she has reached her upper limit of sexual partners and, with a score that is almost double the national average, vows not to sleep with another man unless she thinks he's going to become her husband. After a chance meeting with one of her exes – a reformed slob known only as Disgusting Donald – she realises her best chance of finding Mr Right is by working her way back through all her Mr Wrongs. She hatches a plan to retrace her steps, track down all her ex-lovers and find out if one of them is the perfect soulmate she thinks she may have already let slip through her fingers.

Chris was cast as the charmingly named Disgusting Donald. While the character was now handsome and athletic-looking, Ally remembers him in flashbacks as the fat, mullet-sporting ex she was too ashamed to be seen with in public. In the present-day scenes Chris was expected to deliver a more typically comedic performance, laced with traces of his own natural charm and charisma. But to fully embrace the character's name, during the brief flashback sequence, he donned a prosthetic fat-suit and propelled his creation even further into the realms of grotesque caricature. Anna unexpectedly bumping into Chris's character with stalker-ish regularity becomes a recurring gag through the entire film and these scenes are some of the best in the movie.

The few scenes Chris and Anna share on screen show just

how comfortable they were acting together. In what amounts
to little more than a series of extended cameos – from their first
chance encounter through a sequence of increasingly freaky
coincidental meetings and ending with Ally gatecrashing
Donald's wedding – Chris gets the chance to show off a
surprising number of the acting skills he'd accumulated over
the last few years, ranging from charming to confused, through
fear and ending with outright exasperation.

While *What's Your Number?* undoubtedly contained many
of the same ingredients as its recent predecessors, any subtlety
the script may have had at its inception was long gone by
the time it hit the big screen. By landing in US cinemas just
three months after the considerably wittier and more warm-
hearted *Bridesmaids*, *What's Your Number?* only suffered by
comparison. While *What's Your Number?* focused on one
girl's obsessive search to find the man she wanted to marry,
Bridesmaids seemed more concerned with fully exploiting its
hilarious ensemble of supporting actresses. And while both
movies had more than their fair share of women behaving
badly, *What's Your Number?* lacked the obvious chemistry of
its rival's key players, leaving too much of the comedic 'heavy
lifting' to Anna, its solitary female star.

The movie signalled a professional 'parting of the ways'
for Chris and Anna. Aside from appearing together in 'The
Proposition' – one of the sequences in 2013's sketch-anthology
film *Movie 43* – as of 2015, they would not appear in another
feature film together. Wary of becoming the type of real-life
couple who acted in each other's movies, with a blinkered
and uncritical response to the finished results, Chris told

Entertainment Weekly, 'If we were gonna be doing another movie together, it would really have to be far down the line and a great project.' In fact, just as his film career was beginning to flourish, Anna's was starting to take a back seat and she would only accept a handful of roles before heading to a regular gig on US television.

At the time Chris was about to make a massive career leap, headlining the cast of a major summer blockbuster, Anna took the lead in *Mom*, the latest TV sitcom from *The Big Bang Theory* and *Two and a Half Men* creator Chuck Lorre. The show launched in the US on the CBS network in September 2013, achieving decent ratings and completed airing its second season in April 2015. While this apparent reversal of fortunes might have been a cause for resentment or dissatisfaction among some couples, for Chris and Anna it seemed like a natural progression for both their careers. By concentrating on a series of interesting supporting roles, Chris was now transforming himself into a fully-fledged, well-rounded actor and he was well aware that he had his wife to thank, at least in part, for his current success. Without Anna's full support and understanding he would probably have struggled to maintain any of the momentum his less obvious film choices were generating, giving him little room for growth and leading him along a path littered with a string of progressively older versions of *Everwood*'s Bright Abbott or *Parks and Recreation*'s Andy Dwyer.

In reality, he was now on the brink of his most interesting career progression yet and it was one that would ultimately lead to his transition from being a reliable supporting player to becoming a bankable leading man. But first, juggling two radically different careers, he would spend the next couple of years quietly consolidating his position as a more than capable dramatic actor, while simultaneously monopolising a scene-stealing position in a string of Hollywood comedies. Chris was about to enter – and ultimately rule – 'The Best Friend Zone'.

CHAPTER NINE

THE BEST
FRIEND ZONE

'I just like to gain weight and lose weight. It's a rollercoaster. I just want to do this. I want to touch God.'
CHRIS PRATT, ON HIS 'METHOD-LIKE' APPROACH TO
PHYSICAL TRANSFORMATION – *VULTURE*

Attending the Toronto Film Festival in September 2011, here *Moneyball* premiered at a star-studded Gala Presentation, Chris found himself in a fairly unusual position. Another film in which he had appeared, *10 Years*, was similarly receiving its first public screening as part of the event's Special Presentation programme. While he obviously saw this as a personal triumph, joking in an interview with *AskMen*, 'That's just another thing I have over Brad Pitt. The list goes on and on,' it would be considered an enviable achievement for any young actor. For Chris, it was proof that his decision to focus on interesting character roles was beginning to pay dividends, both professionally and in terms of actually enjoying the work he was doing.

Not only did he have two films showing at the festival that year but they really couldn't have been more different. While *Moneyball* was a multi-million-dollar studio movie, co-starring some of the biggest names in Hollywood, *10 Years* was a truly independent project, made on a shoestring budget and featuring a cast of more than a dozen up-and-coming young actors. The former had been a tough challenge but he'd delivered an assured performance in one of his first wholly dramatic roles. The latter gave him the opportunity to show off his impressive improvisation skills in what appeared to be a far more straightforward comedic role.

10 Years had become a pet project for another young actor whose determination to challenge other people's perceptions of him mirrored Chris's own. Like Chris, Channing Tatum was born and raised by working-class parents, neither of whom had any contacts within the entertainment industry. Tatum had turned to acting after dancing in a music video, which led to spells modelling for the likes of Armani and Abercrombie & Fitch, via a brief spell as a male stripper – a detour that would later inspire his starring role in Steven Soderbergh's *Magic Mike*. Subsequent roles in *Step Up*, *G.I. Joe: The Rise of Cobra* and *Dear John* had brought him considerable success and leading-man status in Hollywood. However, soon he felt sidelined, branded as 'just another Pretty Boy' and wrongly perceived by many as an actor who might struggle to deliver anything other than two-dimensional performances in action movies or as a romantic lead. Tatum's early life and struggles to break into serious acting closely match Chris's own experiences, with both attempting to gain broader acceptance and respect among their peers while realising that diversification was the only way to enjoy any degree of longevity or credibility within the acting profession. *10 Years* would bring them together during the first couple of months of 2011.

Like Chris's earlier project, *Take Me Home Tonight*, *10 Years* takes place over the course of one life-changing night as a large group of former friends meet up to attend their high school's ten-year reunion. Many of them have lost touch during the interim decade, with most of them having left their hometown to make their way in the wider world. The film follows them as they try to reconnect with former classmates and ex-lovers, reminiscing about who they were back then and figuring out how that relates to who they have become since they last saw each other. Tatum became fascinated with the idea of once-close friends becoming strangers and then randomly reuniting years later, following a discussion with a fellow actor who had recently attended his own ten-year reunion. The idea was soon handed to another acquaintance – screenwriter Jamie Linden – and, before long, the project was being considered as a potential starring role for Tatum. As things progressed, he officially came on board to star, also taking an executive producer credit, while Linden's role expanded as he'd decided not only to write the script but also to make this project his directorial debut.

In order to create the right buzz and hopefully raise the necessary funds to turn the concept into a feature-length movie, Tatum and Linden made a short film, simply titled *10 Year*, in the early summer of 2010. It worked. Soon afterwards several producers offered their support and sufficient financial backing to ensure the film was made. Admittedly, the budget was small compared to the average Hollywood movie but it was enough to produce the type of film Tatum and Linden wanted to make. The pair dreamed of bringing together an ensemble cast of actors they'd already worked with, or actor friends they respected, to make a film that might have the same impact and enduring resonance as similarly themed projects, such as *The Big Chill* or *Diner*. By August 2010, reports were circulating about the film's premise and proposed cast. An article in the *Hollywood Reporter* suggested that Tatum and his wife, Jenna Dewan, were set to take the leads, with several of the film's other key roles having been specifically written for some of the couple's actor friends, including Chris, Anna Faris and Chris Pine. The article stated, 'I won't be able to handle all the gorgeousness on one screen,' before adding, 'My favourite on the list has to be Chris Pratt, but maybe I'm still just heartbroken over the gone but not forgotten *Everwood*.'

Unfortunately, the film's limited budget meant the star-power of the project's reported fantasy cast was slightly reduced. Both Anna Faris and Chris Pine were no longer attached and the actors who had signed on were expected to work for a fraction of their usual fee. It was clear that *10 Years* truly had to be a labour of love for everyone involved – no one was going to get rich making this particular movie – but in the end, the *10 Years* team had enlisted an undeniably talented group of friends and like-minded actors, most of whom went on to build extraordinary careers. Among the supporting cast joining Tatum and his wife Dewan were Chris,

THE BEST FRIEND ZONE

Kate Mara, Rosario Dawson, Justin Long, Ron Livingston and Oscar Isaac.

The entire cast and crew was required to relocate to New Mexico for the duration of the shoot, from late 2010 to early 2011. The majority of the film's key scenes were scheduled to be shot in and around the Downtown Albuquerque area, with The Andaluz – a luxurious hotel situated in the heart of the area – serving as one of the movie's principle locations. To everyone's delight, this particularly high-end accommodation would not only be the main setting for the movie, The Andaluz would actually be their new home for the entire three-week shoot. From the outset, this was shaping up to be a particularly enjoyable job for the actors, with Chris telling *Interview* magazine, 'You just roll out of your room in the morning in your slippers and your robe and walk into wardrobe. It's really cool.' This sentiment was echoed by most of the main cast, independently referring to the experience as being like taking part in a 'movie camp'.

Chris plays Cully, one of the key roles in the movie. Cully had been one of the most popular kids in school; he was loud and always ready to party but there was a darker side to him. He had a tendency to become aggressive and developed a reputation as a bully, having tormented the 'freaks and geeks' at school and generally having made their high-school experience far less enjoyable than his own. Cully predominantly sees the reunion as the opportunity to build bridges. He had never moved away, he married his high-school sweetheart and they have a couple of kids. He takes his wife for granted, he eats too much, drinks more than he should and he's carrying a lot of extra weight. The naturalistic feel of the movie meant Chris would actually have to gain weight if he wanted his character to look suitably tubby and out of shape. There was no 'Disgusting Donald' fat-suit for this role.

Chris attacked this task with typical zeal. His eagerness to fatten himself up for the role may have come as a reaction to the strict diet and exercise regime he'd just completed for *Moneyball*. Alternatively, it may simply have been a desire to get back up to his 'Andy Dwyer Weight' for his *Parks and Recreation* gig and that he simply forgot when to stop. Whatever the reason, it was obviously something he was happy to do. He told *Movieline*, 'I went from 220 pounds that I cut down for *Moneyball* to almost 270–280 pounds for *10 Years*,' before adding, 'I would drink dark beer every night. I would have a double order of pancakes every morning, burgers for lunch. Fries, snacks, candy. I ballooned my weight up. It was probably very unhealthy, but it was so fun.'

While there were obvious benefits in following a 'no-limits' diet, he admitted it wasn't all pleasurable and he often struggled to stick to his regime. 'I gained 50lbs for *Ten Years* and got really watery, really fat and pink,' he told *Complex*. 'I'd sleep in every day, be lazy ... But as fun as it was, I never felt nearly as good as when I'm trying to lose weight.' He went on to explain how his teenage athleticism was key to his ability to transform himself so quickly. 'I grew up a wrestler, so working out and cutting weight and dedicating myself to something physical is something that I really love,' before revealing the constant yo-yoing of his weight for film and television roles had forced him into a compromise. 'I try to stay right in the middle, so I'm like six weeks to two months away from whatever weight I want to be.'

With his chosen parallel career paths, as 'the chubby best friend' and 'the more athletic supporting player' interweaving with increasing regularity, he needed to be in control. While he was now in the enviable position of being able to choose the work that interested him from an unusually diverse selection of roles, and he was more than willing to gain or lose the weight accordingly, his frustration came when each project seemed to require a physical transformation contrary to the one he had just made. Chris's 'middle-weight' – let's call it his 'Dwyer-weight' – would prove to be the perfect starting point for the many increases and decreases which were set to follow. Maintaining his 'chunkier' frame also had other benefits. As he would later point out to *Digital Spy*, his wife Anna preferred him heavier. He confided, 'She likes her fat husband better because she gets to feed him.'

Cully's physical appearance wasn't his only responsibility on this project. With the film's director, Jamie Linden, intending to take a much freer approach in terms of how tightly the actors adhered to the script, Chris, like the rest of the cast, had a hand in improvising much of the dialogue for his own character. Linden had made it clear to all the actors that this was not going to be a typical film set; he expected them to be fearless, willing to try anything or say whatever seemed appropriate for their character. He explained on the film's DVD 'Making Of' documentary that what he was looking for was 'a sense of naturalism,' before elaborating, 'I like stuff that feels real and authentic ... I really wanted to create an environment that supported that.' Discussing Linden's style of direction, Chris elaborated, 'He's using the screenplay as a guideline. We all kinda know the main points we have to hit and where we're allowed to improv.' It seemed like his co-star, Scott Porter, was a little less sure about what was going on when he added, 'Is there a script for this thing?'

This approach, however, seemed to work. Soon the cast started to bounce off each other and very quickly the dynamics of the individual couples and cliques loosely written in the script started to emerge for real. While Linden compared the experience of trying to direct scenes with twenty twenty-eight-year-old actors as 'like herding cats... in a good way,' he was undoubtedly thrilled by the results. For much of the shoot, the sizeable principle cast decided to hang out together, on and off set, and over the course of the movie's production built some strong and lasting friendships. Key to this growing camaraderie was the actors having known each other for years, or having worked together on recent projects. For example, among the cast were two of Chris's *What's Your Number?* cast-mates – Ari Graynor, who had played Anna's character's sister, and Anthony Mackie, who had joined Chris's Disgusting Donald on the list of Ally's ex-lovers – while Aubrey Plaza, Chris's *Parks and Recreation* co-star and onscreen wife, made a noteworthy appearance as a typically deadpan and sarcastic party guest.

It would seem these connections were merely the tip of the iceberg. Linden, speculating in an interview with *Entertainment Weekly*, suggested that really talented young actors of the calibre he wanted for the film were very rare in

Hollywood, describing them as 'kind of a small group', before concluding that, under those circumstances, their connections to each other were almost inevitable. 'Everyone knows each other,' he explained. He went on to say, 'There's all sorts of one degree of separation with this cast,' before going a long way towards proving his point by adding, 'There are pictures of Chris Pratt and Rosario Dawson from 10 years ago ... Kate [Mara] and [Anthony] Mackie have known each other for a long time. And Mackie and Oscar [Isaac] went to Juilliard together with [another cast member], Lynn Collins.'

With its friendly vibe and the easy familiarity among its cast, the entire *10 Years* production benefited from its fertile and creative atmosphere. Linden was overjoyed by the level of performance he was getting from the actors; determined not to miss out on any of the unscripted material constantly pouring out of his cast, he set up a second unit to film them wherever they congregated between takes. Roaming the expansive Andaluz set, this crew captured improvised scenes and unscripted conversations during the countless hours the actors spent hanging around the set, either alone or in tightly huddled groups, as they waited for their scheduled scenes to be shot. This technique provided hours of extra footage and encouraged them to fully explore and develop their characters outside the loosely scripted back-story. In turn, this added valuable depth to the characters, filled in underwritten sections of the script and created sub-plots, which would later be interwoven into the screenplay's more relaxed plotting style.

Employing multiple takes to explore different options for

every scene proved to be a masterstroke, with Linden rendered speechless or laughing uncontrollably at unexpected things that would appear on the sixth, seventh or eighth take. He knew it was a risk but a calculated one, stating, 'The trick is, you hire really good actors to do that.'

No one was more at home in this environment than Chris Pratt. This was a way of working he excelled at and a technique he had mastered long ago, finding the perfect outlet for his skills in the shape of Andy Dwyer years before. Many of his cast-mates were in awe of his talents, with Oscar Isaac declaring, 'I think really the reason to come see this movie is Chris Pratt,' before adding, 'I think his performance in this is pretty astounding ... you're watching someone who is truly, truly inspired.' Rosaria Dawson described him simply as 'brilliant', while Jenna Dewan said she shared the entire cast's consensus that Chris was 'full-on stealing this movie' from underneath their noses. It would seem as though creating this particular character and taking part in the *10 Years* experience in general had proved to be one of the most rewarding jobs of Chris's career so far. He described it as 'a blast', before adding, 'It's crazy. It's been six weeks where we've all gotten really close, like acting camp. It's really like a summer camp experience. It's really fun.'

Here, he had found the perfect platform for his dual talents, combining his obvious flair for improvised dialogue and his newfound skills as a dramatic actor. He delivers a performance that, at first glance, appears typically comedic and larger than life but, just below the surface, there's something considerably more real and tragic. While Cully is definitely the life and soul of the party, Chris simultaneously described his character as 'heartfelt and dark'. In the movie, as the night progresses, Cully becomes increasingly desperate to make amends, wildly over-compensating for his behaviour in high school and getting steadily wasted. He soon reverts to his bullying ways, lashing out at his former friends and classmates. Closer to home, his inconsiderate actions begin to irritate his wife, exposing the undercurrent of bitterness and resentment running through his apparently happy marriage. It's undeniably powerful stuff and a very difficult balancing act for any actor to achieve. The fact that the audience retains any degree of sympathy or affection for Cully is testament to Chris's confident and nuanced performance.

A full year after showing at Toronto, *10 Years* received a very limited run in US cinemas. Given the type of 'platform release' employed by most independent movies, intended to slowly build an audience over a period of time, the film opened in only three cinemas in September 2012. A small expansion to a hundred screens ended with it generating a little over $200,000 at the US box office. The film fared even worse outside the US, where it failed to find a distribution deal, finally seeing the light of day on DVD in 2013.

While *10 Years* had failed to find an audience (or perhaps more accurately, the film had been more or less hidden from any audience), the critics who did see it were divided, split fairly evenly between those who loved it and others who were left wondering what all the fuss was about. In the negative camp, *KC Active* questioned Jamie Linden's motives for making the film in the first place, stating, 'This should be a new rule for filmmakers: If the people you're following aren't as interesting as the real folks you know and love, your movie won't be much to leave home for or come home to,' while the *New York Post* was similarly unimpressed with the main characters, asking, 'Is there anything less narratively interesting than a high-school reunion that focuses exclusively on the beautiful and popular crowd?' More positively, the *New York Times* praised the attention to detail and underlying complexity, saying, 'It takes a while to sort out who's who in the gabby high-school reunion comedy *10 Years*. But once you do, the movie that comes together is an unpretentious, well-acted ensemble piece,' before concluding, '[It] settles into a sweet and sad ending, with enough hints of bitterness to keep it from cloying.' Fainter praise was to be had elsewhere, with the *A.V. Club* calling it 'sentimental and unambitious', before adding, 'It has an easy niceness as its foremost quality, which sounds damning, but actually makes it a perfectly pleasant experience, though not a terribly memorable one,' while, over at *Entertainment Weekly*, the film gained a B+ rating with a review that stated, 'Like the conventions of reunions themselves, there's nothing particularly new or deep about *10 Years*.'

But the true legacy of *10 Years* seems to be its role as a virtual show-reel for most of the actors involved. Undoubtedly, it helped pave the way for Channing Tatum's major breakthrough as a more sophisticated dramatic actor in 2012's *Magic Mike* and there's evidence to suggest it similarly showcased the considerable and varied talents of many of its key players. *10 Years* could easily be viewed as an actual first-round audition for several of the extended cast's future roles. Oscar Isaac's turn as the unassuming yet charismatic singer-songwriter Reeves set him up nicely for his role in the Coen Brothers' movie *Inside Llewyn Davis* and Anthony Mackie went on to recreate his wisecracking sidekick persona in countless other movies, including Marvel's *Captain America: The Winter Soldier* and Michael Bay's *Pain & Gain*. Of course, it was Chris who probably came out on top after this particular project and it led very quickly to another 'best friend' role, this time playing opposite Jason Segel and Emily Blunt in the Judd Apatow-produced *The Five-Year Engagement*.

As the title suggests, *The Five-Year Engagement* follows Segel, as Tom Solomon, and Blunt, as Violet Barnes, from the moment Tom decides to propose, through a series of mishaps, break-ups and harrowing crossbow accidents, to the day they finally tie the knot. The audition process was fairly irregular, with Chris merely being asked to attend a read-through of the script, joined by a group of Judd Apatow's friends and various actors he admired. Chris told *Entertainment Weekly*, 'Basically, they're workshopping the script. They're constantly rewriting and evolving,' before finally admitting, 'It wasn't really slated as an audition, but I won the role.' The large supporting cast, recruited the same way, included a few familiar faces and a host of extremely talented – and often criminally underused – supporting players, including *The Office* alum Mindy Kaling, gifted comic actor Chris Parnell, alongside Rhys Ifans, Jacki Weaver, Alison Brie and Kevin Hart.

Chris was cast as Alex, Tom's best friend and co-worker at a high-end San Francisco restaurant. In an interview with *GQ*, he described the character as 'obnoxious' before branding him as 'That guy who was probably a douche in high school, who may have peaked in high school.' He saw Alex as someone who'd wholeheartedly embraced the fact that his best days were already behind him, before asking himself, 'What happens to that guy?' Increasingly with every role, he was attempting to dig a little deeper. He wanted to get under the skin of his characters, exploring the tangled mass of quirks and contradictions we all recognise and accept as key to an individual's personality. No character should be defined as just one thing and viewed as simply 'The Loser', 'The Bully' or 'The Charmer', he believed. By having his creations expose a complex and, often, seemingly opposing array of emotions and behaviours, they would be much more believable and wholly three-dimensional.

Chris was the first to admit that the character of Alex shared many of the best and worst qualities of his other emotionally stunted man-child creation, *Parks and Recreation*'s Andy Dwyer. In both cases, his main aim was to find a way to make the audience bypass their gut reaction to instantly disapprove of the character's behaviour and to find something more engaging and relatable in them. He speculated, 'Typically when someone's obnoxious, they're not likable,' before reasoning, 'What makes the character endearing may be that they're forced to realize that they're not as badass as they used to be,' before concluding, 'And with that comes a sense of sort of a learned humility.' He believed that, by revealing a more humble side to Alex's character early in the film, there was a greater chance of winning the audience over. By forcing them to forgive Alex's faults and share in his future successes, he believed they would be more inclined to accept him, warts and all, saying, 'If you play the character who's learned that lesson, it's really hard to dislike that person.'

Still maintaining much of the additional fifty pounds he'd gained for *10 Years*, Chris reasoned that another key factor was the extra weight his characters carried. He stated, 'Both Andy and Alex are a little bit chubby and schlubby, you know? There's something nice about that.' He theorised that, if either character had been portrayed as an obvious winner in life, an obnoxious jerk handed everything they wanted on a plate, the audience would have rejected them outright. In the early scenes of *The Five-Year Engagement*, Alex is shown to be a bit of a loser, but, primarily, a nice guy. Ultimately, he's someone whose worst character flaws are simply his immaturity and lack of ambition. Chris speculated, 'If Alex had super-ripped abs and came out in the morning and was like, "Yeah, I screwed your sister," you'd be like, "Gross. Ewww. I don't like that guy." But because it's like a major victory for him to have sex with anybody, you're onboard.'

While this character was not a million miles away from others he had played over the last few years, the role had other benefits. He was quickly gaining a reputation as a master improviser and here he was being handed ample opportunity to riff on the material already contained within the script. With permission to take his role to new comedic extremes, Chris spent much of the movie lightly brushing the upper limits of good taste and somehow managing to drift stealthily from charming to extremely creepy and back again during several very funny sequences.

Filming took place in Michigan and on several outdoor locations in San Francisco in early summer 2011 and it proved to be another wholly enjoyable experience. The familiarity and camaraderie among the actors made the set relaxed and productive. In this atmosphere, everyone felt comfortable experimenting and fully developing the characters during the actual shooting of the film. While the script was a little more rigid than that of *10 Years*, the actors were given space to add their own flavour to the dialogue and were actively encouraged by the director, Nicholas Stoller, and his co-writer, Segel, to experiment during multiple takes and improvised extensions to scenes.

Chris was obviously in his element and gives yet another scene-stealing performance. And while he doesn't quite get enough to do to claim the entire movie as his own, he is given plenty of opportunities to shine. Highlights include the speech Alex gives at Tom's engagement party. This is a role Alex takes so seriously that he feels he needs a video projector and microphone headset to achieve the correct level of professionalism. The speech climaxes with Chris performing his own specially written version of Billy Joel's 'We Didn't Start the Fire'. Instead of a long list of historical events and pop-culture moments, this version of the song's lyric now features a seemingly endless parade of Tom's ex-lovers' names.

Chris shares the majority of his scenes with the actress Alison Brie, who plays Violet's sister, Suzie, and their onscreen chemistry is quite astonishing. Like him, Brie has enjoyed an enviably varied film and television career, having been a regular cast member of the acclaimed drama *Mad Men*, as well as having a parallel comedy career in the hit sitcom *Community*. Brie's film appearances have been similarly diverse, ranging from low-budget indie dramas such as *The Kings of Summer* to her appearance in the fourth instalment of the horror/comedy franchise *Scream*. As Alex and Suzie, Chris and Alison are a mismatched couple made in hell but not only do they make this unlikeliest of partnerships hilariously funny but also, somehow, bizarrely plausible.

As virtual strangers, Alex and Suzie only get married after a one-night stand at Tom and Violet's engagement party, which leads to Suzie becoming pregnant. Subsequent scenes in the film paint their relationship as a spiralling, muddled mess of blissful elation and twisted bitterness, with both parties expressing, sometimes in the same breath, overwhelming passion and antagonistic contempt for the other. From the couple's first inappropriately amorous public displays of affection and Chris's frighteningly sincere, deadpan delivery of a traditional Mexican love song at their wedding, through their rollercoaster marriage and ending with the often-confusing mix of affection and disdain they show towards each other and their children, Alex and Suzie are a welcome sideshow in a movie that often stumbles as it attempts to walk a thin line between comedy and drama. While the central plot and characters sometimes fail to deliver the required emotional weight or necessary laughs, Chris and Alison's performances bring their onscreen relationship to life, becoming a rich seam of comedy running through the entire film and managing to bring much-needed wit and surprising warmth when the main plot has taken an unwelcome side road into maudlin drama or misjudged sentimentality.

On release in the US in April 2012, *The Five-Year Engagement* fell way below its predicted opening-weekend box-office target. Universal Pictures was keen to sell the movie to US audiences as 'the next *Bridesmaids*', hammering home the association by emphasising the fact that both films shared a producer and using the same hot-pink-and-white colour scheme on the poster and publicity material. But it was fairly obvious from the film's $11 million opening gross that it was never going to match its predecessor's runaway success. Most reviewers complained that, at just over two hours, it was at least fifteen minutes too long. The *Daily Mail* stated, 'Cut away the flab, and there's probably an adorable hour-long movie in there.' But, in general, the critical response was largely positive, with several of the key cast members being singled out for particular praise. British film critic Peter Bradshaw said in his *Guardian* review, '*The Five-Year Engagement* isn't perfect, but it's a commercial date movie with warmth, sweetness, charm and laughs,' before making a connection to the similarly off-beat and appealing *Four Weddings and a Funeral*, highlighting 'some witty wedding scenes surely inspired by our own Richard Curtis.' The UK's leading critic, Mark Kermode, commented, 'The reliably effervescent Emily Blunt brings a whole lot of charm to this post-*Bridesmaids* romcom,' before concluding that the film offered 'plenty of chuckles.' Singling out Chris and Alison Brie's onscreen chemistry, the *Daily Express* review stated, 'To great comic effect, the Hollywood happy dust is sprinkled over the picture's other couple,' before praising Chris for giving a particularly 'scene-stealing' performance.

The Five-Year Engagement went on to make more than $50 million dollars worldwide, easily recouping its fairly modest $30 million price tag. But its real success was in helping Emily Blunt fulfil her potential as a genuinely funny and engaging lead on the big screen and cementing Chris's reputation as the go-to guy for hapless but undeniably lovable sidekicks.

While on the promotion trail for *The Five-Year Engagement*, Chris spoke about the apparent career transformation he was experiencing since completing *Moneyball*. When asked how he felt about the enviable position he was now in, not only juggling television and film work but also being able to move so effortlessly from comedy to drama, he made it clear he wasn't resting on his laurels or taking anything for granted. He honestly believed he was approaching every new job, funny or serious, with the same level of commitment and drive he'd shown in every job he'd ever had. 'It feels great,' he told *GQ*. 'I'm not sure it feels a whole lot different than maybe the last ten years have felt, you know? Because I feel like the effort and the work is sort of the same. I'm just kind of plugging away, and just more things are lighting up.'

And he was right, of course. He remained, as always, completely focused on creating the most believable version of the character he was being asked to play. Already he'd approached several jobs with 'method intensity', gaining or losing weight on more than one occasion, should the role require it. And while sometimes this merely meant injecting characters with elements of his own personality and humour, he now had the skills to play a little further away from home, bringing a darker or more sombre edge to his performance, if needed.

Chris would get such a chance (quite literally), flexing a few more acting muscles with his next job. He was about to join Kathryn Bigelow's long-gestating 'Hunt for Bin Laden' drama, but, as was becoming something of a recurring theme in his career, he would need to shed a few pounds first.

CHAPTER TEN

GOING DARK

'The only way to survive in Hollywood is to not get caught up in anything. You learn quickly that for all the opportunities there are to raise expectations, they're almost never met.'
CHRIS PRATT, ON KEEPING A LEVEL HEAD IN THE
FILM INDUSTRY – *MOVIELINE*

During the first few months of 2012 Chris was at a crossroads in his life, both professionally and personally. Although he and Anna wouldn't make any official announcements until May, Anna was pregnant with the couple's first child and was due to give birth in October. Chris was about to become a father and, like anyone entering parenthood for the first time, it would signal a fairly dramatic change in his and Anna's lifestyle. As well as their home life, the imminent arrival of the baby would undoubtedly impact on the work they both chose to pursue for the rest of that year and well into the future.

The couple had often talked about having children and, when asked in September 2011 during an *E! Online* interview when they intended starting their family, Anna admitted,

'I don't know... maybe in the next few years. We want to populate!' She wasn't kidding either. Later she elaborated by saying, 'I would love to have eight [kids]!' before adding, 'I don't think I could handle it though!' Anna wasn't alone in her desire to fill the Pratt household with babies, as she told *People* magazine, 'Chris wants a big family,' while also acknowledging the fact that their decision was probably made all the more complicated by their chosen profession, admitting finding the right time to start a family was 'so hard in this industry.'

It appears that by the end of 2011, the couple had reasoned that 'now's as good a time as any.' As was entirely typical of their relationship, their individual thought processes appeared to be perfectly in synch. Although it would seem they had simultaneously arrived at the same 'Eureka! moment', saying, 'Let's have a baby,' they'd apparently got there with very little discussion beforehand. Chris told *People* magazine, 'It started [for us] around the same time and I don't think one of us wanted it any more than the other,' before elaborating further, '[Anna] would say, "How do you feel about that?" and I would say, "Damn, I've been kind of thinking about that too! I think that'd be cool. Let's make that happen."'

There was no denying that he and Anna were in a comfortable place financially. While Chris's ongoing commitment to *Parks and Recreation* tied him to LA for much of the year and limited the amount of time he could spend on other projects, the couple's previous successes meant they were in the enviable position where they could afford to be much more selective about the jobs they took and whether they chose to work at all. But their lifestyle was far from extravagant and they had made it clear that money was no longer the driving force in the roles either of them actively pursued.

Anna was scheduled to shoot a film, *I Give It a Year*, in London during the first half of 2012 but had not committed to any other major roles beyond that. Factoring in a break to have a baby during this particular time would be relatively simple and putting her career on temporary hold would probably never be easier. Chris, on the other hand, was facing up to some harsh realities about the acting profession. His appearance – or more precisely, his weight – was increasingly becoming a deciding factor in the roles he was (and, more importantly, wasn't) being offered. 'I think I was a little naïve when I first started acting,' he told *Glamour*, '[I] didn't quite realise the impact the way you look has on the people who are making casting decisions.' He had chosen to maintain a little extra weight while playing Andy on *Parks and Recreation*, sticking around his own (and Anna's) preferred 220–230lb mark for the last few years. And despite having shown he could easily drop or gain weight if a part required it, he was beginning to feel it limited the work he was being considered for. 'I thought for a while I was going to find a career playing the fat friend, and that was totally fine,' he confessed, before adding with typical deadpan sincerity, 'It keeps you from waiting tables.' But the seeds which had been sown during his time on the *Moneyball* set, of being taken more seriously as an actor and making the transition from supporting player to leading man, were now firmly taking root.

His next role would prove to be a seismic leap forward in

that evolution but he would have been the first to admit it came from left field. Considering he was still carrying much of the excess weight he'd gained for *The Five-Year Engagement*, on the surface at least, Chris was an unlikely choice to play a Navy SEAL. However, the offer to join Kathryn Bigelow's *Zero Dark Thirty* would not only be an important turning point in his career, it also signalled another shift in how he perceived himself as a performer. If nothing else, it highlighted the fact that some very influential people within the industry were starting to sit up and take notice. He recognised that Bigelow and her team were putting a lot of faith in his abilities, sharing the vision he had for his own career. That seal of approval undoubtedly fed into his growing confidence as a dramatic actor. It proved to be all the reassurance he needed to keep following his instincts, to push onwards and keep stretching himself. Now there was little doubt that his enduring self-belief and the continued support of Anna were beginning to pay off.

Kathryn Bigelow had enjoyed an illustrious career as a filmmaker, making her solo directorial debut in 1987 with *Near Dark*. Coming more than twenty years before *Twilight*'s Edward Cullen gave vampires a boy-band makeover, meaning they were more likely to glimmer irresistibly in sunlight than tear you limb from limb, *Near Dark* was a far more visceral and gritty take on the genre. The resulting movie proved to be as exhilarating as it was subversive, not least because it was co-written and directed by a woman. Bigelow proved to be something of a pioneer, forging her way as a screenwriter, producer and director, undaunted by her sex, in a genre largely considered to be a male preserve – the action movie.

While her relationship with fellow filmmaker James Cameron sometimes saw her sidelined and perceived as merely working in his shadow (or at least under his influence), when their marriage failed in 1991, Bigelow's career began to reach new heights. *Point Break* still stands as one of the first truly influential action movies of the 1990s, reinvigorating the careers of Keanu Reeves and Patrick Swayze and becoming Bigelow's most profitable film. However, although its success opened many doors for Bigelow – and, perhaps more importantly in Hollywood, it also opened a few wallets – her subsequent projects as a director failed to find enough of an audience to justify their expense.

1995's *Strange Days* – a bold and prophetic vision of the future that imagined a society strung out on alternate realities and hooked on mind-altering drugs – was critically acclaimed but flopped at the box office. Furthermore, the project was written and produced by her ex-husband, Cameron, and while it may have proved that the couple's working relationship had survived their divorce, it also put Bigelow back in a position where many wondered how much creative influence and control she had on her own work. It was more than a decade later, with *The Hurt Locker* in 2008, when she finally found her true voice and began to receive the respect and credit she deserved.

Set in post-invasion Iraq, the movie follows a small team of bomb-disposal experts during a typically perilous extended tour of duty. Bigelow saw true heroism in these men, where just doing their day-to-day job meant risking their lives on a daily basis. With a relatively low budget of approximately $15 million, the movie became an unlikely challenger to her ex-husband's considerably more expensive 3D spectacular *Avatar* at the 2010 Academy Awards. When Bigelow later picked up the Oscar for 'Best Director' and *The Hurt Locker* was eventually announced as 'Best Picture', Cameron was nothing but gracious in defeat. Perhaps he took solace in the fact that *Avatar* was already the biggest-grossing movie of all time but he was also undoubtedly aware of what a landmark victory this was. As only the fourth woman in history to be nominated for the 'Best Director' Academy Award, Bigelow was already part of an elite group, but to be the first to actually win was something else. She had proved herself as a filmmaker who possessed a singularly distinctive voice and her next project was set to reaffirm her unique position in Hollywood.

Bigelow re-teamed with Mark Boal, the former journalist and war correspondent who had been her screenwriter on *The Hurt Locker*, intending to repeat their winning formula and collaborate on another project based around real events taking place in the Middle East. Initially entitled *For God and Country*, the film was set to focus on the intensive but fruitless search for Osama bin Laden, which took place during two weeks in December 2001.

Bin Laden had become the most wanted man in the world following the terrorist attacks on the World Trade Center in New York on 9/11 and the manhunt triggered by the events of that day was one of the most covert and exhaustive in recent history. Known as The Battle of Tora Bora, the ensuing military campaign was considered a pivotal moment in the US Government's 'War on Terror' and saw the US military and their allies target a well-known cave complex situated in the mountainous region on the Afghanistan/Pakistan border where the al-Qaeda leader was said to be in hiding. The combined military force outmanoeuvred the Taliban opposition but failed to capture or kill bin Laden, allowing him to disappear and remain at large for the best part of the next decade. This project was set to share much of the same DNA as *The Hurt Locker*. Aside from reviving the writer/director partnership of Boal and Bigelow, both films were based on first-hand, factual accounts of recent events and took place in an environment largely hidden from the general public. Both attempted to expose horrors the majority of us will never witness or experience and much of the audience might be forgiven for not believing either of those worlds actually exist.

By the end of April 2011, the film had a completed script and location scouting had begun for the imminent shoot. Then, on 2 May, when news broke that a US military raid had taken place on a compound in Abbottabad, Pakistan and that a team of Navy SEALs had successfully located and killed bin Laden, Bigelow and Boal knew their latest project was effectively dead in the water. 'The minute I heard the news Osama bin Laden had been killed, what we were working on became history,' Bigelow told *Entertainment Weekly*. 'As interesting a story as that would have been to tell, the news redirected our entire efforts. It changed the movie idea forever.' While it was obvious the movie needed to change course and Boal admits he was forced to start the new script from scratch, much of the background research he'd already carried out was still relevant. 'A lot of the homework I'd done for the first script and a lot of the contacts I made, carried on,' he added in the same *Entertainment Weekly* interview. 'The years I had spent talking to military and intelligence operators involved in counterterrorism was helpful in both projects.'

This attention to detail and extensive research would prove to be integral to everything associated with Bigelow's film. She admitted the script could not have been written without Boal's background in journalism. 'There are pieces of this puzzle that you can only discern through in-depth research,' before adding, 'It was Mark's investigative skills and experience in reporting in this space that enabled us to navigate the sheer complexity of the pursuit.' While Boal was keen to tell the untold human story behind the painstaking extended search for bin Laden, he was equally aware that his successful working relationship with Bigelow was based on teamwork and that the director had her own agenda.

First and foremost, Bigelow was a filmmaker. As Mark Strong, the British character actor who would eventually appear in the finished film, states in an on-set interview, 'What I love about Kathryn Bigelow is the juxtaposition of this very charming, supportive, feminine woman and these testosterone-fuelled movies she makes.' Undeniably, her previous films had never strayed too far from the action genre, incorporating a singular and very distinctive visual language. She wanted to make sure this script gave her enough scope to tell a complicated and often challenging story in her typically visually exciting and engaging fashion. But Bigelow didn't want to pigeonhole the project before it had even been made. When asked to define her movie for *Entertainment Weekly*, she said, 'I guess you could call it many things. It's a thriller, it's a drama, it's a mystery, it's historical,' before concluding, 'It's one of the great stories of our time.' She was aiming for greater scope than the average 'action movie', adding gravitas, intrigue and, by shining a light on the type of investigatory work normally carried out 'in the shadows', she aimed to pay tribute to some of the true unsung heroes involved with the decade-long search for bin Laden.

In the end, the real events which had forced major changes to the script acted as a perfect compromise and gave the film a much more dramatic final act. Adding scenes of the covert military operation at the end gave Boal's complex and often wordy script another dimension. It now succeeded in showing a different side to the soldiers and military personnel directly involved with the Abbottabad compound raid and gave Bigelow adequate opportunity to flex her 'action director' muscles. While truth and authenticity might be key to the film's credibility, and the script now had all the necessary ingredients to negotiate a path through its complicated narrative towards a wholly satisfying conclusion, Boal knew, above all else, that their movie also had to entertain an audience. 'I hope the film will portray this story in a way that people find surprising and believable, and moving. And I do think it's moving, emotionally.' He added, 'It's not a documentary. It's a movie.'

For God and Country quickly became *Zero Dark Thirty*. 'It's a military term for thirty minutes after midnight,' Bigelow told *Entertainment Weekly* before explaining its deeper meaning, 'It refers also to the darkness and secrecy that cloaked the entire decade-long mission.' And with the newly titled script complete, she began putting her movie together.

The cast eventually incorporated over a hundred speaking parts, dozens of smaller roles and countless extras.

Leading the cast was Jessica Chastain, hot from her Oscar-nominated turn in *The Help*. Teaming with Bigelow ticked another box on her ongoing 'checklist' of the industry's most visionary directors, following her work in Terrence Malick's *The Tree of Life* and a few years ahead of her role in Christopher Nolan's *Interstellar*. The rest of the cast reads like a 'who's who' of the best actors currently working in films and TV, including Jason Clarke (*Dawn of the Planet of the Apes*), Joel Edgerton (*Exodus: Gods and Kings*), Jennifer Ehle (*Fifty Shades of Grey*), James Gandolfini (*The Sopranos*) and Kyle Chandler (*The Wolf of Wall Street*), among many more. Chris was a relatively late addition to the cast, missing out on most of the upfront casting announcements. Eventually hired to play Justin, one of the Navy SEALs involved in the film's final act, he had been forced to jump through a few hoops to earn his place on the cast list.

When Chris auditioned for the role, he was nowhere near the required fitness level expected for a regular soldier, much less the peak physical condition of a Navy SEAL but he knew that if he could convince Bigelow he had the right attitude and mentality to play the part, the physical transformation would be easy. He told *GQ*, 'I think if you'd asked me or any of my family or friends as a kid, and said, "Hey, Chris is going to be an actor when he grows up. What's he going to do? He's going to play a Navy SEAL, or he's going to play a shoeshine guy who falls down on rollerblades?" I think most people would probably pick the Navy SEAL,' before adding, 'Actually they probably would say, "No, Chris isn't going to be an actor. He's going to be in the armed forces."' He hoped he'd get the same opportunity he'd been given on *Moneyball*, where a little extra coaching had helped him convince the audience that he was a gifted, left-handed baseball player, and his commitment to playing the role as truthfully as possible would be enough to sell it to an audience.

With the thought of being a part of a project from an Oscar-winning director of Bigelow's stature, and with another potentially career-changing role at stake, he embarked on a rigorous and extensive workout and diet regime. Speaking to *E! Online*, he said, 'I worked out really hard and I cut out everything bad for me for a long time and I just focused on trying to become a believable Navy SEAL.' He admitted that his desperation to land the part made him obsess about his weight and pushed him to unhealthy extremes. '[I] was doing 500 push-ups a day, working out at a gym, running five miles a day,' he told *People* magazine. 'But with no food, and I tore my body apart.'

While his weight loss was rapid and dramatic, his technique was far from approved. 'I felt terrible afterwards,' he confessed. '[I] had to get shoulder surgery, and I wore myself down doing that because I didn't have the proper coaching.' His physical transformation was undeniably remarkable. Within a couple of months he had lost the majority of the excess weight he'd been carrying and bulked up with a considerable amount of extra muscle. He certainly looked the part. 'I don't have any delusions,' he told *GQ*. 'I don't think I would make it through Navy SEAL training. Those guys are incredible, amazing physical specimens, but you have to kind of try to at least look like you could go through that,' he confessed, concluding with typically good humour, 'You're not going to see some weird Andy [Dwyer] pratfalls in the middle of the Osama bin Laden raid where I fall down and have pie on my face.'

It would seem Bigelow was suitably impressed. He certainly looked more believable as an elite soldier and she realised the combination of his imposing new physique, coupled with the natural charm he always brings to the audition process, could potentially bring added depth to his character. Chris had officially joined the *ZD30* cast and before long he embarked on a life-changing voyage – one that not only took him to the other side of the globe but also helped him refocus and re-evaluate his entire career.

His home for the next couple of months was one of the movie's main locations in the Arab kingdom of Jordan, where he and his fellow cast-members embarked on a lengthy period of very specific military-type instruction. Stationed at King Abdullah's Special Operations Training Center, where the Jordanian ruler's own security detail were put through their paces, Chris commented in an interview for the 'Making Of' documentary, 'This place is where all the tier-one guys go to compete and to train. It's a state-of-the-art facility.' Joining the cast of actors – which included Chris, Joel and Nash Edgerton, and Callan Mulvey – were some ex-military personnel and a team of stuntmen. Together, they received extensive tuition in every aspect of executing a covert operation from a number of specially hired military experts. As Chris later explained, '[They gave us] ex-Navy SEALs, Dev group guys and Tier One

SAS guys to walk us through, so we could see exactly how these guys do it.'

They took part in weapons training, combat strategy and role-playing raids in simulated battle scenarios. No detail was overlooked as they were taught how to move, hold their weapons and communicate convincingly as a highly trained military unit and all within a suitably realistic, highly pressured atmosphere. It gave the actors a credible context for their characters and the camaraderie that grew among the group perfectly mirrored the close bonds that occur within a Special Forces team, where each man is expected to safeguard the survival of the one standing next to him. Chris was put in charge of looking after his own equipment, including having a thorough understanding of how to dismantle, clean and reassemble his own rifle. With his hunting background and lifelong interest in firearms, this was nothing new but even he was blown away by the level of detail and accuracy. 'All the gear that we got to use was amazing,' he said on the DVD extras. 'It was kinda like playing army, except they were filming it for a movie.'

The whole training experience, working alongside professional soldiers and ex-military personnel, compounded the feelings of respect and gratitude he already held towards the US's service men and woman and it undoubtedly increased the pressure he already felt to deliver an honourable and believable performance. 'It's important that we take real care and real concern to tell the truth about what happened,' he states in an on-set interview, 'They don't do what they do so that we can make movies about them; they do what they do because it has to be done. Someone has to step up and do it.'

In some respects the decision to accept a role in Bigelow's film had been an easy one, but being separated from his wife for a long period of time and at such a distance was tougher than he'd imagined. He told *People.com*, 'Anna was really pregnant and I didn't take it lightly that we would be travelling in the Middle East.' But Chris, with Anna's blessing, had accepted the dangers involved with working in such a potentially volatile and politically unsettled part of the world and, despite the added pressure he was clearly under, he tried to channel everything about the experience into his performance. Without doubt, he now had a much better understanding of what it was like to be stationed in some of the most dangerous areas of conflict around the globe.

'It was this funny thing where I felt like one of the stereotypical soldiers you see in movies,' he said. 'You know, where he is always staring at a picture of his pregnant wife back home.' Fortunately for Chris, he was not under the same restrictions of a real soldier on active duty. Adamant not to miss out on any part of his wife's pregnancy, he was more or less in constant contact with Anna throughout the extended shoot, admitting, 'With Skype and FaceTime, it was a lot easier than I expected it to be.' Thankfully, Anna was not simply left pining for Chris back home in Los Angeles during his entire trip abroad, having accepted a role in the movie *I Give it a Year*. Chris explained to *People*, '[Anna] ended up working in England so on a couple of weekends I was able to travel to London and see her there, which was really great.'

Much of *Zero Dark Thirty* was actually shot in India, with Chandigarh standing in for Lahore and Abbottabad following the production being refused permission to shoot in Pakistan. But the logistics of building full-scale sets and the disruption caused by a 150-strong movie crew meant some considerably more accessible alternative locations were also needed. As part of Bigelow's determined efforts to present a truly accurate recreation of the military raid on the Abbottabad compound, which had been bin Laden's hidden sanctuary for many years, the crew chose to build a life-size replica of the fortress-like structure in a location close to the Black Sea in Jordan. Over the course of three and a half months, with no access to the real location, a team of architectural builders retro-fitted the compound's blueprints from a 3D digital replica. Using plaster-covered cinder blocks and specialist set painters, every detail was painstakingly reproduced – from the exact layout of each room to floor tiles, which were reproduced from images shown in news footage shot on the night of the raid – the end result was undeniably impressive, if a little disconcerting. Chris commented on the movie's DVD extras, 'It was so eerie because this thing, inch by inch, down to [the smallest details], looks like it was there, looks like it was lived in, looks like the place where Osama bin Laden was killed.'

The fact that scenes featuring the Navy SEALs storming the complex were shot on the one-year anniversary of the actual raid also gave the experience added significance. This was the location for much of Chris's work on the film and it proved to be a testing time for everyone involved. Bigelow's insistence on 100 per cent accuracy extended to capturing the actors' initial reactions on entering the set. 'Our first experience seeing the compound was in a raid format,' Chris recalls in a 'behind the scenes' interview. 'We were going to travel all the way there in our Navy SEAL gear so we can pull up to this compound, join up with our teams and do the raid, without ever having seen it.' Bigelow, who intended to shoot the raid 'live', following the real events beat for beat, minute by minute, stated on-set, 'What I try to do with action sequences [like this] is put the audience on the ground, in the middle of the event.' But, as Joel Edgerton remembered, 'Doing the whole raid was a tough experience. We were kind of jumping around the house shooting this piece and that piece. You know it was a lot to keep in your head.'

This sense of confusion and disorientation was obviously useful within the context of portraying the moments of organised chaos, which reportedly occurred during the real events, but it made for a difficult and complicated shoot. The recreation of the compound location was built without the use of removable walls, meaning everything shot on the set had to be done in very cramped conditions, giving the scenes a heightened sense of confinement and adding to the overall intensity of the situation. 'That necessitated a very rigorous shoot in many ways,' Bigelow confessed. 'Spaces were very small. The hallways were very narrow. It was kind of a hot airless structure that when you put 150 people inside, it became even hotter and even more claustrophobic.'

Adding to the stresses of capturing the 'cat-and-mouse' tension of the climactic ground assault were the shooting of some major stunts, involving two stealth helicopters, which formed the explosive centrepiece to the film's final scenes. While the helicopters used in the actual raid remained highly classified, Bigelow's team had designed and built plausible approximations of the real thing. And while transporting each of these replicas, in three easy-to-assemble pieces, from their manufacturing plant to any location would have proved difficult enough, shipping what looked like prototype stealth helicopters through customs into the Middle East was almost impossible. Thankfully, Bigelow and her team had made enough friends in high places along the way and the helicopter parts were duly delivered. This level of co-operation and assistance was typical of the respect she had earned over the course of the seven-month shoot and symbolic of the incredible goodwill directed towards the entire *Zero Dark Thirty* project.

Bigelow later detailed some of the more troublesome aspects of the shoot to *Rolling Stone* magazine: 'Almost zero-light conditions, 150 crew members, twenty-two cast members, and then you bring in the helicopters.' It was these scenes, involving the helicopter flights and crash landing, which would prove to be some of the most intense and gruelling moments of the whole shoot for Chris. 'I'll never complain about flying coach again after shooting those scenes we shot in the helicopters,' he joked in an on-set interview. 'It's hard enough to get twelve Navy SEALs in a helicopter with all their gear and guns but we had twelve Navy SEALs, plus two cameramen, plus two camera loaders and a cable guy. We were sardines for a good week.' But these on-set hardships seemed to be far outweighed by the overall enjoyment he was experiencing in making the film, as he enthusiastically recalls in a 'behind the scenes' interview: 'Life-size Black Hawk helicopters being hoisted from the biggest cranes in Jordan, with stuntmen dangling from them. Lots of lights, wind and gun shots... amazing spectacle.' He had pretty much summed up the entire crew's experience of working on the film and it was one echoed by Bigelow herself. 'I would say working with this cast is one of the great experiences of my life,' she admitted in an interview included on the DVD of the movie. 'Just a phenomenal experience.'

Before a minute of footage had been shot, *Zero Dark Thirty* was being hailed as 'the most controversial movie of the year'. But Bigelow's intentions were clear and, as she would later state in an interview with *Entertainment Weekly*, she hoped her film sparked debate but had no interest in exaggerating real events for the sake of giving it a more dramatic tone. 'This is an amazing story about the triumph of will, dedication and duty,' she insisted. '[It's] about the real-life heroes in the intelligence community who worked behind the scenes day and night on what was perhaps the toughest assignment of their lives,' she added, before concluding, 'As such, it's a story that needs to be told respectfully.'

Screenwriter Mark Boal had taken a similarly adamant stance, 'There's no political agenda in the film. Full stop. Period.' It was a statement substantiated by the fact that the movie clearly avoided promoting the agenda of any one political party and the fact that President Obama never appears on screen, save for a brief moment of actual news footage. It was Boal's clear-cut assertion that he shared Bigelow's view of the film they'd made together – one which celebrated 'people who dedicate themselves to really difficult and dangerous things for the greater good' and was more interested in what happened behind the scenes leading up to bin Laden's death than glorifying Obama's actual decision to launch the attack.

While the film's lack of a clear-cut political message or moral judgement would make it the target for a great deal of criticism in some sections of the media, among most film critics *Zero Dark Thirty* was heralded as a masterpiece. Not only did it became one of the most favourably reviewed films of the year, with the *Rotten Tomatoes* website reporting an average 8.5/10 rating overall, it also scored big with cinema audiences around the world, making it one of the year's most resounding critical and commercial successes. Most reviews praised Bigelow's attempt to present an alternative definition of heroism and examine some of the more covert aspects of modern warfare. *Entertainment Weekly* called it 'A gripping salute to the desk warrior who spent not minutes but years going in for the kill' in an 'A'-grade review, and it was the film's successful blending of all too familiar real-life events and genuine dramatic tension which truly impressed. The review continued, 'Once in a long while, a fresh-from-the-headlines movie – like *All the President's Men* or *United 93* – fuses journalism, procedural drama, and the oxygenated atmosphere of a thriller into a new version of history written with lightning. *Zero Dark Thirty*, Kathryn Bigelow's meticulous and electrifying re-creation of the hunt for Osama bin Laden, is that kind of movie.'

Others applauded the skilful injection of suspense and spectacle into a story where, you had to assume, the majority of cinema audiences were already aware of the outcome. The *Guardian* said, 'Telling a nearly three-hour story with an ending everyone knows, Bigelow and Boal have managed to craft one of the most intense and intellectually challenging films of the year,' while *Time Out* simply proclaimed, 'This is an instant classic.' Many commented on Bigelow's growth as a filmmaker, among them the *Chicago Reader*, which stated, 'Bigelow has widened her reach past the white-knuckle thrills of *The Hurt Locker* and into the darkest currents of American military might.' But it was the overall tone that ultimately frustrated *USA Today*, who declared, 'There's an emotional detachment to the film that undercuts its potency,' something they felt rendered Bigelow's work, 'more technically proficient than emotionally involving,' before concluding, 'The movie audiences are anticipating in *Zero Dark Thirty* takes place in the final half hour.'

When it came to the 2012 'Awards Season', *Zero Dark Thirty* became a front runner in most of the major categories. In the end, the film received countless nominations and won several prestigious awards, including a victory for Jessica Chastain as 'Best Actress' at the Golden Globes and nominations for the film across five different categories at the eighty-fifth Academy Awards. These included Oscar nods for 'Best Picture', 'Best Actress' (for Chastain) and 'Best Original Screenplay'. However, *Zero Dark Thirty* only managed to secure one win, tying with *Skyfall* in the 'Best Sound Editing' category. After a limited US release in just five cinemas in late 2012, it was given a wide release on 11 January 2013, topping the box-office chart with a $24 million opening weekend.

The film went on to accumulate more than $130 million in worldwide box-office receipts, sailing past *Moneyball*'s already impressive $110 million total and becoming (at that point, at least) Chris's highest-grossing movie to date.

For Chris, the film was much more than just a commercial high point. *Zero Dark Thirty* signalled a real change in his attitude towards the work he was capable of doing and saw him continue to build on the unexpected kudos he'd earned after *Moneyball*. That experience had given him the confidence to challenge long-held misconceptions he had about his natural talent as a comedic actor and how those same skills could be harnessed within a more dramatic performance. Chris admitted to the *New York Times*, 'It was another element to myself that I just hadn't seen.' He went on to confess, 'Before *Zero Dark Thirty*, I had played a different version of the same person in every movie,' adding, 'It's been a bit of a survival mechanism my whole life to kind of play the dummy, and get laughs, and goof around.' This type of instant feedback and positive reinforcement had sustained him throughout his tentative first steps as an actor but now he was slowly coming round to the idea that maybe he had a lot more to offer and that it was time to move on to the next level.

As he'd learned during his experiences on set with *Moneyball* director Bennett Miller, successful dramatic acting was more of a collaborative process and Chris was the first to admit, 'It doesn't come as naturally,' before adding, 'The process of drama falls so much more on the filmmaker than with comedy.' He explained that he had always been fairly confident about his own comedic abilities. 'You know when comedy is working,' he told *Movieline*. 'You do a take and in your head you think, "Oh, that's the funniest take of all,"' he said, before elaborating, 'It's a combination of knowing the comedic beat was good – it made you laugh, it made the people on the crew laugh.' However, with drama, he knew he was far less in tune with what he was doing and his relative inexperience often made him doubt himself and left him questioning the effectiveness of the performance he was giving. 'When you do drama you're like, "I have no fucking idea if that was good or not,"' he admitted. 'You do something deep and if your stuff was really effective, the ultimate result is silence.' While he wanted to believe this silence was evidence of the power of his performance and a mark of respect from the cast and crew, the nagging voice in his head always meant there was an element of doubt. He joked, 'Silence is not necessarily [a good thing], that would also be the result if you sucked.'

It had been a long process but he was gradually starting to understand the connections that existed between the different aspects of his work and, with the help of some extremely talented directors, including Bennett Miller and Kathryn Bigelow, he began applying the same rules to every performance. 'I think as long as you're being truthful in whatever role you're playing, people will buy it,' Chris asserted to *GQ*, before adding, 'People can say, "You're making this transition into dramatic roles," but I've been working hard at dramatic roles for a really long time. I just haven't gotten any of them!'

Previously, when he had auditioned for the likes of *Star Trek* and *Avatar*, the self-belief and swagger he normally radiates while playing more comedic roles seemed to mysteriously evaporate and the rejection had left him doubting himself. Unable to shake off the nagging feeling that he'd never have the elusive 'It factor' necessary to become a real 'name above the title' movie star, he had taken a step back – albeit a successful one – into more character-driven supporting roles.

While he admitted he wasn't necessarily being handed any jobs 'on a plate', he now approached each audition, whether it was for comedy or drama, with the same conviction and drive. 'I'm still fighting really hard to get any role I get,' he stressed. 'If it's comedy, I go for the laughs. And if it's drama, I try to tell the truth, and try to play the real stakes of whatever scenario the character's in.' While it may seem like a relatively small step to take – and a simple association to make – the realisation that both strands of his work were intertwined and, in some respects, inseparable was like a thunderbolt moment. 'Doing *Zero Dark Thirty* opened my eyes to the idea that I could be taken more seriously as a leading man character,' Chris confided to *Glamour* magazine. 'So I thought I'd try that.'

While the decision to try out for more lead roles was a relatively easy one, putting it into practice might not be quite so simple and, for the foreseeable future, he was firmly back on familiar territory. Shortly after returning to the US after shooting *Zero Dark Thirty*, he was offered a small role in the latest movie by Spike Jonze – one of Hollywood's most exciting and visionary directors. After almost a decade as a much-in-demand music-video director, Jonze made his directorial debut with *Being John Malkovich* in 1999. This mind-bending comedy set the tone for much of his work, mixing a thought-provoking narrative with dazzling visuals, and sealed his reputation as one of the most unique filmmakers in Hollywood. After his adaptation of the beloved children's classic *Where the Wild Things Are* proved to be a resounding box office misfire, Jonze began developing *Her* as his next project. He served as writer and director on this intriguing sci-fi love story, which became his most commercially successful and critically acclaimed film to date.

Her tells the story of Theodore, as played by Joaquin Phoenix, a lonely office worker struggling to come to terms with his failed marriage, whose life is irrevocably altered when he purchases a new talking operating system (OS). Fitted with intuitive artificial intelligence and voiced by Scarlett Johansson, 'Samantha' is designed to adapt and predict its owner's every whim and offer companionship and comfort whenever it is needed. Theodore soon falls in love with 'Samantha' but things inevitably begin to spiral out of control.

Her is a complex but highly entertaining study of alienation in a society almost completely addicted to technology. It depicts a frighteningly believable world where everyone is slowly losing the ability to communicate effectively or interact with each other without gadgets or machines, giving the film an intriguing mix of seemingly outlandish sci-fi concepts and not-too-far-from-the-truth realism.

Chris plays Paul, Theodore's co-worker, appearing in only a couple of very brief scenes. While his screen time in the film is minimal, it couldn't have done him any harm to be associated with yet another A-list director of Jonze's calibre. *Her* completed his impressive run of appearing in a movie nominated for 'Best Picture' at the Oscars in three consecutive years, following *Moneyball* in 2011 and *Zero Dark Thirty* in 2012. And, although *Her* similarly failed to pick up the main prize, it put Chris into a fairly elite category and prompted comparisons with serial Oscar nominee Meryl Streep. While she may have been nominated a record nineteen times, none of the films Streep has appeared in since 2002's *The Hours* have actually received a nomination in the 'Best Picture' category. These days, it would seem Chris Pratt is a far safer bet for any director wishing to receive Oscar attention for their movie. It was a run of good fortune, which inspired *Hollywood.com* to lead one article with the title WHY DOES EVERY CHRIS PRATT MOVIE GET A BEST PICTURE NOMINATION? before stating, 'Don't be surprised if Pratt starts becoming as much of a fixture on the awards circuit as [Meryl] Streep herself. After all, he does seem to have the better luck with these things.'

For his next major movie, Chris was treading familiar ground. He re-entered 'The Best Friend Zone' by taking the role of Brett in Vince Vaughn's new comedy/drama, *Delivery Man*. It was with some irony that Chris said, when talking to *Glamour* magazine on the *Zero Dark Thirty* publicity trail a few months earlier, 'Who knows, maybe this will be the last movie I'll be in shape for and then I'll go fat again. My wife would appreciate it. She likes me fat.' It appeared as though all Anna's Christmases had come at once. Chris had decided that this particular character needed to be heavy, not just a little on the chubby side but really, REALLY fat. Brett was going to be big and Chris was determined to push his own weight to new, scale-busting extremes.

CHAPTER ELEVEN

TIPPING THE SCALES

'It's a thing when it becomes three peoples'
job to mop sweat off you.'
CHRIS PRATT, ON THE DOWNSIDE OF GAINING
WEIGHT FOR MOVIE ROLES – *ESQUIRE*

2012 proved to be an especially eventful year for Chris, not least because it saw the birth of his and Anna's first child. Their son, later named Jack, was born prematurely on 25 August, arriving nine weeks earlier than expected. Chris announced Jack's arrival on Twitter with typical good humour: 'It's a boy! Thanks for all your kind words. In lieu of gifts we ask that you mouth kiss a stranger,' but in reality, it was a very challenging time for the couple. Anna told *MailOnline*, 'He was born at three pounds and we were told, "OK, you need to be prepared for raising a special-needs child."' Chris and Anna's relationship had proved to be an incredibly strong one, built on communication, honesty and mutual support, and their total commitment to one another had never been more apparent than during the first few months of Jack's life.

Jack's health became the couple's number-one priority and, while his recovery was a slow one, Chris and Anna never lost faith. 'It also felt like, you know, "We can do this,"' Anna recalled, before adding that Chris had been quick to point out, 'He's alive,' and that they should be grateful for every moment they got to spend with their child. After Anna had been allowed to hold her newborn son for only a few precious moments, Jack was required to spend his first month in the hospital's intensive-care unit, closely monitored by the medical staff and with his worried parents never far from his side.

'[Jack] didn't want to be an October baby,' Chris later revealed in a funny and moving speech at the 'March of Dimes' Celebration of Babies Luncheon. 'He wanted to be born in the summer, I guess.' He joked that, at 3lb 12oz, in fisherman's terms at least, his son was 'a decent-sized bass' but admitted he was 'very small for a human.' Chris then elaborated on the extent of Jack's illness. As well as having a hernia operation, 'He had jaundice, so they put a blindfold on him and he slept beneath [a] creepy light and we had a PICC line, which is an IV that runs up his arm into his heart. He had a feeding tube and just wires in and out, and he lived in that incubator. That was his first crib.' He admitted it was a truly testing experience, telling *People* magazine, 'We were scared for so long,' before admitting, 'It showed me who in my life is really close to me. It brought me closer to my family and it restored my faith in God.' He added, 'Not that it needed to be restored, but it really redefined it... We prayed a lot.'

As Jack rallied and began to gain strength, the couple were encouraged to spend as much time as possible with him. During the 'March of Dimes' speech Chris recalled, 'We did this amazing thing called "skin-to-skin" – it was just the best feeling I ever had.' He elaborated, 'My little boy was laying across my neck and chest feeling my heartbeat and feeling my love, and I played him country music and I sang to him and made him promises… in that moment… just about what kind of dad I wanted to be, and I just prayed that he'd be here long enough and he was going to let me keep him.'

It's unlikely there was a single dry eye in the house following Chris's heartfelt speech and it was clear that Jack's arrival had made him count his blessings and reassess his priorities. 'I've done all kinds of cool things as an actor – I've jumped out of helicopters and done some daring stunts and played baseball in a professional stadium, but none of it means anything compared to being somebody's daddy.'

After a couple of anxious months, Jack was now out of immediate danger and Chris and Anna's life regained some degree of normality. Chris was soon back to work. His next acting job was scheduled to start filming in late October but he was eager to reassure everyone who had supported him and Anna during their ordeal and keep them up to date with their son's progress. 'He's totally healthy now,' he said during an appearance on David Letterman's *Late Show*. 'He is just so perfect and I love him so much,' he went on, before adding, 'He's just a ball of joy. He's terrific.' While it must have been difficult to turn his attention to anything other than his family, Chris had already done a lot of preparation for his next role – and he had the 44in waist to prove it!

Delivery Man was a remake of a French-Canadian film, *Starbuck*, which had been released to considerable acclaim towards the end of 2011. Filmed in and around the predominantly French-speaking province of Quebec in Canada, *Starbuck* was co-written and directed by Ken Scott, a Quebec native and former comedian-turned-filmmaker. The film would eventually be the highest-grossing homegrown movie of the year, reaching a worldwide box-office total in excess of $6.3 million and enjoying a rare international breakthrough for a film not in the English language. The American version was also directed by Scott and was set to star Vince Vaughn, with a supporting cast that included Chris and *How I Met Your Mother* star Cobie Smulders.

Vaughn would play the film's central character, David Wozniak, who appeared to be down on his luck but is basically a decent guy. Seen as the black sheep, Wozniak works thanklessly as a deliveryman for his family-owned butcher's shop, while desperately trying to keep the other parts of his life from spinning out of control. With substantial financial debts, he is permanently dodging thugs who are intent on reclaiming what they are owed and his long-term girlfriend has recently announced she is pregnant. Into this chaos comes a bombshell from Wozniak's past: he receives news that, due to a clerical error, the 600 sperm donations he made to a clinic during his college years have been disproportionately assigned to clients, resulting in him being responsible for fathering over 500 children. Wozniak, who made his donations using an alias, 'Starbuck', must fight to retain anonymity as a group of his now grown-up children bring a class-action lawsuit against the clinic in an attempt to find out the true identity of their biological father.

Chris would play Brett, Wozniak's closest friend, and a semi-retired lawyer who wants to use the case as a means to return to the courtroom. We learn early in the movie that Brett has given up his job in order to look after his own brood of four kids but he yearns to escape the everyday stresses that are obviously pushing him to the brink.

From the outset Chris had a very clear idea of who his character was and how he should look. He told the *Huffington Post*, 'He's a sad sack,' before elaborating, 'This was a character who is pretty brash about parenting and talking about "don't have kids" and "kids suck the life out of you and they take all of your time and they take all of your energy and they take all of your money" and "don't be a father, don't do it."' He knew his main challenge was making this character, whose introductory scenes portray him as shallow and fairly offensive, seem relatable and sympathetic, stating, 'It's really important for the comedy and for the tone of this movie that [Brett] be really likeable,' before adding, 'If that character is played by someone cut with six-pack abs, you're like, "That guy is an asshole,"' and he concluded, 'I think the way you make someone ultra-confident and brash really likeable is by making them have outsides that give then away as liars ... I felt, you know, people tend to wear their insides on their outsides.'

As soon as he got the part, Chris had decided Brett's 'outside' needed some extensive padding. He recalls that he set himself an unlikely goal. 'This role came along and I had three months out and I just said, "I'm going to get to 300 pounds!"' While he admits many of his friends and family begged him, 'Don't do it! Don't do it!' he was adamant the character needed to look a certain way and he was determined to see it through. 'I've been sort of gaining and losing weight over the past few years for different roles,' he acknowledged, 'but this was the fattest I ever got... I was like 295 at my highest. So that is a lot for me. That's about fifty pounds higher than my median average.'

Chris had started to gain weight immediately after wrapping *Zero Dark Thirty*, partly to get back to his preferred 'Andy Dwyer Weight' and, as he would later reveal to *SheKnows*, partly due to Anna's condition, 'The first twenty pounds was sympathy weight because my wife was pregnant. I was gaining weight as she was gaining weight,' but he went on to admit that the rest was sheer determination. 'The other thirty-five pounds I did just by declaring that I was going to do it.' While he had gained weight before, he considered this to be his move into the major leagues: 'My rule of thumb became: "If it's there, eat it." And then I would order two entrees at every meal. I would always have desert, and I would drink the darkest beer on the menu.'

Chris was starting from an unusual place, having crash-dieted into shape for his role as a Navy SEAL on *Zero Dark Thirty*, he was already bulkier than normal and he quickly realised things were getting a little out of control. He told the *Huffington Post*, 'I was back on *Parks and Rec* and was eating a whole bunch, going in the opposite swing on that sort of diet pendulum,' before recognising, 'I think it was dangerous. I don't think it's healthy at all to do that.' He concluded, 'I don't imagine I'll do it anytime soon.' Whatever the risks, it appeared that his efforts had paid off. His character, Brett, provides much of the movie's light relief and the scenes he shares with Vaughn are some of the funniest in the whole movie.

The tone of the film was a slight change of pace for Vaughn, almost entirely abandoning the wisecracking, motor-mouthed characters he'd become synonymous with. Instead, *Delivery Man* would explore a far more sentimental and nuanced side to his performance. As Brett, Chris generates most of the big laughs, either with Vaughn or, especially, in the scenes he plays alongside the young actors playing his children. Invariably dressed in sweat pants or a dressing gown, the dishevelled and decidedly chubby Chris sits amid the chaos of dirty dishes, discarded toys and general untidiness. His kids, who are completely disruptive and whom he obviously has no control over, either ignore him or, in one case, relentlessly slap him across the face just to get his attention. While Chris was happy to be appearing in a comedy where the actors were required to adhere more strictly to the actual script, his scenes still retain a certain loose, freewheeling quality. His performance adds a hint of edginess and energy to the overly saccharine aftertaste left by the movie as a whole. It was another scene-stealing performance from Chris. Despite playing second fiddle to Vaughn, there is no doubt that the film acts as a showcase for his developing talents and clearly indicates that he could have easily headlined the movie himself.

On its release in November 2013, *Delivery Man* received

a fairly negative reception. Most critics felt it failed to fully exploit the obvious comedic potential of the story's premise and paled in comparison with the original. However, the *Hollywood Reporter*, in an otherwise lukewarm review, complimented Vaughn by saying it was 'nice to see Vaughn moving out of his fast-talking comfort zone in a role that requires him to be more quietly reactive,' before praising Chris in his attempts to 'comically raise the second-banana bar as a put-upon dad.' Elsewhere, Mark Kermode at the *Observer* complained, 'The tone wavers between the pantomime and the mawkish and while little has been lost in translation, less still has been gained,' while the *Radio Times*' review pointed out, 'It's warm-hearted, certainly, but ultimately undone by a would-be feel-good central conceit that makes less and less sense the more you think about it,' before praising Chris for being considerably 'funnier than the clunky script.'

Delivery Man's critical mauling and Vaughn's rapidly declining status as a bankable leading man resulted in the film's rather lacklustre box-office performance, where it stalled around the $53 million mark. While it couldn't be considered a total failure, *Delivery Man* did little for Vaughn's reputation and seemed a long way down from the dizzy heights he'd reached with *Wedding Crashers* less than a decade previously.

With Jack now out of danger and finally released from hospital, Chris and Anna had very little enthusiasm for anything other than staying home with their new baby. Both actors cleared their schedules to concentrate on making up for the time they'd lost during Jack's extended stay in hospital. While neither accepted any major projects requiring them to be away from home for any prolonged length of time, both kept working – Anna was in the early stages of preparing for her role in the CBS sitcom *Mom*, while Chris completed voice work for Warner Brothers' *The Lego Movie*.

The idea for making a movie based around children's toys was nothing new but it had turned out to be a somewhat risky business. While Michael Bay managed to adapt *Transformers* into a billion-dollar franchise for Dreamworks/Paramount, Peter Berg's *Battleship* and a couple of *G.I. Joe* movies proved it's not always plain sailing, and that the transfer from toy box to the big screen can sometimes go horribly wrong. Lego had already shown some of its potential with a series of very popular and lucrative video games, including various Lego *Star Wars* titles and tie-ins with several other major movie franchises, including *Harry Potter*, *Indiana Jones* and *Pirates of the Caribbean*. It seemed there was already an obvious connection between imaginative, big-screen storytelling and the interlocking, multi-coloured bricks and it wouldn't be long before the basic concept for a movie took shape. After a couple of years in development, the initial script idea attracted filmmakers Phil Lord and Christopher Miller, who were proving to be one of Hollywood's hottest – and uniquely versatile – writing/directing partnerships.

Lord and Miller had made their big-screen debut in September 2009 when their computer-animated adaptation of a popular children's book, *Cloudy with a Chance of Meatballs*, made a somewhat unexpected entry at number one in the US box-office chart on its opening weekend. The film held the top spot for a second week and eventually racked up over $243 million worldwide. But Lord and Miller were not content with limiting their filmmaking output to the world of animation and their next feature saw them turn their attention to producing live-action comedy, *21 Jump Street*. Their adaptation of the late 1980s television show, which had given its lead actor, Johnny Depp, his first big break, was another unlikely hit. After generating another $200 million at the worldwide box office, it's hardly surprising that Lord and Miller were now being given the chance to make whatever movie they wanted. After a *Cloudy* sequel, they turned their attention to writing the first draft of the Lego script, which they also planned to direct. As with their previous work, the resulting screenplay was a highly entertaining subversion of countless classic legends and movie plots. Alongside nods to *The Lord of the Rings*, *The Matrix* and *Star Wars*, there were endless pop-culture references and it even had an anti-establishment/anti-conformity message thrown in for good measure.

Chris was one of the first actors to be attached to the project, at this point known as *Lego: Piece of Resistance*, as announcements were made about casting in early June 2012. 'I've known Chris and Phil for a while now,' he told *Screenslam*. 'They wrote this character and when they talked to me about it I was thrilled... I was beyond thrilled.' Of course, his association with the filmmakers dates back to before the release of the duo's debut feature. With Anna supplying the voice of Samantha 'Sam' Sparks for both *Cloudy* and its 2013 sequel, Chris was well aware of what the filmmakers were capable of. 'I was such a huge fan of theirs and their previous work. I knew anything they did was going to be funny and great.' He added, 'It's not lip service, they are really talented storytellers, really have a unique comedic voice and they work incredibly hard and so with that combination of things I just had to be onboard.'

While he was already sold on the idea, it seemed Lord and Miller thought they still had some persuading to do. Chris continued, 'They showed me some of the original artwork and talked about the character. They said, "What do you think? Do you want to do it?"' His reply was a fairly unanimous 'Are you insane?' before he added, 'I would say "Yes" without seeing any of this stuff.'

Although he had previously done a couple of voice-only roles for television and video games, including Cooper Daniels for *Ben 10* and Obi-Wan Kenobi for *Kinect Star Wars*, this was his first taste of working on an animated feature film. While voice acting for animation can be a tough discipline, having the role more or less written with Chris in mind meant it ended up becoming a perfect fit for his upbeat, everyman persona and 'anything can happen' sense of humour. While it's easy to assume that creating characters in animation might be a very technical and restrictive process for any actor, relinquishing a great deal of control and performance choices to the artists and animators themselves, Lord and Miller encouraged improvisation and riffing on their existing script. Their other casting choices suggested it was not only encouraged but perhaps expected, for Chris was joined by such highly skilled comedic actors as Will Ferrell, Will Arnett, Nick Offerman, Charlie Day and Elizabeth Banks. He approached the creation of his character, Emmet, with the same attitude and commitment he'd used for every other role, relying heavily on the guidance of his directors, Lord and Miller. 'You're doing the voice but you want to understand the world that the character is living inside of,' he explained. 'Chris and Phil do a great job in helping to paint the picture of what's happening all around you ... they were able to show me some of the temporary art and a few of the roughly cut together scenes they had already animated ... They could give me a great sense of where my character was, the world around me, what it looked like and what I was experiencing... that was really helpful.'

Although most of the actors recorded their voice tracks in isolation, with no other cast members present, the calibre of talent involved ensured that these sessions were bursting with creativity. Lord and Miller were always on hand, sitting in the recording room beside the actors, tinkering with the script, adding lines and throwing fresh ideas into the mix. While the actors stood in front of their microphone, Lord and Miller would be constantly coaching them, pushing them to experiment and improvise lines, developing the script organically as the recording process continued. After the initial sessions were completed, they had the difficult task of editing the dialogue into a coherent story before handing their work over to the talented team of artists and animators. Charged with creating the look of the characters based on what the actors had delivered during the voice sessions, the animator's job would be a long and complicated one.

Chris was fascinated by every step of the process. He was particularly intrigued by the attention to detail involved in bringing each individual character to life and the animator's ability to instil some of his personality and physical features into his character. 'When I look at Emmet's little yellow, adorable face, I see myself looking back,' he confessed to *Screenslam*. 'They actually did a good job capturing everyone's facial expressions.' He went on to explain, despite only appearing in animated form, just how much of an integral part each actor played in the final version of their character: 'When you're doing voice work and you're doing the recording sessions, they did have cameras set up all around just to capture, maybe some gestures or facial expressions and they were able to put that into the character,' He added, '[Emmet] does resemble me. It is, by the way, amazing to look at this little Lego figure that's based on you.'

Chris had nothing but praise for his directors. Acknowledging their efforts, he said, '[Lord and Miller] are very, very thorough. So if you have any questions at all, you can just ask them and they will tell you because they have control of everything in the entire movie, right down to the very finest detail and they are so passionate about what they are making.' While Lord and Miller were very hands-on writer-directors, *The Lego Movie* ended up being more of a collaborative effort than the pair's previous work, with former *Robot Chicken* director, Chris McKay, joining them in a supervisory role as work continued throughout 2013. It seemed Lord and Miller's own success had caught up with them. Due to the tight schedules of their lead actors, Channing Tatum and Jonah Hill, they were forced to briefly step away from *The Lego Movie* as they started work on the sequel to their 2012 hit, *21 Jump Street* – imaginatively titled *22 Jump Street*. This left McKay in charge of overseeing the completion of much of the animation work being created by Australian animation studio *Animal Logic* during the later stages of production.

Chris had completed the majority of his work on *The Lego Movie* by the end of 2012 and had yet again declined any other offers of work outside his ongoing commitment to *Parks and Recreation*. It seemed that his decision to take the first half of 2013 off, staying close to home with Anna and looking after Jack, was a logical one. Their son was now fully recovered and, as Chris described him to *People* magazine, had turned out to be a 'strong, smart, happy, funny, beautiful boy,' adding, 'He's such a fighter. He's amazing. He's so open and there's no fear in him, no matter what.' The extended break had also done Chris a lot of good and he entered the New Year with renewed energy and focus on the direction his career would now take. With his name attached as the lead role in a major movie – albeit an animated one – he was attracting a different kind of buzz and his position on the Hollywood 'pecking order' was changing.

The Lego Movie was generating an unprecedented amount of positive feedback and when the executives at Warner Brothers saw the finished movie, they were obviously blown away. The proposed late February 2014 release date was soon scrapped in favour of a 7 February opening. The publicity created by bringing the premiere date forward by almost a full month created a wholly positive buzz and anticipation for the movie started to build.

Critical response to *The Lego Movie* was emphatically positive. The film launched with an exceptional 98 per cent 'Fresh' rating on the *Rotten Tomatoes* website and *Entertainment Weekly* running a feature entitled CAN THE LEGO MOVIE REALLY BE THAT GOOD? *Rolling Stone* said, '[The film] has so much energy it sometimes spins out of control. But the fun is nonstop,' before praising its more subversive and slightly more adult themes. 'The brightly imagined *Lego Movie* is also a wickedly smart and funny free for all, and sassy enough to shoot well-aimed darts at corporate branding.' The review concluded by saying, 'Satirical subversion in family entertainment is an unexpected treat, especially in a movie that also functions as a triumph of product placement.' The film had, indeed, achieved the rarest of feats, appealing equally to the children it was directly aimed at and the adults obliged to accompany them. The *Independent*'s reviewer agreed that 'Adults who go to *The Lego Movie* out of a weary sense of parental duty are in for a pleasant surprise,' adding, 'The Lego characters themselves may be totally inexpressive but this is still a zany and tremendously witty affair.'

As the glowing reviews kept on coming, *The Lego Movie* quickly began to outstrip the industry's box-office expectations. In the regular (and usually reliable) 'Box Office Preview' feature, *Entertainment Weekly* predicted that the film would deliver something in the region of $43 million on the all-important opening weekend, only to report three days later that *The Lego Movie* had actually amassed a staggering $69.11 million. It had achieved the biggest opening of 2014 so far. And with 60 per cent of the audience over eighteen years of age, the film was obviously connecting with a wide audience, hitting the mass-appeal 'sweet spot' and looking likely to keep building – no pun intended! Within a fortnight of *Lego Movie* opening, a sequel had been announced, with a release date eventually set for 2018. Over the coming months, Lord and Miller discussed their plans to create a mini 'cinematic universe', which would include a spin-off movie for Lego Batman, as well as vague plans to produce more tie-ins featuring characters introduced during the first movie.

The Lego Movie eventually generated more than $468 million at the worldwide box office, its profits surpassing those of Warner Brothers' other 'sure-fire' blockbuster, Gareth Edwards' *Godzilla*, by almost $50 million. While no one could have predicted that Edwards' $160 million franchise relaunch would be outperformed by a $60 million kids' movie, it seems even less likely that the film's 350ft titular creature would be cut down to size by an inch-high piece of plastic. While this was undoubtedly Chris's biggest box-office hit to date – and it was made all the sweeter by the fact that his name was very clearly at the top of the cast list – there was no getting away from the fact that it was an animated feature and that only his voice appeared in the film. Fortunately, by the time *The Lego Movie* had hit theatres, his next major movie role was already complete and this particular part would send his career into previously uncharted territory – Chris was about to enter the Marvel Universe and *Guardians of the Galaxy* would change his life forever.

CHAPTER TWELVE

A THIEF, TWO THUGS, AN ASSASSIN AND A MANIAC... WHAT A BUNCH OF A-HOLES

'Just be yourself, and hopefully they can shape an epic space adventure around exactly who you are.'
CHRIS PRATT, EXPLAINING HIS ACTING PROCESS FOR
GUARDIANS OF THE GALAXY – PEOPLE MAGAZINE

When James Gunn was handed the reins to direct *Guardians of the Galaxy* in September 2012 – Marvel Studio's big-screen adaptation of their own cult comic-book series – he was understandably precious about every element of the production. He hadn't been the only director on Marvel's shopping list and he'd fought his way into the driving seat of the movie by proving he had the necessary vision and by enduring a rigorous elimination process to get there. Gunn was something of a maverick filmmaker. He had drifted in and out of the Hollywood mainstream for over a decade, seemingly immune to the intoxicating allure of making big-budget, commercial movies as a director-for-hire for the major studios. But something about directing this particular film struck a different chord. It was the first time he'd felt so passionate about any 'outside' project and he knew instinctively that Marvel Studios would allow him to make the movie exactly as he envisioned it. Marvel had never balked at choosing unexpected or untested directors for their movies – think Jon Favreau's *Iron Man*, Kenneth Branagh's *Thor* and Joss Whedon's *The Avengers*, for example – and while they had enjoyed an almost unbroken run of successes, Gunn didn't want to take any unnecessary risks. So it's hardly surprising that, when Chris Pratt's name came up during early casting discussions for the lead role, Peter 'Star-Lord' Quill, Gunn was a little sceptical.

'[When] somebody first suggested him to me, I thought, you got to be kidding me,' he later explained to *ABC Nightline*. 'This chubby guy from *Parks and Recreation*? There's no way I'm going to make that guy the star of my movie.' Thankfully for Chris, he would later change his mind and that 'chubby guy' would undoubtedly become a key contributory factor in the movie's eventual success, helping it become the highest-grossing film at the US box office in 2014.

Aside from a couple of *Hulk* movies, which didn't quite hit the mark, the transition of Marvel's most popular comic-book superheroes to the big screen had resulted in some of the highest-grossing movies of the previous decade or so, including blockbuster franchises featuring *Iron Man*, *X-Men*, *Spider-Man*, *Captain America* and *Thor* and culminating in the assembly of several key figures from their extended universe in 2012's *The Avengers*. According to *boxofficemojo.com*, this impressive run had seen Marvel characters generate over

$9 billion at the worldwide box office – a total accumulated from just fourteen of their movies released between May 2008 and May 2014. However, the *Guardians* project already had several ingredients that didn't automatically add up to mainstream success and Gunn obviously felt it might be seen as reckless to consider making any risky casting decisions.

Aside from the fact that the first *Guardians* comics appeared as far back as 1969 – a good twenty years before the typical summer blockbuster's target audience was even born – and enjoyed little more than cult status, this band of unlikely heroes had to hit the ground running. *Guardians* would not benefit from a series of lead-in movies to introduce its key characters the way *Iron Man*, *Captain America* et al. had fed into *The Avengers*. Also taking into account that two of *Guardians*' main characters would have to be completely computer-generated (CG) – Rocket, a genetically modified, talking racoon and Groot, a tree-like creature with a three-word vocabulary – it would seem that he felt the project had its own mountains to climb.

From its earliest inception the *Guardians of the Galaxy* movie had looked like a somewhat risky proposition. News of the project's 'green light' from Marvel had been received with a combination of scorn and general indifference. Most entertainment-news outlets were baffled by the source material's basic premise and brief character bios, while the more discerning fan-boys and comic-book aficionados doubted that even Marvel could do justice to these beloved and undeniably cultish characters. It seems many feared the worst and presumed *Guardians* would end up under-served by a hack filmmaker and suffer the same fate as obvious misfires like *Blade: Trinity*, *The Punisher* and *The Fantastic Four*. As speculation grew and unsubstantiated stories filled the fan-boy message boards, the film was soon attracting the same vague stench of 'turkey' that had surrounded *John Carter*, Disney's previous attempt to launch a space-opera franchise set within a largely unfamiliar universe. Only a few months earlier, that particular 'experiment' had lost Disney close to $100 million. So, even before a single frame of film had been shot, *Guardians* was being talked about as Marvel's biggest gamble to date and many asked, 'Is Marvel setting up its first genuine box-office flop?' Things didn't really improve when Kevin Feige – Marvel President and *Guardians*' producer – announced, after a long and protracted search, that James Gunn had been hired to direct the project.

At first glance, Gunn's previous feature films could be seen as an acquired taste and somewhat cultish, to say the least, and neither his 2006 directorial debut, *Slither*, or 2010's *Super* made much of a splash at the US box office. Added to the fact that he was well known as the screenwriter for such universally derided fare as 2002's *Scooby-Doo*, its subsequent follow-up, *Monsters Unleashed*, and an ill-advised (but not nearly as bad as you'd think) *Dawn of the Dead* remake from 2004, things didn't exactly bode well. But by reassessing his previous work as a writer-director, it's easy to see that Feige and Marvel were on to something. Closer analysis reveals a far more interesting filmmaker at work. Both *Slither* and *Super* achieve a rare balancing act, retaining a subversive and edgy quality while simultaneously being far more engaging and entertaining than their lack of commercial success suggests. Both scripts possess moments of rare ingenuity and imagination, alongside some genuinely witty dialogue and funny one-liners. And, undoubtedly, Gunn had shown that he was an accomplished director, creating irresistible images and using ingenious visual effects, despite both films being made for a fraction of the price of a typical Hollywood blockbuster.

Marvel had already received a first-draft script for *Guardians* from Nicole Perlman, a graduate of the studio's own (now defunct) screenwriting programme, when Gunn's name came up. This draft was subsequently rewritten by Chris McCoy, an up-and-coming writer who had already placed three scripts on the legendary 'Black List' – Hollywood's annual list of the best unproduced screenplays. So, when Gunn was first approached to direct *Guardians*, he wasn't particularly interested, especially if he was being asked to direct someone else's script. But something else was holding him back. It seemed a natural self-defence mechanism, cultivated by years of disappointments and false starts as a filmmaker, had already kicked in.

'I used to think that my success in this industry was due to not giving a shit,' he told *fastcocreate.com*. 'I would be fully committed to something and completely unattached to it. I would go in and pitch a movie and I would work really hard on a monologue so that I'd know exactly what I'm pitching, and at the same time I would not care if it got made.' Despite knowing that Kevin Feige was a fan of his earlier movies, Gunn's casual indifference seems to have stemmed from his assumption that, out of all the directors still in the running, he was merely there to make up the numbers. He told *Geek* magazine, 'I thought I was probably just an interesting person to meet with as opposed to someone that they would actually hire.' Once he realised that Marvel were genuinely interested, his attitude changed. 'They pitched me pretty hard,' he told *Screen Rant*, 'They showed me art that had been done for Comic-Con that year, and that really spoke to me.' Suddenly his usual detachment dissolved and he admitted, 'This is the first time in my career I know that I cared, which was terrifying to me because I really did care.' On leaving the meeting, he returned home and began to formulate a plan. 'It just sort of came to me, not the story at all but the visuals of it. I really saw how I visually could see this film and how I could add my own voice to that and really create something different with it that still had some familiarity.' He wrote a twenty-page document outlining his idea for Marvel.

Gunn imagined a visual style that combined the everyday grit and grime of the worlds created in movies like *Blade Runner* and *Alien* with the boldness and bright colours of 1950's and 1960's more pulpy space serials and science-fiction films – 'the beauty mixed with the ugliness.' His approach seemed to chime with Marvel's own vision and the contract to direct *Guardians of the Galaxy* was duly signed. While he was now fully committed – and, by his own admission, uniquely possessed by the idea of making the movie – he wasn't convinced by the Nicole Perlman/Chris McCoy versions of the screenplay he'd initially been given to work with. Marvel decided to put its money where its mouth was and allow Gunn to scrap the previous scripts and write his own from scratch.

While the key-character line-up and some of the basic story elements and plot structure remained from Perlman's draft – enough for her to retain a co-writing credit on the finished film – *Guardians* was going to be 100 per cent 'a James Gunn film'.

On completion, Gunn was understandably nervous about submitting his first draft. 'I wanted to be as weird and wonderful and exciting as possible without knocking people off balance,' he told *Badass Digest*. 'I want them to get off on the novelty of it and get off on what's cool about it without it being so odd or weird or out there that they can't relate to the characters.' Above all else, Gunn's main objective was to create well-rounded characters – whether they are human, alien or something in between – whose relationships to each other were grounded in reality and whose actions and emotional responses to the situations they found themselves in were not only justifiable but wholly believable. 'I knew going in that the core of *Guardians* was the characters,' Gunn told *fastcocreate.com*. 'If you care about the characters and you care about the story, and you love who they are, then all those rollercoaster moments are going to be all the more meaningful and exciting.' It would seem his fears were unfounded, though. Marvel was delighted with the direction the movie was taking and the main feedback seemed to be, 'We want more James Gunn in it.'

While Marvel's output had always contained an element of humour – most notably through the involvement of Robert Downey Jr. in the *Iron Man* role and Joss Whedon's light comic touch in *The Avengers* – Kevin Feige addressed Gunn's unique voice within the subsequent drafts of the *Guardians* script. He told *Neontommy.com*, 'There was very little irony, very little cynicism,' adding, '[but] what James did was he had the sarcasm [as well as] the humour,' before concluding, 'We always want films to connect on an emotional level of some kind, and I think this film does particularly well, thanks to James.' Given full approval by Marvel, the final script was exactly the movie Gunn had wanted to make – a space-opera adventure with epic scale and moments of pure adrenalin rush but grounded in drama and featuring characters the audience rooted for and wanted to spend time with. 'This was intentionally my version of *Star Wars*,' he explained to *Den of Geek*. 'Not just *Star Wars*, but *Raiders of the Lost Ark*, and other movies like that. The stuff I loved as a kid. I wanted to make a movie that made people feel the way they made me feel.' He concluded, 'Marvel wanted to make the same movie that I wanted to make. There's no way anybody but Marvel would've hired me for a movie like this, and I'm so grateful to them for that.' For Gunn, it was undoubtedly a giant leap forward in terms of scale of production, and the idea of being answerable to a major studio hadn't always sat well with him. But it seemed like he felt adequately prepared for the change of pace. 'I always wanted to make big movies!' he stated. 'I always felt restrained by lower-budget films. I enjoyed making them and I felt fulfilled, but I really did always want to make bigger movies.'

His next job was to get the pre-production underway and find his cast of intergalactic freaks. Key to the success of the movie was building a strong ensemble cast and, from the outset, he knew the tone of his writing dictated the casting of a certain type of actor. 'I really like people who can do both drama and comedy,' Gunn told *Screen Rant*, 'I'm not talking about some guy who does these bland dramedies all the time. I'm [talking] about people that have done heavy drama and who have done heavy comedy.' While the main thrust of the movie was centred on recruiting the unlikely team of misfits who would form the titular *Guardians*, one character in particular held the entire story together. Peter Quill, the half-human, half-alien bounty hunter and self-appointed leader of the *Guardians*, was the most relatable character in the movie. Seeing things through his eyes was the audience's ticket to understanding much of what was going on in a wholly unfamiliar universe. The search for the actor to play the pivotal role was on and it would take Gunn several months and countless auditions before he found the perfect actor to play his 'Star-Lord'.

When Chris was first pitched the idea of auditioning for *Guardians*, he was understandably reticent. It was late 2012 and he'd just finished making *Delivery Man* in New York and was still carrying most of the extra weight he'd gained for the role. Since returning from the shoot, he had been telling himself he'd get back to the gym and start dieting once he'd got through the holiday period. So at that particular moment, he knew he wasn't in the right state of mind to audition for anything. 'I said, "I don't think so,"' he told *Esquire*. 'I just didn't picture myself getting the role. I didn't want to go and embarrass myself.' He knew he didn't exactly look like a superhero and he worried that history was going to repeat itself. 'I auditioned for *G.I. Joe* a couple of years previously,' he explained. 'And halfway through I saw the director's eyes just glaze over. It made sense, I was a little heavy and out of shape... I did not look like a G.I Joe action figure come to life.'

After initially turning down his agent's request, Chris eventually relented and agreed to take the meeting with Marvel. Gunn, who by this time had seen countless actors for the role – both famous names and newcomers – was beginning to think his search would never end. Among the twenty or so serious contenders were a host of fast-rising stars, including Eddie Redmayne, hot from his role as Marius in *Les Misérables* and just ahead of his award-winning performance as Stephen Hawking in *The Theory of Everything*, fellow Brits Jim Sturgess (*Cloud Atlas*) and Jack Huston (*Boardwalk Empire*) and several more established actors, such as Chris's *Zero Dark Thirty* co-star Joel Edgerton, *Breaking Bad*'s Aaron Paul and Joseph Gordon-Levitt (*Looper*, *The Dark Knight Rises*, *Inception*). While many of these actors screen-tested, most were deemed unsuitable.

It was with a little indignation that Gunn initially dismissed any notion that THE Chris Pratt, THE Andy Dwyer from *Parks and Recreation*, could ever play the lead in his movie. 'I didn't really even want to see him,' he admitted to *GQ* but, on finally meeting the actor, he was forced to reconsider and changed his mind almost immediately. 'I'm not kidding,' he told the *Los Angeles Times*, 'maybe thirty seconds he was doing his character, I knew he was the guy. I liked his performance so much that even if he stayed chubby, I knew that we'd have to go with it; it would just have to be a new take on a superhero who was a little bit heftier.'

Chris had a similarly positive initial reaction, telling the *Huffington Post*, 'For me it felt like a perfect fit right off the bat. I felt like at my very first audition that I nailed it... I knew he had my spirit,' before admitting, 'But I was afraid that I wasn't physically right for it.' Later he would joke with *GQ*, 'You can make a talking racoon that looks real, why can't I just be fat?' but he knew it wasn't that simple. He left feeling that, despite his weight, he'd made enough of a good impression, telling the *Huffington Post*, 'If they could just believe in me, then I can lose the weight, then I'll get this role.' But as with any audition process, he knew there would have to be several more meetings before any final decision was made and he'd already resigned himself to the answer being a polite but definite 'not this time'. At that very moment, he made a choice that would have a dramatic impact on the rest of his life and – in retrospect – it would probably be the most important decision he would ever make in his career.

Years before, he had seemingly given up worrying about how he looked, or how his appearance might dictate the type of jobs he was being offered, when he'd chosen to concentrate on bringing as much truth and as many elements of his own character to whatever roles he played. He told the *New York Times* he'd experienced 'an identity crisis as an actor' after being told he wasn't really suitable physically for most leading-man roles but had made his peace with it and was content to swing back and forwards between 'fat character guy and in-shape character guy.' But in the last couple of years, following his marriage to Anna – and especially after the birth of Jack – his priorities had changed.

Talking to the *Irish Independent*, Chris admitted he'd belatedly come to realise the 'sad reality' that, in Hollywood at least, 'physical appearance plays a great deal in the roles you get.' He went on to explain that the opportunities to move his career onto a whole new level had increased following the work he'd done on *Moneyball* and *Zero Dark Thirty* and he was feeling the pressure to seize the moment: 'For me, trying to tighten it up and look as good as I possibly can for the next few years is the best way for me to achieve the type of success I need to live my dream of getting out of LA. Taking my son and wife and living in the country somewhere.' *Guardians* felt like one of those opportunities but, weighing in at around the 280lb mark, he felt it may have come along at exactly the wrong moment.

'I had a feeling [I was carrying] a little too much weight to expect any person to lose,' he told the *Huffington Post*, before acknowledging that there was a voice in his head telling him to start making changes as soon as possible. 'I was like, well, you know what, if I'm not going to get this, that's fine. But no one is ever going to tell me that I'm too fat for a role again … So I started getting in shape right away.' In the meantime, it seems he had the full support of *Guardians*' director James Gunn, who had been loudly championing the actor since his first audition. He told *Wired*, 'I knew I wanted Chris to get the gig, so I just tried as much as I could to help him do his thing.' Chris had lost ten or so pounds by the time he got the next call and this time he was to meet with Marvel President, Kevin Feige. Heading into the centre of LA from his home in the Manhattan Beach area, he suddenly felt optimistic about his chances, joking with the *Irish Independent*, 'That's like a forty-five minute drive. If they were bringing me in to tell me I didn't get it, I would've been like "Fuck you!"' It was good news. Feige and Gunn both agreed that Chris was the perfect fit to play Peter Quill but, as always in Hollywood, 'perfect' wasn't quite good enough. Chris explained, 'They held up the selfie from *Dark Thirty* and said, "You're too fat for Star-Lord. How long will it take you to look like this?"' before adding, 'They gave me five and a half months. I did what I had to do.'

While this wasn't the first time Chris had gotten into shape for a role, this time the stakes were higher than ever before. He would be the lead in *Guardians*, on-screen for most of the movie, and he knew much of the success (or failure) of the entire project rested on whether the audience bought into the character of Quill and were invested enough in his journey. With filming due to begin at London's Shepperton and Longcross Studios in July, nothing could be left to chance. Thankfully, Marvel would be there to help, giving him access to his own team of fitness experts, and this time there would be no dangerous crash diets or extreme workouts.

Alongside an intense physical-training regimen put together by personal trainer Duffy Gaver, Chris worked with nutritionist Phil Goglia to create a perfectly balanced diet plan, which helped him lose weight while still supplying him with the necessary fuel to complete his workouts. Gaver told *Men's Fitness*, '[Chris] wanted more muscle, to be much leaner, and to be more fit,' adding, 'He wanted to do justice to the role.' Gaver's programme was broken down into three distinct sections. For the first two months, Chris would focus on some fairly intense bodybuilding, eventually switching to equal parts bodybuilding and conditioning during the next couple of months. In the final month before shooting began, his efforts would more or less be concentrated on conditioning exercises, which included cardio circuits, swimming, mountain biking and intensive timed workouts. He was definitely putting in the hours, training with Gaver for up to four hours at a time, at least four or five times a week, and sometimes doing extra sessions in his home gym when he felt up to it.

Gaver had nothing but praise for his client, saying, 'Chris's athleticism is amazing, he's incredibly disciplined and his work ethic is phenomenal,' before explaining, 'He isn't the client you have to push; he is the type of client you have to pull down. If you were to walk into the gym when he was training, you would have thought for sure you've got a guy getting ready for the NFL [National Football League].'

In order for his body to keep up, Chris also needed to completely change his diet. Nutritionist Phil Goglia devised a healthy eating plan to help him reach his desired training goals. He bumped up Chris's calorie intake to around 4,000 per day, urged him to stop drinking alcohol completely and insisted he drank a lot more water – an ounce of water for every pound he weighed – something which had an unwelcome side-effect for Chris. 'I was peeing all day long, every day,' he told *Men's Fitness*. 'That part was a nightmare.'

Goglia's approach to controlling your weight harnesses the body's natural fat-burning properties, making sure it receives the correct type of foods, rather than limiting food intake.

Chris told *Business Insider*, 'My body hadn't been in starvation mode,' before adding, 'I actually lost weight by eating more food, but eating the right food, eating healthy foods.'

As July approached, Chris's weight was being closely monitored by Gunn and the studio, both directly and in more subtle ways. The studio sent someone to take his measurements on a weekly basis and asked for photographs to be sent of every costume or prop fitting. Sometimes props would be sent directly to Chris's home, rather than have him come to the studio's costume department, and he was expected to send photographs back, apparently to show how he looked holding a certain prop, or if a particular accessory matched the rest of his costume. But Chris was convinced it was the studio's way of keeping track of his weight loss, telling *Screen Rant*, 'All I was worried about was, "I'm going to send them pictures of me holding this gun and they're going to think I'm too fat and fire me."' He elaborated on this theory while talking to *ABC News*: 'They would send me prop guns ... I would take a picture ... so they could see how it looked in my hand. Meanwhile, what they're secretly doing is, "How fat is Chris, still?"' he said, before joking, 'They're like, "Oh, we also need you to try on these gloves. Make sure it's a full body shot with the glove on." Oh, yeah, thanks.'

If Chris's progress and physical transformation was initially a concern at all for the studio, any residual anxiety immediately evaporated when he posted a picture of himself on his Instagram account at the start of July, just as principle photography on the movie began. Under the caption, 'Six months no beer. #GOTG Kinda douchey to post this but my brother made me,' the shirtless picture showed a distinctly different Chris Pratt from the one most people knew as Andy Dwyer on *Parks and Recreation*. The picture quickly went viral, with many 'before and after' type comparison photos appearing online. Suddenly, Marvel's decision to cast him was not looking quite so left field and at last the movie was starting to pick up the merest hint of positive publicity.

With Chris now confident he had the right look, he began to concentrate on creating the personality of Peter Quill. While Kevin Feige's idea of who Peter Quill was reportedly lay somewhere between *Star Wars*' Han Solo and *Back to the Future*'s Marty McFly, Chris felt the real essence of the character should be more original and more grounded in his own personality. 'I'm different than anyone else, just like our mothers all tell us we're all very special and unique and we are,' he told *Screen Rant*, 'And I think if an actor can stick to trying to make the character resemble something from their own spirit it will automatically be unique.' He went on to explain, 'I talk and I listen and I feel things and I have a certain rhythm to my spirit, all of which, all of those things I can manipulate [in my performance].'

It seemed Chris had the full backing of his director and Gunn was quick to show his support. 'He's got all the classic movie star things and the ability to do humour,' Gunn told the *New York Times*. 'He's like Gary Cooper, he's like John Wayne.' While these particular reference points might fly over the heads of much of *Guardian*'s intended audience, Gunn had a point. Chris's general demeanour as an actor, trying to channel elements of his own spirit into every character and the use of his well-honed, quick-witted humour would influence many of the acting choices he made on set and ultimately lifted his performance beyond even Gunn's high expectations.

As the majority of the film was to be shot in the UK, including months of filming at London's Shepperton Studios, Chris faced leaving home and being away from Anna and Jack for close to six months. It was the longest time he had spent away from his new son and, despite earlier discussions and agreements he and Anna had made about the requirements of the job they were both doing, it was obviously troubling him. Discussing the thought of seeing his son again after such a long time away, he told *People* magazine, 'I was worried that he wasn't going to recognize me.' In reality, he managed to stay in touch with his family via Skype and his time away felt more like an incredible adventure than an agonising separation.

Just walking onto the enormous studio complex was a breathtaking experience for Chris. He recalls seeing countless drawings and concept paintings, alongside hundreds of storyboards mapping out the entire movie on the walls in front of him. Chris told the *Empire* podcast, 'Some of the wardrobe concept artwork had my character, they were pencil sketch drawings, and they had my face on them. That was one moment I will never forget.' As filming got underway, he was particularly awestruck by the scale and meticulous attention to detail of the entire production. From the huge cavernous sets, bursting with tiny design elements, which were unlikely to be captured on film, to the exactness of the costumes and props, it all went to make his job a lot easier. He told *Screen Rant*, 'I would just get out of hair and makeup and have my costume on and look in the mirror and I would just not even see myself staring back. I would see Peter Quill.'

Once he began working on set with Gunn and the other actors, Chris realised he was experiencing something completely new and that making a movie on this scale was altogether more complex and painstakingly planned out.

Gunn had spent a long time getting his *Guardians* screenplay into shape, working with all the actors during fairly intense rehearsal periods and ironing out any misgivings they had prior to actual shooting. When they eventually got to the set, as Chris confirmed to *Screen Rant*, the director expected them to treat the script 'like the Holy Bible' but he was also open to suggestions and willing to make adjustments when necessary. 'There were changes that were made,' Chris recalled. 'It's always an evolution. But for the most part, it was pretty damn good to begin with.'

While this relatively strict adherence to what was on the page meant there was little room for improvisation, Gunn had obviously hired Chris for a reason, knowing the type of energy and experimentation his methods could bring to a particular scene, and the director gave him some room to manoeuvre, where appropriate. 'I've been trying pretty hard to stick to the lines,' Chris admitted, 'because you don't want to blow a three-hundred thousand dollar crane, dolly or helicopter shot or something because you wanted to poke a little fun and they're like, "What are you doing? Noooooo! It's going to take us like five hours to reset this shot."'

Almost immediately after shooting began, it became very clear that he and James Gunn had developed a strong and intuitive bond during the preparations for the movie. This camaraderie helped them evolve their own comedic shorthand and soon they were pushing each other's ideas in unplanned directions. This to-and-fro became a constant source for subtle tinkering and embellishment, enhancing the humour already present within the script. 'I think James is really, really funny,' Chris declared. 'It's really rare that someone makes me consistently laugh out loud, and he really does. We have a similar sense of humour, and a really great relationship and banter on set that probably could be seen as inappropriate, but it's really keeping us both sane.'

As filming continued and the pressures on Gunn increased, the mood was undoubtedly lightened by Chris's on-set antics and the general tone of the movie seemed to be shifting into fairly unique territory. The original script had its share of humorous situations and one-liners but the footage coming off the set was funny. And not just amusing – it was hilarious. With Gunn and the actors making minor changes and elaborating on the jokes as they went along, *Guardians of the Galaxy* was beginning to find its own voice.

'I think all the best big adventure movies have comedy, like all the *Indiana Jones* movies and like a *Romancing the Stone*,' Chris stated, acknowledging that the film was following a fairly well-worn path, but he knew that by pushing the comedy to new extremes, they were creating something special. Speculating on how this twist on an existing formula was something that would truly set the film apart, Chris said, 'I think comedy is very, very important, especially in this film. I mean, if we pull this off right, it's going to be hard for other movies to come out that are like this,' adding, 'They're going to seem pretty unfunny compared to our movie.'

While Gunn echoed Chris's thoughts, unquestionably happy that the film was benefiting from the comedic talents of his main actor and simultaneously reflecting his own work in terms of the humour contained in his previous movies as a writer-director, he knew the film he was making was not an out-and-out comedy. 'At its core it's an action adventure film,' he told *Screen Rant*. 'There's also a lot of comedic elements and there's a lot of dramatic elements,' he added, before concluding, 'It's been a balance but it feels pretty comfortable ... I think it's a really different movie for a tent pole, big, huge film to have as much comedy and drama as it has. I think it's very unusual.'

It was these more dramatic and emotional aspects of the story that Gunn was especially keen to preserve, insisting it would be such moments that would ultimately pull the audience into the central story, make them believe these seemingly disparate characters could pull together as a team and compel them to join the *Guardians* on their incredible adventures. 'I think people are gonna be surprised,' he stated. 'It really is dramatic. I think that was important to me from the beginning and I think it's something that helps to ground the movie in a way.' He insisted that, despite the movie containing more than its fair share of aliens and incredible creatures, at its very core it was a human story.

'*Guardians* is about emotions and caring,' he told *Vulture*. 'That aspect of the film is actually more important than the humor.' He went on to say, 'I think both the humor and the emotions come from the exact same place because it's based in character and relationships.' It was while capturing these more serious moments that Gunn began to appreciate the full extent of Chris's skills as an actor, his potential to become one of the biggest movie stars of his generation and just how important his apparent evolution on the *Guardians* set would be to the finished film.

'He had to learn the potency of just being,' Gunn told the *New York Times*. 'It was very difficult to get him to trust that.' But with the director's help, Chris began to realise how much of his authority and allure on the big screen came from somewhere other than his ability to make people laugh. It was something he later described as finding 'the willingness to not make a joke, the willingness to not have to charm.' Ignoring his natural instinct to play the clown and recognising that he didn't always have to go for the laugh, Chris was ready to exploit fundamental aspects of his real-life persona, which had gone largely untapped in previous film roles. By embracing his inherent likeability and mixing it with the quiet masculinity and a solemn stillness that seemed to lie just beneath the surface, he was soon giving a much more focused, authoritative and emotionally vulnerable performance.

As shooting progressed through the summer, Chris's schedule was becoming insanely busy. While some of the actors were enjoying short breaks away from the set, he seemed to be working around the clock. Part of the problem was his ongoing commitment to *Parks and Recreation*, which was about to start filming the opening episodes for its sixth season. He was still under contract and *Guardians*' extended shooting schedule went way beyond the show's usual three-month break in production. While NBC had allowed him the time off to travel to London and make the movie, he still intended to appear in as much of the season as possible. 'That was something that NBC and Marvel worked out beforehand,' he told *MTV*. 'They said, "We'll let him out for some episodes, but he does have to come back." NBC was awesome to let me out and I'm missing probably six episodes.' It ended up being a case of 'If Mohammed can't come to the mountain' when part of *Parks and Recreation*'s cast and crew relocated to London to film two episodes for the season-six premiere, incorporating Chris's temporary relocation into Andy's storyline. Chris loved his *Parks and Recreation* family and, despite the demands on his free time, the extra workload involved in travelling back and forth and the strain it put him under, he was determined to do whatever it took to make it work. During another break in his *Guardians*' schedule, Chris was able to fly back to LA to do a ten-day stretch on another episode before finally rejoining the production immediately after the end of the *Guardians*' shoot in October 2013.

As time on the set came to an end and principal photography was completed, Chris started to fantasise about the food blowouts he'd have once the film was done and he started to readjust to life as Andy Dwyer again. But in reality, once the shoot was over he remained fairly committed to his new, healthier lifestyle. With his determination to look a certain way for the foreseeable future still intact, he avoided his usual Andy Dwyer-inspired weight gain and maintained a far healthier 240lb baseline, instead of leaving London carrying an extra 20lbs or so. In fact, all he took away from his extended stay in the UK was a newfound love for the reality show *The Only Way Is Essex*. He told *Empire*, 'We love garbage on TV,' before treating everyone to some uncanny Essex-boy banter.

While Chris's job was done for the time being, Gunn still had a lot of work to do to get his movie ready for its proposed 1 August 2014 release date. While the director had been at the helm of several productions, none of his previous films had come close to the mammoth scale of *Guardians*. His last feature film as writer-director, *Super*, had been shot over a mere twenty-four days and, while it may seem like an easier proposition – to complete a low-budget movie in a short space of time as opposed to bringing a $170 million summer blockbuster to the big screen – Gunn insisted that nothing could be further from the truth. He explained how shooting to a tight deadline with a limited budget was far more stressful and that the key to completing a large-scale movie was money and the time it bought.

'This movie, I shot over five months,' he told *Collider*. 'It's actually easier.' While he may have found it less harrowing, Gunn admitted it had taken its toll on him in other ways, 'It's a marathon because I've done nothing else for two years, really truly, I've had very little life.' He joked, 'I've lost two girlfriends during the two years.' This was, without doubt, his most complex project to date and his next task was 'finding the film' in the cutting room. Achieving the right balance between the different aspects of the film – countless special-effects shots, the introduction of a dozen or more new characters and propelling the story forward while keeping the narrative structure clear and grounded in reality – would be quite a juggling act. Gunn had a very unusual way of looking at the overall structure of the film, telling *Collider*, 'I always like to think that I make movies that are like Nirvana songs.' He went on to elaborate, 'They have a slow verse and then they pop into high gear and then they go back into slow and then they pop into high gear again.'

Unorthodox maybe but he seemed to be on the right track and his film was shaping up nicely. Gunn had somehow managed to make his unorthodox and almost entirely alien cast of characters incredibly human and relatable. The film satisfied as a full-throttle space adventure, without scrimping on the more tender emotional moments, and delivered big belly laughs without diminishing the dramatic beats of the story. It seemed that Marvel's initial faith in Gunn was well-founded and as the film slowly started to come together in the editing room, everyone realised that the finished movie was going to be a bit of a game-changer. Apparently, Marvel were so pleased with what they were seeing, they green-lit the sequel almost immediately. With Gunn signed to direct, *Guardians 2* was officially announced at the San Diego Comic-Con in July 2014, a full three years in advance of its proposed 28 July 2017 release date and a couple of weeks before the first *Guardians* film had even hit US theatres.

It was at this same event where Gunn and a few of *Guardians'* cast and crew unveiled a short 'sizzle reel' to an understandably ecstatic crowd. Consisting of glimpses of some of the movie's key action scenes and including newly finished effects shots of the entirely CG Rocket and Groot, the footage was undeniably impressive. While wowing a Comic-Con audience might seem like preaching to the converted, they can be notoriously withering if they sense someone is about to mess up one of their beloved titles. Everyone seemed to agree that the footage presented was fairly mind-blowing and it appeared Marvel had swiftly won over a sizeable percentage of *Guardians'* target audience. It would be over six months later before a broader audience would get to see anything of Gunn's finished work.

When the first trailer was eventually unveiled by Chris on the *Jimmy Kimmel Live!* TV show on 18 February, the response was nothing short of phenomenal. As soon as the trailer aired, the Internet went crazy. Instantly, any last seeds of the doubt that had plagued the production from its initial announcement were completely eradicated in two and a half minutes. With obvious nods to *Raiders of the Lost Ark* and *Star Wars* – a specially-filmed-for-the-trailer criminal line-up sequence used to introduce the main characters, glimpses of the incredible production design and a healthy dose of the edgy humour which infused the entire movie – *Guardians of the Galaxy* was suddenly the most anticipated movie of the summer.

The trailer was viewed almost 23 million times during its first twenty-four hours online and the song used so successfully as the main sound-bed – 'Hooked on a Feeling' by Blue Swede – saw an extraordinary 700 per cent upswing in sales the next day. Using a wholly unexpected and eclectic clutch of classic 1970s pop songs to soundtrack a futuristic space saga proved to be one of Gunn's unpredictable masterstrokes, adding yet another unforeseen dimension to *Guardians'* eventual success.

The film's soundtrack, *Awesome Mix Vol.1*, was one of the biggest-selling albums of 2014 in the US, becoming the first soundtrack album consisting exclusively of previously released songs to top the Billboard album chart.

As with most summer tent-pole releases, work continued on *Guardians* right down to the wire. With less than a fortnight before the planned world premiere at the Dolby Theatre in Hollywood, Gunn triumphantly announced that he had finally finished work on *Guardians of the Galaxy* on 7 July. In the weeks leading up to the film's completion, he had posted his thoughts about calling time on the production via his Facebook page. 'I think Marvel producers are starting to understand my almost psychotic inability to be happy with anything, and to pick things apart to the very bitter end,' he wrote, before adding, 'They're going to have to tear this movie from my bloody grip.'

A few days later, it appeared that Marvel had somehow managed to stop him tinkering with his film and the final word came via a Twitter message to fellow filmmaker Peyton Reed, who was about to start shooting Marvel's next major project, *Ant-Man*. Reed had recently been announced as the director who would replace Edgar Wright on this long-delayed and much-discussed production. The tweet simply said, '@ MrPeytonReed Take this baton, my friend! :)' and it's easy to speculate that the 'baton' in question was the mantle of 'Marvel's Next Gamble' as much as anything else.

Later on Facebook, Gunn went into a little more detail about the final preparations for the release of his movie, seeing the last visual-effects shots to be completed ('amazing'), finalising the 3D conversion ('exciting') and how he felt about the whole experience of making the film ('Best experience of my life'). Looking ahead to the imminent release, he went on to say, 'I couldn't be feeling more gratitude and love for all the people who have helped create this film. However the audience take it, there's not a single dishonest or impure bone in *Guardians*' cinematic body – and that's a hell of a thing for a spectacle film of this size with so many people involved.'

Gunn's labours actually making the film might have been over but he was immediately on the move, heading off to join members of the cast for the extensive press tour, which was scheduled to last for the next month at least. He first joined Zoe Saldana (Gamora) and Dave Bautista (Drax) in Singapore for the first leg of the promotional tour, with Chris eventually joining them as the entire team made further jaunts across Europe and the United States. Chris was determined to make this part of the process as painless as possible. During one particularly memorable interview, he was happy to confirm his skills as a hairstylist by French braiding a member of the interview team's hair. The story went viral online and while he confessed it was a skill he'd picked up from his sister years before and perfected while working on his wife, even he couldn't have expected it to be so useful during the process of promoting a multi-million-dollar Hollywood movie.

It was the end of July before he had finally completed all his press duties for the film and as he headed back to the US, he turned his attention to help promote something other than his latest movie. Chris's social-media statistics had increased fairly dramatically over the last few months and he decided to use his boost in online status to help raise awareness for some good causes. Aside from the ALS Ice Bucket Challenge – where Chris joked he would drink a Blue Ice vodka miniature and a bottle of Smirnoff Ice instead of taking the challenge before enduring five separate soakings, with the sound of Anna laughing hysterically in the background – he used his Twitter feed to highlight several charities and even posted links to stories involving individual cases.

One such article involved an eleven-year-old boy named Joe Henson. Joe's struggle to fight terminal brain cancer was obviously one that particularly touched Chris. As Joe began treatment, he shared news of his progress. Chris later became a huge supporter of the subsequent 'Fear Isn't Real' campaign, which was set up to help raise funds and awareness to fight the disease, filling his Facebook and Twitter feeds with photos, updates and retweets with the hashtag #fearisntreal for several months. Chris's increased profile before the film had even opened was remarkable but if he felt his life had changed by merely joining the extended Marvel Universe, he was in for quite a surprise when *Guardians of the Galaxy* actually opened in the US in August 2014.

To say *Guardians* over-performed against everyone's expectations on its release might just be the biggest understatement since 'Li'l Sebastian? It's a little horse. I just don't get it'. Maybe it had something to do with the initial scepticism surrounding the film's potential as a summer blockbuster or the general shoulder-shrugging that had greeted the project's announcement back in 2011, but when the critics finally saw the finished film, the majority of their reviews were resoundingly positive, while many could be seen as utterly glowing. While 'Marvel Fatigue' was being recognised as a genuine medical disorder in some circles, the ever-expanding superhero-movie market meant multiplexes were virtually bursting at the seams with brooding anti-heroes and crime-fighters in tights. Hollywood's persistent reliance on 'more of the same, only bigger and better' dictated the production of endless reboots and sequel after sequel of anything remotely perceived as a box-office hit. With each instalment getting progressively 'darker' and 'more serious', this usually translated as 'less entertaining' for the audience. *Guardians*, it appeared, was a much-needed push of the reset button. It was a complete throwback to a much more carefree type of blockbuster, set in a whole new universe – even if it did contain a few familiar faces. Bold and brash, it was an explosion of colour, which was downright psychedelic in places.

Aside from its obvious touchstones – *Star Wars*, *Indiana Jones*, *Blade Runner* – *Guardians* seemed to have more in common with the camp excesses of 1980's *Flash Gordon* movie and Jane Fonda's classic 1960's sci-fi romp *Barbarella* than with *2001: A Space Odyssey* or even the various incarnations of *Star Trek*. Most of all, *Guardians* was fun. And it was the feel-good factor, which came with an unexpected whirl of refreshing, uncluttered joy, most critics responded to with unanticipated delight. *Rolling Stone*'s Peter Travers wrote, '*Guardians of the Galaxy* does the impossible. Through dazzle and dumb luck, it turns the clichés of comic-book films on their idiot heads and hits you like an exhilarating blast of fun-fun-

fun,' before concluding, 'It's insanely, shamelessly silly.' He had particular praise for Chris, noting, 'Pratt nails every beat in the role – comedy, drama, action and six-pack-baring stud appeal,' adding, 'Want to see Pratt become a full-fledged movie star? This is where it happens.' Over at the *Chicago Tribune*, Michael Philips was similarly impressed, stating, 'The film owes its relative buoyancy above all to Chris Pratt,' adding, 'There are moments in *Guardians of the Galaxy* when Pratt seems to be growing into a quirky action hero before our eyes, the way Robert Downey Jr. did in the first and best *Iron Man*.'

Entertainment Weekly's A+ review matched others' approval. 'He's such a natural, you can't help but wonder why it took so long,' before turning their attention to Marvel, praising the studio's desire to overturn their own winning formula. 'Give Marvel props, even with all of its mega-success; the studio's still willing to take chances,' they wrote. 'Here, that risk pays off big-time. The film's a giddily subversive space opera that runs on self-aware smart-assery.' The reviewer concluded, 'I've been pretty mixed on Marvel movies over the years – some have dazzled me, others have left me depressed. But *Guardians* is the first one that feels excitingly unpredictable.' This sentiment was echoed by the *Washington Post* review, 'It's the funniest of any Marvel movie yet, lending the film a lightness that goes a long way toward deflating the grandiosity that sometimes inflates and bloats the studio's film. *Guardians of the Galaxy* goes down like cotton candy: colourful, sweet, nutrition-free, melting in your mouth.' They concluded, 'It manages the trick of being both an unironic sci-fi action-adventure and a zippy parody of one. It's exciting, funny, self-aware, beautiful to watch and even, for a flickering instant or two, almost touching.' The review also commented on the revelatory nature of Chris's performance, saying, 'The actor exerts the disarming superpower of charm.'

Director James Gunn was also high on many critics' list of *Guardians*' most noteworthy components, with *Vulture* stating, '[Gunn] has a great eye, not necessarily for pretty pictures, but for images of emotional grandeur.' On the other end of the spectrum, the rare negative reviews seemed to dislike the film's irreverent tone and more frivolous approach to the space-opera genre. Stephanie Zacharek at the *Village Voice* said, 'It's just a little too self-aware, too pleased with itself, to work,' while in his one-star review in the *New York Post*, Kyle Smith wrote, '*Guardians of the Galaxy* brings to mind some of the most unforgettable sci-fi event movies of the last thirty years,' before adding, 'Alas, those films are *Howard the Duck* and *Green Lantern.*'

While no one within the film industry was expecting the film to fare quite as badly, financially at least, as either of those notorious flops, expectations were a little muted – perhaps anticipating the audience's unfamiliarity with the source material might limit its 'must-see' appeal. In *Entertainment Weekly*'s respected Box Office Preview feature, Lindsey Bahr predicted *Guardians* would score a healthy $75 million on its opening weekend in the US, a figure that now seems incredibly conservative when, on its debut, the film's ticket sales actually soared to an estimated $94 million. The film had not only won that weekend's box office, it had achieved a new record for the highest August debut, simultaneously becoming Marvel's ninth consecutive number-one movie and the seventh-highest grossing opening weekend ever for a non-sequel. Having already earned a further $66 million in overseas territories, *Guardians* had gone from being Marvel's ultimate gamble to almost earning back its entire production budget in three days. The film maintained a strong position at the US box office for the next couple of months and was soon declared the number-one movie of the summer, eventually topping the US year-end money-making chart with a staggering $333 million domestic gross, narrowly beating the third instalment of the *Hunger Games* series, *Mockingjay – Part 1*. Worldwide, the movie had to settle for third place, with its $772 million haul failing to match the final totals achieved by Peter Jackson's final instalment of his *Hobbit* saga, *The Battle of the Five Armies* ($788 million), or Michael Bay's fourth *Transformers* movie, *Age of Extinction*, which had exceeded $1 billion by the end of the year.

For Chris, the effect of the movie's success was beyond anything he could have imagined and it had all happened at an incredible pace. Suddenly, he was the subject of countless magazine articles, mostly featuring a variation on the 'Zero to Hero' tag line, and his online profile went through the roof. Within a couple of weeks of the film's opening, he was approached to host the season premier of legendary late-night comedy show, *Saturday Night Live*. With his connections to former *SNL* stalwarts – his *Parks and Recreation* buddies Amy Poehler and Michael Schur – and the fact that his wife Anna had already hosted the show twice (in 2008 and 2011), this was obviously a great honour. And he announced with typical good humour via his Twitter feed, 'Hosting *SNL*! That was high on the bucket list! Right up there with hunting human.'

It had been a wild and insanely busy few months for Chris and it looked likely the madness would continue for some time to come. The *Guardians'* press-tour had taken him on a seemingly endless promotional trip around the world and there had also been the small matter of shooting his next big movie project. While he had been announced as the lead in the forthcoming *Jurassic Park* sequel at the beginning of the year, almost six months before *Guardians* opened, suddenly, with the newly crowned 'Hottest New Star on the Planet' on board, *Jurassic World* was looking like a much bigger deal.

CHAPTER THIRTEEN

PARKS AND DINO-MUTATION

'Oooh, ahhh! That's how it always starts.
Then later there's running and screaming.'
JEFF GOLDBLUM AS IAN MALCOLM –
JURASSIC PARK: THE LOST WORLD

A couple of days earlier than expected, on 25 November 2014, filmmaker Colin Trevorrow quietly unveiled the first full-length trailer for his forthcoming movie via a two-word message on his Twitter account. It simply read, 'Coming Attraction'. His movie, *Jurassic World*, would be the first instalment in a proposed franchise reboot of 1993's *Jurassic Park*, Steven Spielberg's dinosaur spectacular adapted from Michael Crichton's bestselling novel of the same name.

Spielberg's film had become a global phenomenon, thrilling audiences with the director's usual edge-of-your-seat action sequences mixed with state-of-the-art special effects and eventually spawning two sequels, 1997's *The Lost World* and a third, simply entitled *Jurassic Park 3*, in 2001. It was a fairly low-key introduction for a $150 million movie, especially one starring Hollywood's latest 'Man of the Moment', Chris Pratt. Chris had just been named 'Man of the Year' by *GQ* magazine and the previously untested blockbuster headliner had recently helped turn Marvel's *Guardians of the Galaxy* into a box-office champion. The understated nature of its arrival had less to do with the clip's content than a result of bad timing. The *Jurassic World* trailer's proposed day-after-Thanksgiving release date, when traditionally just about everyone in the world is sitting in front of a computer screen trawling the Internet, wishing they had something cool to watch, was about to be hijacked by a certain Mr J.J. Abrams and the first teaser trailer for his own, much anticipated franchise relaunch, *Star Wars: The Force Awakens*. It seemed that someone at Disney – the new home for all things *Star Wars* since their purchase of Lucasfilm from George Lucas in May 2011 – was trying to give *Jurassic World* a fighting chance and had given Trevorrow a heads-up about their plans to take over the Internet during the holiday period. Kim Kardashian may have famously failed to 'break the Internet' with her bottom but a new *Star Wars* teaser just might manage it.

Spectacular as it is, it's highly unlikely that two minutes and forty seconds of *Jurassic World* would have stood much of a chance against a mere eighty-eight seconds of new *Star Wars* footage. To put it into perspective, the first trailer for *Pan* – Joe Wright's Peter Pan reboot starring Hugh Jackman – was released at exactly the same time as the *Jurassic World* clip. It's unlikely that many people chose to watch the guy in green tights squaring off against Wolverine, in heavy eyeliner and a sword in place of his adamantium claws, instead of feasting on some giant sea monsters, genetically modified dinosaurs and a handful of motorbike-chasing velociraptors. While this potential scheduling clash was narrowly avoided, it could be seen as merely the last of many mishaps and false starts that had befallen the fourth instalment of the *Jurassic Park* franchise over the years.

When *Jurassic Park III* hit US cinemas in July 2001, it arrived with fairly low expectations and many critics felt it struggled to even meet those. *JPIII* was the first of the franchise not directed by Steven Spielberg, helmed instead by Joe Johnston, a former special-effects pioneer at Lucasfilm's ILM (Industrial Light and Magic), who had turned to filmmaking more than a decade earlier. The film accumulated a more-than-acceptable $368 million at the worldwide box office but lacked much of the expected visual flair, excitement and inventiveness of its predecessors. While financial success meant a fourth instalment was more or less assured, Spielberg's enthusiasm to direct any further instalments of the saga had all but disappeared. However, he agreed that there was still potential to tell more stories based around the ideas contained in Crichton's original novels. Years passed with no concrete news of a follow-up, despite many very talented screenwriters and directors showing interest. Among those attempting to resurrect the franchise with their own ideas were writer/director John Sayles and director Alex Proyas, who came closest to kick-starting a new *Jurassic Park* in the mid-2000s. Their extraordinary script treatment was said to involve gun-carrying, genetically engineered human-dinosaur hybrids created to hunt dinosaurs that had escaped from offshore islands onto the mainland but it was soon scrapped when concept art was leaked online and the story idea rejected by Spielberg.

All went quiet for a few years until Spielberg himself hinted, at the 2011 San Diego Comic-Con, that *I Am Legend* and *Thor* screenwriter Mark Protosevich was working on a couple of possible *Jurassic Park IV* scripts and that he was extremely happy with the drafts he'd seen. Almost a full year later, an official announcement from Spielberg and Universal Pictures confirmed that the film was definitely going ahead and the screenwriting team, Rick Jaffa and Amanda Silver, had now been hired to complete a draft of the script. Jaffa and Silver, having recently completed their *Rise of the Planet of the Apes* screenplay, seemed like a perfect fit.

With plenty of knowing references to the original saga, *Rise* had successfully relaunched the long-dead *Apes* franchise and unexpectedly accumulated almost $500 million at the worldwide box office in 2011. The film had successfully walked a very thin line, pleasing a whole new audience – many of whom were presumably unfamiliar with the 1968 original – while captivating existing fans with an ingenious twist on the existing *Ape* saga's mythology and origin story. All of this seemed like good news for the *Jurassic Park* franchise and the fans patiently waiting during the decade-long search for a suitable fourth-instalment script.

With everything falling neatly into place, at the beginning of 2013 Universal Pictures confidently announced that *Jurassic Park IV* would be shot in 3D and was scheduled to hit theatres on 13 June 2014. *JPIV* finally had a story idea (from Protosevich), a working script (from Jaffa and Silver), producers (long-time Spielberg collaborator Frank Marshall and *Bourne* franchise veteran Patrick Crowley) and, probably most importantly, Spielberg's blessing. Unfortunately, the thing it didn't have was a director and it was this final hurdle that would send the whole production crashing back to square one.

It is unlikely that anyone could have predicted the announcement of Colin Trevorrow as the director of *JPIV* on 14 March, coming so far from left field you could virtually hear the entire Internet shrugging its shoulders and saying, 'Who?' While Trevorrow's directorial debut, *Safety Not Guaranteed*, had been a runaway hit at the 2012 Sundance Film Festival, it was estimated to have been made for a mere $750,000 and handing him the reins of a billion-dollar franchise seemed to be a considerable leap of faith on behalf of Spielberg and Universal.

Safety Not Guaranteed had been a long-gestating pet project for Trevorrow and his screenwriter partner, Derek Connolly, and its completion and subsequent success cemented a working relationship that would prove to be both long-lasting and extremely fruitful. The pair had become close friends many years before, during their time at NYU, where they had taken film-production and comedy-writing classes together, and *Safety Not Guaranteed* was their first major collaboration. While the script for *Safety* would eventually win the Waldo Salt Screenwriting Award for Connolly at Sundance, its origins were far less auspicious. Connolly's script was based on an idea suggested by a real classified ad placed in Oregon's *Backwoods Home* magazine more than a decade earlier. The ad simply read, 'WANTED: Somebody to go back in time with me. This is not a joke...You'll get paid when we get back. Must bring your own weapons. Safety not guaranteed. I have done this one before'.

On further investigation, Trevorrow and Connolly discovered that the ad had been written by one of the magazine's senior editors, John Silveira, simply to fill unsold space on the classified ads pages, and duly optioned the short passage of text as if it were a novel. Silveira received a flat fee for the rights (a sum which the film's director later told *Entertainment Weekly* was 'certainly more than I got'), as well as a brief cameo in the film and the screen credit 'Time Travel Consultant'. The resulting film – which starred Chris's *Parks and Recreation* co-star Aubrey Plaza and *New Girl*'s Jake Johnson as journalists trying to track down the man who placed the ad, Kenneth (as played by *The Mindy Project* and *Togetherness*'s Mark Duplass) – was equal parts romantic comedy and sci-fi drama, with the burning question of whether Kenneth is simply mad or a time-travelling genius left unanswered until the closing moments.

Riding a wave of positive reviews, and a 91 per cent 'fresh' rating on *Rotten Tomatoes*, *Safety Not Guaranteed* managed to gross over $4 million at the US box office and would soon help pave the way for the pair's journey to *Jurassic World*. Over the next twelve months there would be a few high-profile projects under discussion. Trevorrow unveiled plans to direct an original project he was working on with Connolly called *Intelligent Life*, which he described to *View London* as 'a sci-fi romantic thriller with comedy' but this never materialised.

The pair's names were linked to a big-budget remake of the 1986 science-fiction comedy *Flight of the Navigator* for Disney and there were persistent rumours of the duo's involvement in the early development of *Star Wars: Episode VII*. In the end, none of these came to fruition and Trevorrow and Connolly's next project would in fact be as director and co-writers on the proposed *Jurassic Park* sequel.

Trevorrow explained that, once he and Connolly were officially on board, their brief was relatively simple: 'I know Steven [Spielberg] didn't want me to make a carbon copy of the earlier films,' he told *Entertainment Weekly*. 'So we're going for it.' It was soon very apparent that the pair wanted a complete rewrite on the previously approved Jaffa and Silver script, so they entirely abandoned much of the work that had been done up to that point and began creating their own script from scratch. Together they shared a vision of when and where the new story should take place, imagining an expansive site on *Jurassic Park*'s original Isla Nublar location. They envisioned a resort that had been fully functional for the last twenty years or so, with Trevorrow telling *SlashFilm.com*, 'It's the realization of John Hammond's dream.'

Then they began to list the greatest inventions and changes mankind had experienced over the last couple of decades and started to build their story from the ground up. Firstly, Trevorrow stated, 'Our relationship with technology has become so woven into our daily lives, we've become numb to the scientific miracles around us. We take so much for granted.' He wondered, 'What if the parks customers were becoming increasingly blasé about what was on display?' Trevorrow added, 'We imagined a teenager texting his girlfriend with his back to a T-Rex behind protective glass ... For us, that image captured the way much of the audience feels about the movies themselves. "We've seen CG dinosaurs. What else you got?"'

Secondly, Trevorrow imagined that the park's new owners, The Masrani Global Corporation, would do anything to keep their investment profitable, whether it was ethically sound or not. 'Money has been the gasoline in the engine of our biggest mistakes,' he stated. 'If there are billions to be made, no one can resist them, even if they know things could end horribly,' and thus, he and Connolly envisioned the park's geneticists being asked to create a new hybrid dinosaur to thrill the somewhat jaded audience. Trevorrow teased that their creation would not only be something no one had ever seen before, but with the fact scientists had felt the need to make it at all would be called into question, 'This creation exists to fulfil a corporate mandate – they wanted something bigger, louder, with more teeth. And that's what they get.'

When early story leaks suggesting Trevorrow was planning to introduce genetically altered dinosaurs – The D-Rex – into the mix of authentic and verified species, they were met with a combination of scepticism and downright disapproval. So much so that Trevorrow had been forced to defend the idea in several interviews. He told *SlashFilm*, 'I know the idea of a modified dinosaur put a lot of fans on red alert, and I understand it.' He explained the concept of his 'D-Rex' as being completely founded in nature, insisting, 'This animal is not a mutant freak. It doesn't have a snake's head or octopus tentacles,' before stating that the idea was grounded within the original source material. 'We aren't doing anything here that Crichton didn't suggest in the novels,' he said, before concluding, 'It's a natural evolution of the technology introduced in the first film.'

Gripped by the endless possibilities, Trevorrow and Connolly soon concluded that their story concept was far more complicated than they'd previously imagined. With the proposed June 2013 release date a little over a year away, they felt more time would be needed to fully realise their vision and bring the film they wanted to make to the big screen. Trevorrow later explained to *Entertainment Weekly*, 'There are a lot of bold new ideas in this movie,' before adding, 'I'm pushing it as far forward as I can.' After discussion with Universal Pictures, it was decided to postpone the film for a full year – a decision that caused much online speculation and suggested it was slipping back into the previous decade-long 'development hell'.

Universal were quick to scotch any unfounded rumours, releasing a full statement to explain their actions. It stated, 'In coordination with filmmakers, Universal has decided to release *Jurassic Park 4* at a later date giving the studio and filmmakers adequate time to bring audiences the best possible version of the fourth instalment in Universal's beloved franchise.' The studio went on to show their full support for the creative team they'd entrusted with making the film by saying, 'We could not be more excited about the vision that Colin Trevorrow has created for the film, and we look forward to watching as he and the producers create another great chapter in this franchise's storied history.'

While this failed to stop all the Internet chatter, it certainly made Universal's position very clear. Within three months it seemed Trevorrow and Connolly had done most of the heavy lifting on their script, prompting Universal to announce on 10 September that the film not only had a new release date of 12 June 2015 but a confirmed title: *Jurassic World*. Confident all the pieces were now in place, Trevorrow began the long process of casting his movie – something that was to prove as problematic and protracted as every other element of putting the film together.

The first cast member officially confirmed was Bryce Dallas Howard, as Claire, the park's operations manager. Daughter of acclaimed filmmaker Ron Howard, the talented young actress had made her startling breakthrough as the blind protagonist, Ivy, in M. Night Shyamalan's *The Village* in 2004. She has since worked with such esteemed directors as Lars von Trier and Kenneth Branagh, as well as taking over the role of Victoria in *The Twilight Saga: Eclipse* and receiving several 'Best Supporting Actress' nominations for her portrayal of the controversial racist character, Hilly Holbrook, in 2011's *The Help*.

Next on board was Ty Simpkins, who, at only thirteen years old, had already shown his ability to shine opposite Robert Downey Jr. in *Iron Man 3* and in the key role of Dalton Lambert in the ongoing horror franchise, *Insidious*. Around the same time, Josh Brolin was said to be in talks to take the lead male role but lengthy negotiations proved to be fruitless. While later reports suggested 'salary and scheduling' issues, it has to be said that the actor, who had previously been Oscar-nominated for his turn as Dan White in Gus Van Sant's *Milk*, was suffering a particularly brutal string of box-office flops and misfires, including Jason Reitman's *Labor Day*, Spike Lee's *Oldboy* remake and the belated *Sin City* sequel, *A Dame to Kill For*, all of which must have taken some of the shine off his potential to lead the *Jurassic Park* franchise into its next chapter.

In an interview with the *New York Times*, Trevorrow admitted he was looking for a particular type of actor. 'If someone is strong enough to play the lead in a movie like this, you need to know it at first sight.' It seemed that, with *Guardians for the Galaxy* already completed, Chris Pratt's name was suddenly attracting the kind of buzz that suggested he might have the necessary charisma and gravitas Trevorrow was looking for.

While it is unclear if the director, or anyone else in his team, had seen completed footage from *Guardians of the Galaxy* prior to Chris's name being thrown into the hat, it's very easy to speculate that they'd been privy to some sort of sneak preview. By the time the first *Guardians* trailer arrived in mid-February, Universal had already confirmed, after months of speculation, that Chris Pratt would, indeed, be headlining the cast of *Jurassic World*. The announcement came via a picture of Chris alongside Bryce Dallas Howard at a red-carpet event uploaded to Ron Howard's Twitter feed on 13 January. Obviously bursting with fatherly pride, the caption read, 'Bryce and Chris meet for the 1st time on red carpet they will be co-stars in the next Juraissic.' Apart from a fairly inexcusable spelling mistake, Howard had leaked the news a little earlier than planned, forcing Universal to release an official statement the following day.

Chris couldn't have been more excited. On a visit to Legoland California, while promoting *The Lego Movie*, he told the *Peace River Gazette* how much the original *Jurassic Park* had impacted on his childhood. 'I lined up at the theatre to see it, I saw it opening night, I saw every sequel, I've seen it a whole bunch of times ... for me that was my big movie, I think I was thirteen or fourteen when it came out,' he enthused, before adding, 'It was my *Star Wars*.' He went on to say, 'It's a big deal for me to be any part of that, let alone this part I'm going to be playing. I'm thrilled about it.'

Later, talking to the *Daily Mirror*, Chris made it clear that he understood Trevorrow's updated vision for the franchise by saying, 'This is new and cutting edge, it has a point of view about how society has changed since the original came out.' But as a devoted fan of the original trilogy, he was quick to reassure his fellow enthusiasts, 'Dude, it's going to be good. I'm precious about *Jurassic Park* and I would not want them to fuck it up.'

He had been hired to play Owen, a member of the resident research staff who specialises in studying the behaviour of the park's velociraptors. Trevorrow was keen to point out that, while Owen has a very special relationship with the raptors, their bond is complex and they shouldn't necessarily be considered as tame or friendly. 'They aren't trained, they can't do tricks,' he told *SlashFilm*, '[Owen is] just trying to figure out the limits of the relationship between these highly intelligent creatures and human beings.'

Talking to *Empire*, Trevorrow went on to say, 'These are nasty and dangerous and they'll bite your head off if you make the wrong move,' before explaining his thought process further. 'There are men and women out there today who have forged tenuous connections with dangerous predators ... That's interesting territory to me.'

Assuming his character was expected to be in fairly good shape and with little doubt the shoot would prove to be an arduous one, Chris had decided to try and maintain the strict diet and workout regime he had put in place in the lead up to filming *Guardians*. While this was not as much of a challenge as his previous efforts to bulk up or slim down, it did mean that he would have to avoid certain indulgencies. With the production scheduled to start filming in Hawaii, before eventually moving on to spend its final six weeks shooting in New Orleans, he was worried he wouldn't be able to resist the traditional – and far from slimming – local Creole cuisine.

'I would love to eat it,' Chris explained to the *New York Times*, presumably imagining plates of the local stew (gumbo), po'boys (a giant sandwich stuffed with beef or fried seafood) or beignets (the popular French pastry that now forms a key element of Creole cooking), before adding, 'I personally can't allow myself to eat it. I know what it translates to. I would see a plate of food, and, if I spin my eyes, I see a treadmill.' While fighting culinary temptation might prove as difficult as out-witting the genetically modified residence of *Jurassic World*, it seemed as though Chris's *Guardians*-inspired fitness drive had knocked the shine off one of his former indulgences, as he admitted, 'Turns out I don't like beer anymore.'

Jurassic World was scheduled to start filming in Hawaii on 10 April, moving to several different locations between then and the start of June. Remarkably, for a project so far blighted with multiple setbacks and issues over the years, everything was reported to have gone pretty much as planned for most of the two-month shoot. A veil of secrecy had descended over every aspect of the production as Trevorrow understandably attempted to keep as much of the film's key plot points and creature designs firmly under wraps. But in the age of instant Twitter updates and fevered online speculation, the director was also keen to drip-feed the fans' excitement with teasing on-set photographs and behind-the-scenes titbits. Soon, shots featuring some of the cast in their costumes surfaced online and Trevorrow attempted to dispel any lingering doubts about his intentions to preserve the original film's legacy. Officially sanctioned images seemed to indicate that the entire production was maintaining a staggering level of authenticity and attention to detail, revealing some tantalising shots of (presumably) dinosaur-induced carnage, which included a bloody handprint on the side of a mobile veterinary unit and a smashed-up maintenance van. Unfortunately, these glimpses 'behind the curtain' were not enough for some and the production suffered a series of unauthorised leaks and intentional online plot spoilers.

Rather than shy away from these potentially damaging rumours, Trevorrow attacked the problem head on, contacting the *Slashfilm* website and giving a full interview to confirm and clarify the reported details. Obviously disappointed that key components of his film were already in the public domain, he said, 'Last week was discouraging for everyone on our crew – not because we want to hide things from the fans, but because we're working so hard to create something full of surprises.' He went on to lament the fact that much of the film's potential audience was merely reading about major story elements from a computer screen, rather than experiencing it on the big screen in a darkened theatre. Bemoaning the current obsession with spoilers, he said, 'When I was a kid, you got to discover everything at once, it washed over you and blew your mind,' before adding, 'Now it only takes one person to spoil it for everyone else.'

With this cloud of disappointment hanging over them, the *Jurassic World* cast and crew soon relocated to New Orleans, where they settled in to complete the remainder of principal photography. During this period of filming, Chris experienced an enormous personal loss: the death of his father, Dan, after a long battle with multiple sclerosis (MS). With his excessive smoking cited as a possible contributory factor, Dan had been diagnosed with the disease over twenty years earlier and while MS is fairly common and its symptoms can be managed with specialist care, there is still no cure.

Chris had wanted to keep his dad's struggle with the disease a private matter for many years but *Radar Online* revealed soon after Dan's death that he had been nothing but supportive towards his father during his extended illness. A 'family insider' revealed that Chris had said, 'Don't worry, Dad, I got this,' before helping him financially when the family's medical insurance fell short of his dad's treatment costs. While Chris had left home long before his father's passing and there had been reports of the strain he had been put under by the entire family's 'money troubles', he had retained strong links with his parents and all his siblings.

The Pratts were working-class people with very little money to spare and Chris's recent success had reportedly eased some of the financial pressure they had been dealing with for much of their lives. Chris had reportedly bought a house for his parents and was always keen to take his siblings' kids on hunting trips and adventure holidays whenever he had time to spare. According to *Star Magazine*, the family's problems with money had begun to spiral out of control some time before, with Chris's parents filing for bankruptcy in 2003 and both his siblings filing Chapter 13 – the US legal term for court-mandated debt assistance – in the last couple of years.

Chris had remained fairly close to his sister Angela, now a sales rep in Washington, and his brother Cully, a California-based freelance artist, and it's hardly surprising that he felt increasing pressure to help them out during their respective periods of hardship. The *Star* quoted a family friend as saying, '[Chris] hates to see them struggle, but he doesn't like the expectations that he'll provide for them financially,' adding, 'The whole situation is a strain on Chris.' It was obviously a difficult situation and one that caused a degree of tension for everyone involved. Thankfully, while Chris seems to have remained adamant about not necessarily becoming a financial crutch for his extended family, the Pratts remained supportive towards each other and Dan's death only seemed to pull the whole family closer together again.

It was Chris and Anna's fifth wedding anniversary shortly

after Dan's funeral and as Chris was still on location in New Orleans, the couple hatched a plan to combine this occasion with an elaborate dinner, which might also form part of Dan's commemoration. Chris's mother, Kathy, was flown in from Lake Stevens especially and acted as the event's guest of honour. The group descended on a very fancy local restaurant, where they indulged in a fifteen-course menu. Apparently, while each course had its own specially chosen wine, it seemed Kathy was far from accustomed to this style of extravagant dining and ordered a light beer instead. Chris later described the occasion to the *New York Times* as 'like my two worlds colliding' but admitted it had all gone beautifully, saying, 'It all worked out.'

The celebratory dinner acted as a brief respite for Chris before the punishing shooting schedule resumed. As hard as it was, both he and Trevorrow were apparently having the time of their lives. The director revealed to *Entertainment Weekly*, 'Yesterday I was under a construction crane with Chris, covered with dirt, eyeballing the exact height of the dinosaur trying to kill him,' before adding, 'We both cracked up laughing. Sometimes you just have to stop and let the joy take over.'

On 5 August 2014, Trevorrow announced via Twitter that principal photography on *Jurassic World* was completed. Almost immediately, he and the rest of his crew settled in for the long process of post-production and perfecting the numerous special-effects shots needed to bring the park's main attractions to life. Almost four months passed before the world got the chance to take a closer look inside *Jurassic*

World, with the first trailer eventually surfacing online on 25 November. It had been a long wait for the fans – albeit one cut short by the clip's arrival a couple of days earlier than expected – and, despite earlier official and unofficial revelations, there was plenty to get the Internet buzzing.

Opening with the rather prophetic line, 'Remember, if something chases you... run!' the trailer went on to show the enormous scale of the resort, the public's close interaction with its living and breathing attractions and ended with a shot of a motorcycle-riding Chris Pratt racing alongside a pack of velociraptors – definitely enough to whet the appetite of even the most critical *Jurassic Park* fan. Also included was the first look at the giant sea-dwelling dinosaur, the mosasaurus, which Trevorrow and Connelly had discussed during their first script meeting. The scene opens with the shot of a great white shark suspended above a giant aquatic arena. Soon we can see a huge shape moving under the water and as it breaks the surface, the giant creature swallows the shark in one bite. Trevorrow explained to *Empire*, 'I thought it would be cool if we had this massive animal and the park used one of our most fearsome modern predators as food,' before adding, 'There could be a whole facility where they used shark DNA to mass-produce them to feed the bigger beast.' While the trailer also revealed that Chris's character was firmly against the idea of lab-created dinosaur hybrids, stating categorically that it was 'probably a bad idea', most arguments against the concept seemed to be silenced by the first sight of Trevorrow's fully realised creation. A brief glimpse of the awe-inspiring 'D-Rex' suggested something much bigger and far more terrifying than the original trilogy's T-Rex and, more importantly, it all looked undeniably cool.

For Trevorrow, it must have been a massive relief to finally get the chance to quash some of the harsher criticisms being thrown his way. The clip also went a long way towards letting the hardcore fans see that he understood how important the franchise was to them and how precious he was about maintaining the original film's legacy. Trevorrow might have been taking this movie in a slightly different direction but that didn't necessarily mean he wasn't protecting the overriding concept; in fact, he insisted he was merely expanding upon it. He told *Empire*, 'There is no shortage of awesome [real] dinosaurs. We could have populated this entire story with new species that haven't been in any of these movies. But this new creation is what gave me a reason to tell another *Jurassic Park* story.' He concluded by saying, 'It's a bonkers idea, but I'm comfortable going to Crazytown, because I used to live there when I was a kid.'

For Chris, the end of the *Jurassic World* shoot meant a well-earned rest. He had been working more or less non-stop since early 2012 and, as Jack approached his second birthday, he settled back into his family life, back in Los Angeles. He and Anna had bought a new home in early 2013 – a $3.3 million house in the Hollywood Hills area – and he relished the thought of spending time relaxing by the pool with his wife and young son. His work schedule was fairly light for the next few months, with only one confirmed project in the works – as *Parks and Recreation* prepared to shoot its final season, he would be making one last trip back to Pawnee, Indiana.

CHAPTER FOURTEEN

GO BIG OR
GO HOME

'So now what happens?'
AUBREY PLAZA, AFTER FILMING HER LAST
SCENE ON *PARKS AND RECREATION* –
ENTERTAINMENT WEEKLY

Only days after completing work on *Jurassic World*, when it would have been reasonable to assume he'd earned the right to kick back and take a break, Chris was, in fact, heading off on a lengthy press tour scheduled to coincide with the 1 August release of *Guardians of the Galaxy*. While most actors agree that promoting a film can be the most tedious part of the movie-making process, it must be even worse if you've just spent the last few months a couple of thousand miles away from home on another movie set. To make things worse, wrapping up his promotional commitments for *Guardians* also signalled the end of his regular *Parks and Recreation* hiatus, meaning he'd be going straight back to work on the show's seventh season. While he wouldn't normally be unhappy about regrouping with his Pawnee family, this time he knew he'd be returning to play Andy Dwyer for the last time.

This year's reunion would be bittersweet for the whole team as NBC had already confirmed that the upcoming season of *Parks and Recreation* would be its last. Chris had not been surprised by the news. He told *Entertainment Weekly*, 'I think people are ready for it to be done.' While he had only praise for everyone involved in bringing the show to life, he realised it had been a struggle. Commenting on the fact that the series had already aired over a hundred episodes, he said, 'That's a lot of work. Day in, day out they're writing episodes and trying to create stories that can somehow stay fresh with the same core group of characters.' His co-star Adam Scott added, 'I think the show had a couple more seasons in it, but all the more reason to stop.'

For Mike Schur, *Parks and Recreation*'s co-creator and long-term show runner, plans to end the show had begun germinating during early preparation work for season six. Talking with the show's star, Amy Poehler, Schur had asked the question, 'What's our endgame here?' Most of the actors' contracts ended after the seventh season and, with the main cast increasingly in demand, negotiations would undoubtedly have been tricky. Poehler summed up the dilemma she and Schur faced to *Entertainment Weekly*, 'I would have done this show for more years, but the cast is busy, they're getting pulled in directions, because they're so good,' before adding, 'It's a lot to commit to the show, and people have a million other things they're working on.' They both agreed that the smartest thing to do was to start creating an exit plan. After repeated struggles just keeping the show on air, narrowly avoiding cancellation year after year – Schur and the scriptwriters had created series finales for seasons three and four, as well as two for season five (episodes fourteen and twenty-two) when they were unsure if they would even get a full season pick-up – somehow they'd managed to go from strength to strength critically, if not in the ratings.

Schur and Poehler reasoned that the show – and everyone involved in putting it together – deserved to finish with dignity. 'We both felt like all we really cared about was that we wanted to be the people who ended the show when we wanted to end it,' Schur told *Entertainment Weekly*. 'For whatever reason, our gut was saying: One more season.' He later admitted that the strongest argument he and Poehler could make in defence of continuing was, 'But we won't get to hang out all the time!' Discussions with the network were brief and Schur suggested that both sides seemed to be on the same page. 'It was a thirty-second conversation,' he told *Entertainment Weekly*. 'We felt very lucky.' NBC's mandate was more or less, 'We're happy to go along with however you want to play it'. With that, Schur began mapping out a season-six finale, which would also act as stage one of the show reaching its appropriate conclusion.

'Moving Up', the last episode of season six, unveiled a monumental twist in its closing moments. The events unfolding in the final scene were revealed to be taking place in the near future, setting up the entire final season as a leap forward to Pawnee, circa 2017. Schur, Poehler and the writers saw it as a great opportunity to reposition every character into whatever situation they wanted, giving them a new starting point from which to bring each story arc to a satisfactory end.

Poehler admitted the concept seemed risky. 'I was kinda scared at first,' but was won over by Schur's belief in the extra scope it would give the writers. Schur told *Entertainment Weekly*, 'Everywhere we looked, it gave us possibilities to drop in interesting things for the characters.' While *Entertainment Weekly*'s Dan Snierson described the decision to move three years into the future as 'a mouth-agape game changer', Schur was adamant that it was really the best chance they had to go out with a bang. 'We decided, "Well screw it... go big or go home,"' he told *Entertainment Weekly*. 'And we're going home, so go big anyway.'

After seeing the scripts, Chris had his own spin on what was about to take place in the show's future-set episodes. 'It's like a *Twilight Zone* episode of *Parks and Rec*,' he exclaimed to *Entertainment Weekly*. 'It's super-meta. It's going to fuck people's brains out.'

When the time came to actually start work, he was a little more rational about the whole thing. 'It's going to be sad,' he told the *Independent* a couple of weeks prior to returning to *Parks and Rec*'s LA set. 'I can't even bring myself to think about it,' he went on to say, 'I guess all good things come to an end,' before joking, 'We are a good group of people, no one has turned into an a-hole.' And he wasn't alone: Aubrey Plaza, his onscreen wife, was similarly upset about the show coming to an end but had decided to count her blessings. She told the *New York Times* she was happy to be reconnecting with her 'TV husband', especially after his recent success meant she hadn't seen him so much in the last year. 'I am glad to have him all to myself because if anyone tries to get with him, I will destroy them,' she joked, before adding, 'I love him and now he has rock-hard abs. Which is just a bonus.'

For the next four months, the *Parks and Recreation* team were hard at work completing the thirteen episodes that would form the show's final swansong. For Chris, it was a relief to finally be closer to home after almost two years of constant travelling and working in far-flung locations. While he was sad to think that his time as Andy Dwyer would soon be over, he was definitely looking forward to taking a break.

'The plan come January when *Parks and Rec* wraps is that Anna is going to be working on her TV show, *Mom*, and I'm going to be playing the role of dad at home,' he told the *Independent*. 'It's going to be awesome.'

As the key cast members gathered for the first read-through of the series finale, the reality of the situation started to hit home. 'It's not often that I'm speechless,' Chris told *Entertainment Weekly*. 'I always have some shit coming out of my mouth. But I was a little speechless. I just didn't know quite how to handle it.' He recalled the mood changed once the actors had read through the very last page of the script. 'No one wanted to get up after the table read was over,' he said. 'Then we all walked away and said, "That wasn't too bad." And it's like, "Oh yeah – that's just the very beginning of saying goodbye. The table read is over but there's shooting an entire episode still."'

As production started to wind down, each day brought the final day on set for one of the many regular actors in the cast.

As the main cast filmed their last group scenes together, the mood on set was both light-hearted and sombre. Everyone was doing all they could to keep the jokes flying but mostly to stop the tears coming. 'We're really making this ending tantric,' Chris joked with *Entertainment Weekly*. 'Slowing it down, enjoying every thrust, breathing deeply, looking into our lover's eyes...' While Aubrey Plaza wasn't coping quite so well: 'I can't take it. I'm going to kill myself when it's over.'

As someone who had gone through a similar experience when leaving *Saturday Night Live* after many years as a core cast member, Poehler was philosophical. 'I know a little more about how rare this experience is, how lucky we are,' before adding that she was coping by 'just kind of pretending it's not ending.'

Sadly, there was no getting away from it, and on 12 December 2014, the cameras stopped rolling on the show's 125th and final episode. The cast and crew soon took to Twitter to announce that the very last scenes for the series finale had been completed. Under the hashtag #ThankYouParksCrew, Aziz Ansari posted, 'I'm gonna miss this glorious cast and crew very much,' while Aubrey Plaza wrote, 'Last day. goodbye Pawnee. you are all the loves of my life. I HATE GOODBYES.'

Chris summed his experience up neatly by saying, 'Today we wrapped @parksandrecnbc for good. Lots of years, lots of tears, lots of love, lots of gratitude.' With the majority of the show's cast and crew gathered for a farewell party, he left his Mouse Rat bandmates behind to deliver a (literally) show-stopping solo performance of '5,000 Candles in the Wind', bringing the curtain down on his time in Pawnee.

Season seven premiered on 13 January 2015, with NBC airing two back-to-back episodes in the show's new 8pm time slot. NBC had decided to air double episodes every week in an attempt to give the show 'event TV' status ahead of the 24 February two-part finale. The 2017 setting threw out countless unexpected changes in the lives of most Pawnee residents but also highlighted that a lot of them had comfortingly stayed exactly the same. In the future, Chris's character, Andy Dwyer, has found fame on public-access television as a children's entertainer, hosting the 'Johnny Karate Super Awesome Musical Explosion Show'. He and April are still married but struggling to come to terms with the idea that they might actually be growing up. Worried they are getting boring and old before their time, Andy and April vow to shake things up. They try to buy a house together but insist on only looking at properties that are completely inappropriate or virtually uninhabitable. Andy describes one house – in a viewing hosted by guest-star realtor Werner Herzog – 'Says here there are twelve closets, three bomb shelters, five dumbwaiters, two and three-eighths baths, no kitchen. So, fairly standard layout.'

The first pair of episodes saw the series achieve a small ratings increase over the previous season's September debut. At 3.5 million viewers, it was slightly disappointing for a season premiere but it was still the highest-rated comedy to air that night, beating *New Girl*, *Mindy Project* and *Marry Me*. Obviously, no one was expecting *Parks and Recreation* to suddenly become a huge ratings hit – least of all NBC if you take their two-episodes-at-a-time blowout as a sign of their eagerness to move on to other things – but it would seem the show was still hitting the right nerve with most of its biggest fans.

Entertainment Weekly gave the series premiere a B-rating and came down largely in favour of the show's new time-jump premise: the tiny glimpses into the world of 2017 – where Shia LaBeouf now designs wedding dresses and Kevin James is the new Jason Bourne – and Pawnee's own techno-gadget revolution provided a rich vein of comedy. However, certain aspects of the new set-up were ringing alarm bells. A Leslie-Ron feud and April experiencing a mid-twenties career crisis had reviewer Jeff Jenson stating, 'The last thing I want from the last season of this gem of a show is to leave me wishing it ended one season earlier.' On the whole, it appeared the gamble had paid off. As the season progressed, the show took great delight in filling in the three-year gap with titbits of missing information about the characters' lives and made sure there were still plenty of obstacles standing in the way of their 'Happy Ever After'.

Schur explained, 'By the time the series finale is over, the characters will have gone through as much upheaval and change as in the previous six seasons.'

What was Chris's personal take on how the show should end? He told *Entertainment Weekly*, 'Dinosaur attack. *Jurassic World* crossover. They are killed by dinosaurs... in space.'

However the show chose to end its seven-year run, no one could deny it had been a crazy ride and a lot of fun.

Virtually no other show on television could claim to have created such an expansive fictional world and filled it with an incredibly rich cast of supporting characters. From the lovable (Li'l Sebastian, Pawnee's much-loved and much-missed celebrity miniature horse) to the downright crazy (Tammy 1, Tammy 2 and Marcia Langman, the very vocal member of the Society for Family Stability Foundation), over seven seasons *Parks and Recreation* had given birth to some truly iconic comic creations. Perhaps only *The Simpsons* came close, with the town of Springfield playing host to a similarly diverse and colourful cast of characters. But of course the only real advantage *The Simpsons* producers had over Schur and his crew was the fact that no one in Hollywood was trying to pull their cast apart, steal the key players and set them up in their own multi-million-dollar movie franchises. The show's real legacy would probably be similar to that of its main character, Leslie Knope: it never gave up. Amy Poehler described the show's fighting spirit to *Entertainment Weekly*: 'We stuck to our fundamentals, we put our head down and played our game,' adding, 'We didn't get distracted by the noise.'

For Chris, his time on *Parks and Recreation* had coincided with some major changes in his life. He had got married, had a child... and then there was the small matter of him becoming one of the biggest movie stars on the planet. He was incredibly appreciative of everything his time on *Parks and Recreation* had taught him – and not only as an actor – and he was painfully aware of how unique an experience it was. *Deadline Hollywood* reported on an NBC press conference where Chris said, 'I hope that I could have the good fortune of finding another group of people like this, but I don't expect I ever will.' He went on to joke, 'I would never fucking leave this show,' before his co-star, Aziz Ansari, burst his bubble by saying, 'We're all leaving now.'

Chris's last thoughts on the final season were suitably optimistic. 'This year they're going to know they're writing a series finale,' he reasoned to *Entertainment Weekly*. 'So I think they can really look at it as a graceful and appropriate ending to a wonderful show full of characters that we all loved playing.'

Staying with one television show for seven seasons is quite a commitment but he viewed it as part of an invaluable learning experience and fundamental to his development as an actor. As shoe-shine Andy Dwyer he had literally been studying at the feet of some true masters of comedy. Being 'locked into' a long-running series can be a frustrating situation for some actors, but for others it provides financial security and the freedom to accept jobs they wouldn't normally be able to pursue, such as low-paid independent films or stage work. It's a situation Chris's *Jurassic World* co-star Jake Johnson seemed to understand better than most. After playing Nick Miller in *New Girl* for the last four years, Johnson admitted that having a regular television gig definitely affected the choices of any actor. He told the *Huffington Post*, 'As an actor, you act in order to make a living. Then, when you can make a living, you start acting because you want to do what you love to do. I need to remind myself of that a lot. *New Girl* is how I make my living, and if I'm going to do a movie it's because I really, artistically want to do it.'

This seems to have been Chris's thought process for some time now. In terms of finances, with the way his movie career had been progressing lately, it looked as though he and Anna had nothing to worry about for the considerable future. And now, with *Parks and Recreation* ending, he would have a lot more free time on his hands and ample opportunities to pick and choose the projects he wanted to work on. While his first priority was to take a little time off, it seemed that he was more or less in complete control of what he wanted to do next.

CHAPTER FIFTEEN

SPREAD YOUR WINGS AND FLY

'The truth is, Chris Pratt is the biggest movie star in the world. It's just people don't know it yet."
JAMES GUNN – *NIGHTLINE, ABC NEWS*

As 2015 began, Chris was enjoying a well-earned rest. Production on the final season of *Parks and Recreation* was over and he'd chosen not to accept any other offers of jobs for the time being. While Anna went to work, filming new episodes of her sitcom, *Mom*, he was content to stay at home with his baby son, Jack. *Forbes Magazine* had recently published an article that named him the highest-grossing male movie star of 2014. His roles in *Guardians of the Galaxy* and *The Lego Movie* had amassed $1.2 billion at the box office, placing him just behind Jennifer Lawrence's $1.4 billion. It's testament to the type of man Chris had become; that despite the position he found himself in as one of the most in-demand actors in Hollywood, he was happy to just take a moment to enjoy the fruits of his recent labours. He splashed out on a new truck, took a few short trips to visit old friends and relatives and generally took the time to settle back into his 'normal' life – as a husband to Anna and a father to Jack.

None of this gave much of a clue as to what he would do next. There were obvious commitments – *Guardians 2* had already been announced and he was almost certain to return in any proposed *Lego Movie* or *Jurassic World* sequel – but news of where his career was headed was less forthcoming than Ron Swanson at a local-government public forum. Chris was in a fairly unique and enviable position; he could take as long as he wanted to make his next move and he could probably secure a green light for any project with his name attached. He has talked about producing his own projects, stating that he likes the idea of being in charge on set and relishes the thought of having more input with the movies he makes.

'I'm always biting my tongue,' he told *GQ*. 'If I could tell everyone what to do, it would be great, and it would be done faster. And so that's what I'm working towards. I want control.' But with all due respect, it feels like he is a few years away from becoming an actor-director-writer-producer to rival George Clooney and he himself is the first to admit he has work to do. 'I have to get better at writing, because the stuff that I have written, no one bought,' he revealed, before acknowledging the newfound power that comes with his recent success. 'Maybe they'll buy it now, because they can put my name on it, but I'd be in a bad movie that I wrote.'

It was this determination to maintain a certain level of quality control that seems key to Chris's hesitation to accept roles merely to keep working. There were rumours, of course, but nothing had been officially announced since he wrapped on *Jurassic World*. In November of 2014 Chris's name was being mentioned as a possible replacement for Mark Wahlberg in a big-screen adaptation of the video game *Uncharted*. The film was being written by Mark Boal, who had previously worked alongside Chris as the screenwriter for *Zero Dark Thirty*. But shortly after news broke that Chris had been approached to play Nathan Drake, *Uncharted*'s Indiana Jones-style fortune-hunter lead, the *Hollywood Reporter* stated that he had, in fact, declined the offer. The following month, in early December 2014, *Deadline Hollywood* reported that he was in early talks to join Denzel Washington in a remake of 1960s Western *The Magnificent Seven*, which would be directed by Antoine Fuqua.

While it's easy to imagine him starring in either of these projects, the truth is it's becoming almost impossible not to imagine Chris in virtually any role. When the trailer for Bennett Miller's *Foxcatcher* first appeared, with Channing Tatum starring as former Olympic wrestling champion Mark Schultz, Chris seemed an utterly feasible replacement. Perhaps it had something to do with the subject matter, his former life as a high-school wrestler or, indeed, his former associations with both Miller and Tatum. But, in reality, it has more to do with his fairly unique stature as an actor. Watch almost any trailer, for indie comedies or big-budget sequels, and you'd have no trouble at all in placing him logically somewhere in the film's cast list. He has more than proven himself as a nimble and accomplished comedy performer and his forays into dramatic acting have resulted in an impressive run of subtle and truthful performances. By finding traces of his own personality in every role, he manages to project a relatable truth and believability into every character he plays. We believe him because, at least partly, he is playing someone he truly knows well and who actually exists... himself.

With the enormous success of *Guardians of the Galaxy* and *Jurassic World*, Chris's status as a leading man is more or less secured and perhaps the most interesting casting suggestion involves him taking the title role in Disney's planned relaunch of the Indiana Jones franchise. This particular development in his career would see him reach exactly the same threshold that a similarly versatile young actor found himself on in the late 1970s/early 1980s.

Like Chris, Harrison Ford found fame in a blockbuster sci-fi movie franchise, after almost a decade working as a jobbing actor in Hollywood and being told on a regular basis he lacked the 'It factor' to become a successful leading man. Ford has a similarly acute understanding of how to mix comedy and drama, something that stood him in good stead while negotiating the 'you can write this stuff down, but you can't say it' absurdities of the first *Star Wars* script. Most of all, he possesses the same old-school Hollywood star quality that James Gunn attributed to Chris when listing the reasons he hired him to play Peter Quill in *Guardians*.

Like Chris, Ford has been likened to Gary Cooper, Jimmy Stewart and Peter Fonda, exuding undeniable but muted masculinity; equally comfortable playing everyman lawyers and cops as he is playing space pirates and whip-cracking adventurers. Subsequently, over the course of his fifty-year career, Ford has faced similar questions about how much of what the audience sees on the big screen is acting and how much of it is the man himself. But while Ford seemed to avoid the type of roles that win actors major awards – he has only been nominated at the Oscars once, for his role in *Witness* – he has gone on to work with some of the world's most acclaimed directors and filmmakers. Alongside some of Hollywood's biggest names – the likes of Steven Spielberg, Ridley Scott, Mike Nichols, Robert Zemeckis and Wolfgang Petersen – Ford managed to collaborate with several more independently-minded filmmakers, including Roman Polanski, Peter Weir, Sydney Pollack, Alan J. Pakula and Kathryn Bigelow. Perhaps this is the route Chris is more likely to take. If so, I'm sure Ford would be the first to advise him to accept more *Star Wars*', *Indiana Jones*', *Witness*'s, *Working Girl's* and *The Fugitive's* than *Cowboys and Aliens*', *Hollywood Homicide's* and *Sabrina's*.

The similarities with Ford extend beyond the two actors' profession – Ford shares Chris's disdain for most of the excesses and intrusions that seem to go hand and hand with working in Hollywood, rejecting much of the lifestyle and removing himself from the public eye between jobs. And while Chris finds escape in disappearing into the wilderness for fishing and hunting trips, Ford famously used carpentry and his woodworking skills as a means to depressurise and avoid the stress of his sometimes demanding job. Chris also shares his basic outlook on acting. Ford always saw himself as the essential down-to-earth element of every story; the relatable character entrusted with drawing the audience in and making them accept anything they might be asked to believe or experience along the way.

'They have had in my company some significant experiences,' he told *Vanity Fair*. 'I am, of course, just part of it. In *Star Wars*, it was George [Lucas] who created the rocket ship to go through the heavens which gave the movie technological scale, and it was John Williams who created the music which gave it operatic scale, but I gave it human scale.'

Perhaps it is this ability to encapsulate 'human scale' that will also be Chris Pratt's greatest asset. Fat or thin, funny or serious, his future career is destined to be one of the most unpredictable and fascinating to watch unfold. And of course if it all goes wrong, he can always pick up the guitar to front his own Pearl Jam tribute band, take up shoe-shining or fall over a few times on rollerblades... that stuff always gets a laugh.